WHAT TH
THE JOB

MW01602947

". . . A superior series of jo... ....

**-Cornell University
Career Center
WHERE TO START**

"A timely book for Chicago job hunters follows books from the same publisher that were well received in New York and Boston...A fine tool for job hunters..."

**-Clarence Petersen
THE CHICAGO TRIBUNE**

"Job hunting is never fun, but this book can ease the ordeal...The Southern California Job Bank will help allay fears, build confidence and avoid wheel-spinning."

**-Robert W. Ross
THE LOS ANGELES TIMES**

"This well-researched, well-edited job hunter's aid includes most major businesses and institutional entities in the New York metropolitan area...Highly recommended."

**-Cheryl Gregory-Pindell
LIBRARY JOURNAL**

"Here's the book for your job hunt...Trying to get a job in New York? I would recommend a good look through the Metropolitan New York Job Bank..."

**-Maxwell Norton
NEW YORK POST**

"Help on the job hunt...Anyone who is job-hunting in the New York area can find a lot of useful ideas in a new paperback called The Metropolitan New York Job Bank..."

**-Angela Taylor
THE NEW YORK TIMES**

"If you are looking for a job...before you go to the newspapers and the help-wanted ads, listen to Bob Adams, editor of The Metropolitan New York Job Bank."

**-Tom Brokaw
NBC TELEVISION**

"No longer can job seekers feel secure about finding employment just through want ads. With the tough competition in the job market, particularly in the Boston area, they need much more help. For this reason, The Boston Job Bank will have a wide and appreciative audience of new graduates, job changers, and people relocating to Boston. It provides a good place to start a search for entry-level professional positions."

**-from a review in
THE JOURNAL OF
COLLEGE PLACEMENT**

What makes the JOB BANK SERIES the nation's premier line of employment guides:

With vital employment information on thousands of the nation's largest companies, the **JOB BANK SERIES** is the most comprehensive and authoritative set of career directories available today.

Each of the entries provides contact information, telephone numbers, addresses and a thumbnail sketch of the firm's business. Many entries also include a listing of the firm's typical professional job categories, the principal educational backgrounds sought, and the fringe benefits offered.

All of the reference information in the **JOB BANK SERIES** is as up-to-date and accurate as possible. Every year, the entire database is thoroughly researched and verified, first by mail and then by telephone. More local **JOB BANK** books come out more often than any other comparable publications.

In addition, the **JOB BANK SERIES** features important information about the local job scene--forecasts on which industries are the hottest, overviews of local economic trends, and even lists of regional professional associations, so you can get your job hunt started off right!

Looking for a particular kind of employer? Each **JOB BANK** Book features a comprehensive cross-index, which lists entries both by industry and, in multi-state job markets, by state. This means a person seeking a job in, say, finance, can identify major employers quickly and accurately.

Hundreds of discussions with job-hunters show they prefer information organized geographically, because most people look for jobs in specific areas. The **JOB BANK SERIES** offers sixteen regional titles, from Minneapolis to Houston, and from Washington, D.C., to San Francisco. The future employee moving to a particular area can review the local employment data and get a feel not only for the type of industry most common to that region, but also for major employers.

A condensed, but thorough, review of the entire job search process is presented in the chapter, 'The Basics of Job Winning', a feature that has received many compliments from career counselors. In addition, each **JOB BANK** directory is completed by a section on resumes and cover letters **The New York Times** has acclaimed as "excellent".

The **JOB BANK SERIES** gives job-hunters the most comprehensive, most timely, and most accurate career information, organized and indexed to facilitate the job search. An entire career reference library, **JOB BANK** books are the consummate employment guides.

The
Minneapolis-St. Paul
JobBank
1992

Managing Editor: Carter Smith

Associate Editor: Peter Weiss

Editorial Assistants:
Michelle Bevilacqua
Sharon Cook
Elizabeth Gale
Lynne Griffin

BOB ADAMS, INC.
P U B L I S H E R S
Holbrook, Massachusetts

Top career publications from Bob Adams, Inc.:

THE JobBank SERIES:

The Atlanta JobBank ($12.95)
The Boston JobBank ($12.95)
The Chicago JobBank ($12.95)
The Dallas-Ft. Worth JobBank ($12.95)
The Denver JobBank ($12.95)
The Detroit JobBank ($12.95)
The Florida JobBank ($12.95)
The Houston JobBank ($12.95)
The Los Angeles JobBank ($12.95)
The Minneapolis-St. Paul JobBank ($12.95)
The New York JobBank ($12.95)
The Ohio JobBank ($12.95)
The Philadelphia JobBank ($12.95)
The Phoenix JobBank ($12.95)
The San Francisco JobBank ($12.95)
The Seattle JobBank ($12.95)
The St. Louis JobBank ($12.95)
The Washington DC JobBank ($12.95)

The JobBank Guide to Employment Services (covers 50 states: $129.95)
The National JobBank ($199.95)

CAREERS

Campus-Free College Degrees ($9.95)
Careers and the College Grad ($12.95)
Careers and the Engineer ($12.95)
Careers and the MBA ($14.95)

The Complete Guide to Washington Internships ($12.95)
Cover Letters that Knock 'em Dead ($7.95)
The Elements of Job Hunting ($4.95)
Harvard Guide to Careers in Mass Media ($7.95)
How to Get a Job in Education ($6.95)
International Careers ($12.95)
Job Search Handbook ($6.95)
Knock 'em Dead with Great Answers to Tough Interview Questions ($6.95)
The Minority Career Book ($9.95)
Over 40 and Looking for Work ($7.95)
Resume Handbook ($5.95)
Resumes that Knock 'em Dead ($7.95)
Which Niche? (Answers to the Most Common Questions About Careers and Job Hunting) ($4.95)

To obtain a copy of any of these books, please check your local bookstore. If unavailable, please call 1-800-USA-JOBS toll free. (In Massachusetts call 617-767-8100).

HOW TO USE THIS BOOK

A copy of *The Minneapolis-St. Paul JobBank* is one of the most effective tools you can find for your professional job hunt. Use this guide for the most up-to-date information on most major businesses in the Twin Cities. It will supply you with specific addresses, phone numbers, and personnel contact information.

Separate yourself from the flock of candidates who answer the help-wanted advertisements "looking for a job." The method this book offers, direct employer contact, boasts twice the success rate of any other. Exploit it.

Read and use *The Minneapolis-St. Paul JobBank* to reveal new opportunities. Here's how:

Read the introductory economic overview section in order to gain insight on what the overall trends are for the Twin Cities' economy.

Map out your job-seeking strategy by reading the "Basics of Job Winning" section. It's a condensed review of the most effective job search methods.

Write a winning resume and learn how to sell yourself most effectively on paper, by using the "Resumes and Cover Letters" section.

Focus your career goals by reading the "Jobs in Each Industry" section. This chapter features descriptions of many of the most common professional occupations, as well as background requirements, and forecasts for future growth.

Formulate a target list of potential employers in your field. Consult the company listings in the "Primary Twin Cities Employers" section. Use that information to supplement your own research, so that you'll be knowledgeable about the firm - before the interview.

Increase your knowledge of your field, as well as your connections within it, by using our listings of some of Minnesota's major professional and trade associations.

Whether you are just out of college starting your first job search, looking for a new position in your current field, or entering an entirely new sector of the job market, *The Minneapolis-St. Paul JobBank* will give you an idea of the incredible diversity of employment possibilities in one of the the country's most dynamic employment centers. Your ultimate success will largely depend upon how rigorously you use the information provided herein. This one-of-a-kind employment guide can lead you to a company, and a job, that would otherwise have remained undiscovered. With a willingness to apply yourself, a positive attitude, and the research within these covers, you can attain your career objective.

TABLE OF CONTENTS

INTRODUCTION/11

A complete and informative economic overview designed to help you understand all of the forces shaping the Twin Cities job market.

PART ONE: THE JOB SEARCH

The Basics of Job Winning/17

A condensed review of the basic elements of a successful job search campaign. Includes advice on developing an effective strategy, time planning, preparing for interviews, interview techniques, etc.

Resumes and Cover Letters/33

Advice on creating a strong resume. Includes sample resumes and cover letters.

PART TWO: OCCUPATION PROFILES

Jobs In Each Industry/51

Descriptions of many of the most common professional positions, with forecasts of their growth potential for the 1990's.

PART THREE: WHERE THE JOBS ARE

Primary Twin Cities Employers/109

Greater Minneapolis-St. Paul organized according to industry. Includes the address, phone number, description of the company's basic product lines and services, and for most firms, the name of the contact person for professional positions.

Professional Employment Services/237

Includes the address, phone number, description of each company's services, contact name, and a list of positions commonly filled.

Professional & Trade Associations/251

Includes both local and national addresses and phone numbers for professional and trade associations in each field.

INTRODUCTION

INTRODUCTION

For job seekers willing to brave the chill of Minnesota winters, the Twin Cities of Minneapolis and St. Paul present some terrific opportunities. As the de facto capital of the Upper Midwest region that stretches from Montana to Michigan, the Twin Cities play a dominant role not only regionally, but nationally as well.

Historically, Minneapolis gained prominence as an old milling town, and serves today as headquarters for the world's four largest grain milling companies. Minneapolis' economy is also boosted by a number of high-tech manufacturers and a wide array of professional and business services.

St. Paul has traditionally been an axis of transportation, and a hub for the entire Midwest. Today, it is a government town (home to the state capital, state offices, affiliated associations, and many lobbyists), and a college town (home to Hamline University, Macalester, St. Thomas, St. Catherine and Concordia colleges, as well as the University of Minnestota's St. Paul campus -- which is literally in Falcon Heights. St. Paul also specializes in non-profit businesses, with Minnesota Public Radio, KCTA Public Television, and the Wilder Foundation located there.

The Minneapolis-St. Paul metro area has one of the lowest unemployment rates in the country. Businesses are attracted to the secure, productive and proficient labor force of nearly one million persons, with low absenteeism and low turnover. Major corporations include: 3M, Honeywell, General Mills, Control Data, Pillsbury, Bemis, Dayton Hudson, and Northwest Airlines.

In addition to its prime geographic location in the heart of the Upper Midwest, the Twin City area is also graced with a solid transportation infrastructure. Equally beneficial has been the state of Minnesota's commitment to improving welfare programs, education, and highway systems, helping in turn to create an excellent working and living environment.

A Population Profile

The Twin Cities metro area has a population of over 2.4 million residents, making it the 14th largest metropolitan area in the country. Throughout the 80's, the city attracted people from across the state, region and nation. Between 1986 and 1989 alone, the city grew at an annual rate of 1.5% percent.

Minneapolis-St. Paul has a fairly young population, with a relatively affluent labor force dominated by that 25-44 year old age group. A major reason that Twin Cities incomes tend to be higher than the national average is because the city is home to so many high-tech firms and corporate headquarters. Ethnically, the area is highly homogenous -- over 95% white.

With blacks making up only 2% of the population, the Twin Cities fall well below the national average of 14%.

A 1980's Boomtown

In recent years, the Twin Cities have enjoyed prolonged prosperity and economic expansion because venture capitalists have helped to establish it as a pre-eminent location to invest substantial sums of capital. Burgeoning entrepreneurship during the 1980s did wonders for the entire region. Today, over 30 billion dollar corporations operate in the area.

To a large degree, the 1980s brought about a shift in the metro area's economy, moving it away from dormant farming, mining, and heavy durable goods manufacturing industries toward the lucrative high-tech field. In fact, fully one quarter of the workforce is now engaged in either a professional career or an occupation related to electronics or computers. Over 1200 firms in the area are involved in intensive technology, including Cray Research, Unisys, Honeywell, and the previously mentioned Control Data.

High Tech: A Temporary Slowdown

As instrumental as Minneapolis-St. Paul's high tech growth has been in turning around the Twin Cities economy, the local service industries have been the economy's stabilizer. Just as the city's durable goods-concentrated manufacturing sector was hit hard by the 1982 recession, shakeouts in the computer industry have again pushed manufacturing employment down. Between 1986 and 1989, computer-related employment dropped at an annual 1.1% rate. Luckily, Minnesotans in the computer field have been somewhat insulated from the national downturn in the industry. Analysts believe this is due largely to Twin Cities employment in headquarters offices and in research and production facilities.

Three events in Minneapolis-St. Paul's computer sector, however, have highlighted recent difficulties. In 1989, Control Data discontinued its super-computer operations, restructured and downsized its computer products operations, discontinued training and education, and reduced its corporate staff. The second event was the closing of ETA Systems and the spin off of Cray Computer by Cray Research. The impact of these moves will continue to be felt in the short-term. And thirdly, Unisys recently reduced its staff as well -- about half of the cuts coming from a simplification of the company's U.S. organizational structure.

The U.S. Department of Defense has also been one of the Twin City high-tech and general manufacturing industries' leading benefactors. Minneapolis-St. Paul ranked 18th among the nation's top 100 metro areas in terms of defense contract awards. With possible defense cutbacks looming, only time will tell whether the region's position can be maintained.

Analysts predict that problems in the computer industry will continue over the next several years to dampen expansion. In the long term, the prominence of high-tech manufacturing -- an expected rapid-growth area nationally -- will be a boon to the Minneapolis-St. Paul economy. The labor force is among the best educated in the country, providing an excellent business environment for manufacturers in computer related industries, with low energy costs as an added bonus.

The Services Explosion

Most of Minneapolis-St. Paul's growth during the past few years has come from its expanding role as the financial center of the Midwest, and from large numbers of nationally recognized firms that have established headquarters there. These companies have substantially increased the demand for financial and business services. All this has taken place despite the decline in the computer industry.

Business and financial services growth, not particularly impressive during the early 1980s, ended the decade strongly. Finance, insurance, and real estate companies have been leading the way. Over the next few years, the insurance industry will be one of the fastest growing segments of the economy.

The Capital of America's Breadbasket

Although the Twin Cities economy has shifted away from its historic reliance on agriculture, since Minneapolis-St. Paul is home to some of America's largest food processing companies, that industry will continue to hold major importance. In fact, the region's trade sector remains heavily dependant on farm production. Unfortunately, recent mergers and aquisition activity in the food processing industry have hurt the Twin Cities economy, cutting jobs in company headquarters.

The Retail Market

Minneapolis-St. Paul is the nation's 11th largest retail market, and the largest in the Upper Midwest. Minneapolis retailers not only attract local residents, but also those from around Minnesota, as well as from Wisconsin, North and South Dakota, and Iowa. The metro area is home to such retailing giants as Dayton-Hudson, Target, Lechmere, and Mervyn's.

Largely because of manufacturing declines in 1986 and early 1987, retail sales dropped 2.4% during 1987. Between the years 1986 and 1989, Minneapolis-St. Paul's retail market grew by 4.9%, placing the city's retail growth in the bottom quarter of the top 100 metro area rates. During the years since 1987, however, the retail market has been steadily improving. This process has been sped along by the 1987 Canadian Free Trade Agreement, upon which the city has been able to capitalize. As a result of the agreement, exports through Minneapolis' port of exit more than doubled between 1986 and 1988 alone, from $221.7 million to $469.7

Prognosis for Jobseekers

Despite short-term troubles in the computer industry, the Twin Cities are poised to remain the center of the Upper Midwest's economy for the foreseeable future. With a very favorable long term outlook for computer manufacturing, when that industry does regain strength, the manufacturing sector should return, removing one of the area's main economic obstacles. Meanwhile, the retail and wholesale trade sector and business and financial services should continue to show solid growth through the next several years.

In short, despite the somewhat slowed growth rate that has started off the 1990's in Minneapolis-St.Paul, the Twin Cities should remain one of the jobseeker's best bets as we head toward the 21st Century.

PART ONE:
THE JOB SEARCH

The Basics of Job Winning

The best way to obtain a better professional job is to contact the employer directly. Broad-based statistical studies by the Department of Labor show that job seekers have found employment more successfully by contacting employers directly, than by using any other method.

However, given the current diversity, and increased specialization of both industry and job tasks it is possible that in some situations other job seeking methods may prove at least equally successful. Three of the other most commonly used methods are: relying on personal contacts, using employment services, and following up help wanted advertisements. Many professionals have been successful in finding better jobs using one of these methods. However, the Direct Contact method has an overall success rate twice that of any other method and it has been successfully used by many more professionals. So unless you have specific reasons to believe that another method would work best for you, the Direct Contact method should form the foundation of your job search effort.

The Objective

With any business task, you must develop a strategy for meeting a goal. This is especially true when it comes to obtaining a better job. First you need to clearly define your objectives.

Setting your job objectives is better known as career planning (or life planning for those who wish to emphasize the importance of combining the two). Career planning has become a field of study in and of itself. Since most of our readers are probably well-entrenched in their career path, we will touch on career planning just briefly.

If you are thinking of choosing or switching careers, we particularly emphasize two things. First, choose a career where you will enjoy most of the day-to-day tasks. Sure, this sounds obvious, but most of us have at one point or another been attracted by a glamour industry or a prestigious sounding job without thinking of the most important consideration: Would we enjoy performing the everyday tasks the position entailed?

The second key consideration is that you are not merely choosing a career, but also a lifestyle. Career counselors indicate that one of the most common problems people encounter in job seeking is a lack of consideration for how well-suited they are for a particular position or career. For example, some people, attracted to management consulting by good salaries, early responsibility and high level corporate exposure, do not adapt well to the long hours, heavy travel demands, and the constant pressure to produce. So be sure to determine both for your career as a whole and for each position that you apply for, if you will easily adapt to both the day-to-day duties that the position entails and the working environment.

The Strategy

Assuming that you have now established your career objectives, the next step of the job search is to develop a strategy. If you don't take the time to develop a strategy and lay out a plan you will probably find yourself going in circles after several weeks making a random search for opportunities that always seem just beyond your reach.

Your strategy can be thought as having three simple elements:

1. Choosing a method of contacting employers.

2. Allocating your scarce resources (in most job searches the key scarce resource will be time, but financial considerations will become important in some searches too.)

3. Evaluating how the selected contact method is working and then considering adopting other methods.

We suggest you give serious consideration to using the Direct Contact method exclusively. However, we realize it is human nature to avoid putting all your eggs in one basket. So, if you prefer to use other methods as well, try to expend at least half your effort on the Direct Contact method, spending the rest on all of the other methods combined. Millions of other job seekers have already proven that Direct Contact has been twice as effective in obtaining employment, so why not benefit from their effort?

With your strategy in mind, the next step is to develop the details of the plan, or scheduling. Of course, job searches are not something that most people do regularly so it is difficult to estimate how long each step will take. Nonetheless, it is important to have a plan so that your effort can be allocated the way you have chosen, so that you can see yourself progressing, and to facilitate reconsideration of your chosen strategy.

It is important to have a realistic time frame in mind. If you will be job searching full-time, your search will probably take at least two months and very likely, substantially longer. If you can only devote part-time effort, it will probably take four months.

You probably know a few people who seem to spend their whole lives searching for a better job in their part time. Don't be one of them. Once you begin your job search on a part-time basis, give it your whole-hearted effort. If you don't really feel like devoting a lot of energy to job seeking right now, then wait. Focus on enjoying your present position, performing your best on the job, and storing up energy for when you are really ready to begin your job search.

Those of you currently unemployed should remember that job hunting is tough work physically and emotionally. It is also intellectually demanding -- requiring your best. So don't tire yourself out by working on your job campaign around the clock. It would be counter-productive. At the same time, be sure to discipline yourself. The most logical approach to time management is to keep your regular working hours.

For those of you who are still employed, job searching will be particularly tiring because it must be done in addition to your regular duties. So don't work yourself to the point where you show up to interviews appearing exhausted and slip behind at your current job. But don't be tempted to quit! The long hours are worth it - it is much easier to sell your skills from a position of strength (as someone currently employed).

If you are searching full-time and have decided to choose a mixture of contact methods, we recommend that you divide up each week allowing some time for each method. For instance, you might devote Mondays to following up newspaper ads because most of them appear in Sunday papers. Then you might devote Tuesdays, and Wednesday mornings to working and developing the personal contacts you have, in addition to trying a few employment services. Then you could devote the rest of the week to the Direct Contact method. This is just one plan that may succeed for you.

By trying several methods at once, job-searching will be more interesting for you, and you will be able to evaluate how promising each of the methods seems, altering your time allocation accordingly. Be very careful in your evaluation, however, and don't judge the success of a particular method just by the sheer number of interviews you obtain. Positions advertised in the newspaper, for instance, are likely to generate many more interviews per opening than positions that are filled without being advertised.

If you are searching part-time and decide to try several different contact methods, we recommend that you try them sequentially. You simply won't have enough time to put a meaningful amount of effort into more than one method at once. So decide how long your job search might take. (Only a guess, of course.) And then allocate so many weeks or months for each contact method you choose to use. (We suggest that you try Direct Contact first.)

If you are expected to be in your office during the business day, then you have an additional time problem to deal with. How can you work interviews into the business day? And if you work in an open office, how can you even call to set up interviews? As much as possible you should keep up the effort and the appearances on your present job. So maximize your use of the lunch hour, early in the morning and late in the afternoon for calling. If you really keep trying you will be surprised how often you will be able to reach the executive you are trying to contact during your out-of-office hours. The lunch hour for different executives will vary between 12 and 3. Also you can catch people as early as 8 AM and as late as 6 PM on frequent occasions. Jot out a plan each night on how you will be using each minute of your precious lunch break.

Your inability to interview at any time other than lunch just might work to your advantage. If you can, try to set up as many interviews as possible for your lunch hour. This will go a long way to creating a relaxed rapport. (Who isn't happy when eating?) But be sure the interviews don't stray too far from the agenda on hand.

Lunchtime interviews will be much easier for the person with substantial career experience to obtain. People with less experience will often find that they have no alternative other than taking time off for interviewing. If you have to take time off, you have to take time off. But try to do this as little as possible. Usually you should take the whole day off so that it is not blatantly obvious that you are job searching. Try to schedule in at least two, or at the most three, interviews for the same day. (It is very difficult to maintain an optimum level of energy at more than three interviews in one day.) Explain to the interviewer why you might have to juggle your interview schedule -- he/she should honor the respect you are showing your current employer by minimizing your days off and will probably appreciate the fact that another prospective employer is showing an interest in you.

Once again we need to emphasize if you are searching for a job, especially part-time, get out there and do the necessary tasks to the best of your ability and get it over with. Don't let your job search drag on endlessly.

Remember that all schedules are meant to be broken. The purpose of a schedule in your job search is not to rush you to your goal, its purpose is to map out the road ahead of you and evaluate the progress of your chosen strategy to date.

The Direct Contact Method

Once you have scheduled a time, you are ready to begin using the job search method that you have chosen. In the text we will restrict discussion to use of the Direct Contact method. Sideboards will comment briefly on developing your personal contacts and using newspaper advertisements.

The first step in preparing for Direct Contact is to develop a check list for categorizing the types of firms for which you would prefer working. You might categorize firms by their product line, their size, their customer-type (such as industrial or consumer), their growth prospects, or, of course by their geographical locations. Your list of important considerations might be very short. If it is, good! The shorter it is, the easier it will be to find appropriate firms.

Then try to decide at which firms you are most likely to be able to obtain employment. You might wish to consider to what degree your particular skills might be in demand, the degree of competition for employment, and the employment outlook at the firm.

Now you are ready to assemble your list of prospective employers. Build up your list to at least 100 prospects. Then separate your prospect list into three groups. The first tier of maybe 25 firms will be your primary target market, the second group of another 25 firms will be your secondary market, and remaining names you will keep in reserve.

DEVELOPING YOUR CONTACTS

Some career counselors feel that the best route to a better job is through somebody you already know or through somebody to whom you can be introduced. The counselors recommend you build your contact base beyond your current acquaintances by asking each one to introduce you, or refer you, to additional people in your field of interest.

The theory goes like this: You might start with 15 personal contacts, each of whom introduces you to 3 additional people, for a total 45 additional contacts. Then each of these people introduces you to three additional people which adds 135 additional contacts. Theoretically, you will soon know every person in the industry.

Of course, developing your personal contacts does not usually work quite as smoothly as the theory suggests because some people will not be able to introduce you to several relevant contacts. The further you stray from your initial contact base, the weaker your references may be. So, if you do try developing your own contacts, try to begin with as large an initial group of people you personally know as possible. Dig into your personal phone book and your holiday greeting card list and locate old classmates from school. Be particularly sure to approach people who perform your personal business such as your lawyer, accountant, banker, doctor, stockbroker, and insurance agent. These people develop a very broad contact base due to the nature of their professions.

This book will help you greatly in developing your prospect list. Refer to the primary employers section of this book. You will notice that employer listings are arranged according to industry, beginning with Accounting, followed by Advertising, and so on through to Utilities. If you know of a firm, but you're unsure of what industry it would be classified under, then refer to the alphabetically ordered employer index at the rear of the book to find the page number that the firm's listing appears on.

At this stage, once you have gotten your prospect list together and have an idea of the firms for which you might wish to work, it is best to get to work on your resume. Refer to formats of the sample resumes included in the Resumes and Cover Letters section that follows this chapter.

Once your resume is at the printer, begin research for the first batch of 25 prospective employers. You will want to determine whether you would be happy working at the firms you are researching and also get a better idea of what their employment needs might be. You also need to obtain enough information to sound highly informed about the company during phone conversations and in mail correspondence. But don't go all out on your research yet! At some of these firms you probably will not be able to arrange interviews, so save your big research effort until you start to arrange interviews. Nevertheless, you should plan to spend about 3 or 4 hours, on average, researching each firm. Do your research in batches to save time and energy. Go into one resource at a time and find out what you can about each of the 25 firms in the batch. Start with the easiest resources to use (such as this book.) Keep organized. Maintain a folder on each firm.

If you discover something that really disturbs you about the firm (i.e. perhaps they are about to close their only local office) or if you discover that your chances of getting a job there are practically nil (i.e. perhaps they just instituted a hiring freeze) then cross them off your prospect list.

If possible, supplement your research efforts with contacts to individuals who know the firm well. Ideally you should make an informal contact with someone at the particular firm, but often a contact at a direct competitor, or a major supplier or customer will be able to supply you with just as much information. At the very least try to obtain whatever printed information that the company has available, not just annual reports, but product brochures and anything else. The company might very well have printed information about career opportunities.

Getting The Interview

Now it is time to arrange an interview, time to make the Direct Contact. If you have read many books on job searching you have probably noticed that virtually all tell you to avoid the personnel office like the plague. It is said that the personnel office never hires people, they just screen out candidates. In some cases you may be able to identify and contact the appropriate manager with the authority to hire you. However, this will take a lot of time and effort in each case. Often you'll be bounced back to personnel. So we suggest that you begin your Direct Contact campaign through personnel offices. If it seems that in the firms on your prospect list that little hiring is done through personnel, you might consider an alternative course of action.

The three obvious means of initiating Direct Contact are:

-Showing up unannounced
-Phone calls
-Mail

Cross out the first one right away. You should never show up to seek a professional position without an appointment. Even if you are somehow lucky enough to obtain an interview, you will appear so unprofessional that you will not even be seriously considered.

Mail contact seems to be a good choice if you have not been in the job market for a while. You can take your time to prepare a careful letter, say exactly what you want, tuck your resume in, and then the addressee can read the material at leisure. But employers receive many resumes every day. Don't be surprised if you do not get a response to your inquiry. So don't spend weeks waiting for responses that never come. If you do send a cover letter, follow it up (or precede it) with a phone call. This will increase your impact, and underscore both your interest in the firm and the fact that you are familiar with it (because of the initial research you did.)

Another alternative is to make a "Cover Call." Your Cover Call should be just like your cover letter: concise. Your first sentence should interest the employer in you. Then try to subtly mention your familiarity with the firm. Don't be overbearing; keep your introduction to three sentences or less. Be pleasant, self confident and relaxed. This will greatly increase the chances of the person at the other end of the line developing the conversation. But don't press. When you are asked to follow up "with something in the mail" don't try to prolong the conversation once it has ended. Don't ask what they want to receive in the mail. Always send your resume and a highly personalized follow-up letter, reminding the addressee of the phone conversation. Always include a cover letter even if you are requested to send a resume. (It is assumed that you will send a cover letter too.)

Unless you are in telephone sales, making smooth and relaxed cover calls will probably not come easily. Practice them on your own and then with your friends or relatives (friends are likely to be more objective and hence, better participants.)

If you obtain an interview over the telephone, be sure to send a thank you note reiterating the points you made during the conversation. You will appear more professional and increase your impact. However, don't mail your resume once an interview has been arranged unless it is specifically requested. Take it with you to the interview instead.

DON'T BOTHER WITH MASS MAILING OR
BARRAGES OF PHONE CALLS

Direct Contact does not mean burying every firm within a hundred miles with mail and phone calls. Mass mailings rarely work in the job hunt. This also applies to those letters that are personalized -- but dehumanized -- on an automatic typewriter. Don't waste your time or money on such a project; you will fool no one but yourself.

The worst part of sending out mass mailings or making unplanned phone calls is that you are likely to be remembered as someone with little genuine interest in the firm, as someone who lacks sincerity, and as somebody that nobody wants to hire.

HELP WANTED ADVERTISEMENTS

Only a small fraction of professional job openings are advertised. Yet a majority of job seekers -- and a lot of people not in the job market -- spend a lot of time studying the help wanted ads. As a result, the competition for advertised openings is often much more severe.

A moderate-sized Manhattan employer told us about an experience advertising in the help wanted section of a major Sunday newspaper:

It was a disaster. We had over 500 responses from this relatively small ad in just one week. We have only two phone lines in this office and one was totally knocked out. We'll never advertise for professional help again.

If you insist on following up on help wanted ads, then research a firm before you reply to an ad so that you can ascertain if you would be a suitable candidate and that you would enjoy working at a particular firm. Also such preliminary research might help to separate you from all of the other professionals responding to that ad, many of whom will only have a passing interest in the opportunity. That said, your chances of obtaining a job through the want-ads are still much smaller than they are if you use the Direct Contact method.

Preparing For The Interview

Once the interview has been arranged, begin your in-depth research. You have got to arrive at the interview knowing the company upside down and inside out. You need to know their products, their types of customers, their subsidiaries, their parent, their principal locations, their rank in the industry, their sales and profit trends, their type of ownership, their size, their current plans and much more. By this time you have probably narrowed your job search to one industry, but if you haven't then you need to be familiar with the trends in this firm's industry, the firm's principal competitors and their relative performance, and the direction that the industry leaders are headed. Dig into every resource you can! Read the company literature, the trade press, the business press, and if the company is public, call your stockbroker and ask for still additional information. If possible, speak to someone at the firm before the interview, or if not, speak to someone at a competing firm. Clearly the more time you spend, the better. Even if you feel extremely pressed for time, you should set aside at least 12 hours for pre-interview research.

If you have been out of the job market for some time, don't be surprised if you find yourself tense during your first few interviews. It will probably happen every time you re-enter the market, not just when you seek your first job after getting out of school.

Tension is natural during an interview, but if you can be relaxed you will have an advantage over the competition. Knowing you have done a thorough research job should help you relax for an interview. Also make a list of questions that you think might be asked in an interview. Think out your answers carefully. Then practice reviewing them with a friend. Tape record your responses to the questions he/she raises in the role as interviewer. If you feel particularly unsure of your interviewing skills, arrange your first interviews at firms in which you are not very interested. (But remember it is common courtesy to seem excited about the possiblity of working for any firm at which you interview.) Then practice again on your own after these first few interviews. Go over each of the questions that you were asked.

How important is the proper dress for a job interview? Buying a complete wardrobe of Brooks Brothers pinstripes, donning new wing tip shoes and having your hair trimmed every morning is not enough to guarantee your obtaining a career position as an investment banker. But on the other hand, if you can't find a clean, conservative suit and a narrow tie, or won't take the time to polish your shoes and trim and wash your hair -- then you are just wasting your time by interviewing at all.

Very rarely will the final selection of candidates for a job opening be determined by dress. So don't spend a fortune on a new wardrobe. But be sure that your clothes are adequate. Men applying for any professional position should wear a suit; women should either wear a dress or a suit (not a pant suit.) Your clothes should be at least as formal or slightly more formal and more conservative than the position would suggest.

Top personal grooming is more important than finding the perfect clothes for a job interview. Careful grooming indicates both a sense of thoroughness and self-confidence.

Be sure that your clothes fit well and that they are immaculate. Hair must be neat and clean. Shoes should be newly polished. Women need to avoid excessive jewelry and excessive makeup. Men should be freshly shaven, even if the interview is late in the day.

Be complete. Everyone needs a watch and a pen and pad of paper (for taking notes.) Finally a briefcase or folder (containing extra copies of your resume) will help complete the look of professionalism.

Sometimes the interviewer will be running behind schedule. Don't be upset, be sympathetic. He/she might be under pressure to interview a lot of candidates and to quickly fill a demanding position. So be sure to come to your interview with good reading material to keep yourself occupied. This will help increase your patience and ease your tenseness.

The Interview

The very beginning of the interview is the most important part because it determines the rapport for the rest of it. Those first few moments are especially crucial. Do you smile when you meet? Do you establish enough eye contact, but not too much? Do you walk into the office with a self-assured and confident stride? Do you shake hands firmly? Do you make small talk easily without being garrulous? It is human nature to judge people by that first impression, so make sure it is a good one. But most of all, try to be yourself.

Often the interviewer will begin, after the small talk, by proceeding to tell you about the company, the division, the department, or perhaps, the position. Because of your detailed research, the information about the company will be repetitive for you and the interviewer would probably like nothing better than to avoid this regurgitation of the company biography. So if you can do so tactfully, indicate to the interviewer that you are very familiar with the firm. If he/she seems intent on providing you with background information, despite your hints, then acquiesce. But be sure to remain attentive. If you can manage to generate a brief discussion of the company or the industry at this point, without being forceful, great. It will help to further build rapport, underscore your interests and increase your impact.

Soon (if it didn't begin that way) the interviewer will begin the questions. This period of the interview falls into one of two categories (or somewhere in between): either a structured interview, where the interviewer has a prescribed set of questions to ask; or an unstructured interview, where the interviewer will ask only leading questions to get you to talk about yourself, your experiences and your goals. Try to sense as quickly as possible which direction the interviewer wishes to proceed and follow along in the direction he/she seems to be leading. This will make the interviewer feel more relaxed and in control of the situation.

SOME FAVORITE INTERVIEW QUESTIONS

Tell me about yourself...

Why did you leave your last job?

What excites you in your current job?

What are your career goals?

Where would you like to be in 5 years?

What are your greatest strengths?

What are your greatest weaknesses?

Why do you wish to work for this firm?

Where else are you seeking employment?

Why should we hire you?

Many of the questions will be similar to the ones that you were expecting and you will have prepared answers. Remember to keep attuned to the interviewer and make the length of your answers appropriate to the situation. If you are really unsure as to how detailed a response the interviewer is seeking, then ask. Query if he/she would prefer more details of a particular aspect.

As the interview progresses, the interviewer will probably mention what he/she considers to be the most important responsibilities of the position. If applicable, draw parallels between your experience and the demands of the position as seen by the interviewer. Describe your past experience in the same manner that you did on your resume: emphasizing results and achievements and not merely describing activities. If you listen carefully (listening is a very important part of the interviewing process) the interviewer might very well mention or imply the skills in terms of what he/she is seeking. But don't exaggerate. Be on the level.

Try not to cover too much ground during the first interview. This interview is often the toughest, with many candidates being screened out. If you are interviewing for a very competitive position, you will have to make an impression that will last. Focus on a few of your greatest strengths that are relevant to the position. Develop these points carefully, state them again in other words, and then try to summarize them briefly at the end of the interview.

Often the interviewer will pause towards the end and ask if you have any questions. Particularly in a structured interview, this might be the one chance to really show your knowledge of and interest in the firm. Have prepared a list of specific questions that are of real interest to you. Let your questions subtly show your research and your knowledge of the firm's activities. It is wise to have an extensive list of questions, as several of them may have already been answered during the interview.

Do not allow your opportunity to ask questions to become an interrogation. Avoid bringing your list of questions to the interview. And ask questions that you are fairly certain the interviewer can answer (remember how you feel when you cannot answer a question during an interview.)

Even if you are unable to determine the salary range beforehand, do not ask about it during the first interview. You can always ask about it later. Above all, don't ask about fringe benefits until you have been offered a position. (Then be sure to get all the details.) You should be able to determine the company's policy on fringe benefits relatively easily before the interview.

Try not to be negative about anything during the interview. (Particularly any past employer or any previous job.) Be cheerful. Everyone likes to work with someone who seems to be happy.

Don't let a tough question throw you off base. If you don't know the answer to a question, say so simply -- do not apologize. Just smile. Nobody can answer every question -- particularly some of the questions that are asked in job interviews.

Before your first interview, you may have been able to determine how many interviews the employer usually has for positions at your level. (Of

YOU'RE FIRED!!

You are not the first and will not be the last to go through this traumatic experience. Thousands of professionals are fired every week. Remember, being fired is not a reflection on you as a person. It is usually a reflection of your company's staffing needs and its perception of your recent job performance. Share the fact with your relatives and friends. Being fired is not something of which to be ashamed.

Don't start your job search with a flurry of unplanned activity. Start by choosing a strategy and working out a plan. Now is not the time for major changes in your life. If possible, remain in the same career and in the same geographical location, at least until you have been working again for a while. On the other hand, if the only industry for which you are trained is leaving, or is severely depressed in your area, then you should give prompt consideration to moving or switching careers.

Register for unemployment compensation immediately. A thorough job search could take months. After all, your employers have been contributing to unemployment insurance specifically for you ever since your first job. Don't be surprised to find other professionals collecting unemployment compensation as well. Unemployment compensation is for everybody who is between jobs.

Be prepared for the question, "Why were you fired?", during job interviews. Avoid mentioning you were fired while arranging interviews. Try especially hard not to speak negatively of your past employer and not to sound particularly worried about your status of being temporarily unemployed. But don't spend much time reflecting on why you were fired or how you might have avoided it. Look ahead. Think positively. And be sure to follow a careful plan during your job search.

course it may differ quite a bit within one firm.) Usually you can count on at least three or four interviews, although some firms, such as some of the professional partnerships, are well-known to give a minimum of six interviews for all professional postions.

Depending on what information you are able to obtain you might want to vary your strategy quite a bit from interview to interview. For instance if the first interview is a screening interview then try to have a few of your strengths really stand out. On the other hand, if later interviews are primarily with people who are in a position to veto your hiring, but not to push it forward (and few people are weeded out at these stages), then you should primarily focus on building rapport as opposed to reiterating and developing your key strengths.

If it looks as though your skills and background do not match the position your interviewer was hoping to fill, ask him or her if there is another division or subsidiary that perhaps could profit from your talents.

After The Interview

Write a follow-up letter immediately after the interview, while it is still fresh in the interviewer's mind. Then, if you have not heard from the interviewer within seven days, call him/her to stress your continued interest in the firm and the position and to request a second interview.

A parting word of advice. Again and again during your job search you will be rejected. You will be rejected when you apply for interviews. You will be rejected after interviews. For every job you finally receive you will probably have received a multitude of rejections. Don't let these rejections slow you down. Keep reminding yourself that the sooner you go out and get started on your job search and get those rejections flowing in, the closer you will be to obtaining the better job.

Resumes and Cover Letters

RESUMES AND COVER LETTERS

THIS SECTION CONTAINS:

1. Resume Preparation

2. Resume Format

3. Resume Content

4. Should You Hire A Resume Writer?

5. Cover Letters

6. Sample Resumes

7. General Model For A Cover Letter

8. Sample Cover Letters

9. General Model For A Follow-up Letter

RESUMES/OVERVIEW

When filling a position, a recruiter will often have 100 plus applicants, but time to interview only the 5 or 10 most promising ones. So he or she will have to reject most applicants after a brief skimming of their resume.

Unless you have phoned and talked to the recruiter -- which you should do whenever you can -- you will be chosen or rejected for an interview entirely on the basis of your resume and cover letter. So your resume must be outstanding. (But remember -- a resume is no substitute for a job search campaign. YOU must seek a job. Your resume is only one tool.)

RESUME PREPARATION

One page, usually.

Unless you have an unusually strong background with many years of experience and a large diversity of outstanding achievements, prepare a one page resume. Recruiters dislike long resumes.

8 1/2 x 11 Size

Recruiters often get resumes in batches of hundreds. If your resume is on small sized paper it is likely to get lost in the pile. If oversized, it is likely to get crumpled at the edges, and won't fit in their files.

Typesetting

Modern photocomposition typesetting gives you the clearest, sharpest image, a wide variety of type styles and effects such as italics, bold facing, and book-like justified margins. Typesetting is the best resume preparation process, but is also the most expensive.

Word Processing

The most flexible way to get your resume typed is on a good quality word processor. With word processing, you can make changes almost instantly because your resume will be stored on a magnetic disk and the computer will do all the re-typing automatically. A word processing service will usually offer you a variety of type styles in both regular and proportional spacing. You can have bold facing for emphasis, justified margins, and clear, sharp copies.

Typing

Household typewriters and office typewriters with nylon or other cloth ribbons are NOT good for typing the resume you will have printed. If you can't get word processing or typesetting, hire a professional with a high quality office typewriter with a plastic ribbon (usually called a "carbon ribbon.")

Printing

Find the best quality offset printing process available. DO NOT make your copies on an office photocopier. Only the personnel office may see the resume you mail. Everyone else may see only a copy of it. Copies of copies quickly become unreadable. Some professionally maintained, extra-high-quality photocopiers are of adequate quality, if you are in a rush. But top quality offset printing is best.

Proofread your resume

Whether you typed it yourself or had it written, typed, or typeset, mistakes on resumes can be embarrassing, particularly when something obvious such as your name is misspelled. No matter how much you paid someone else to type or write or typeset your resume, YOU lose if there is a mistake. So proofread it as carefully as possible. Get a friend to help you. Read your draft aloud as your friend checks the proof copy. Then have your friend read aloud while you check. Next, read it letter by letter to check spelling and punctuation.

If you are having it typed or typeset by a resume service or a printer, and you can't bring a friend or take the time during the day to proof it, pay for it and take it home. Proof it there and bring it back later to get it corrected and printed.

RESUME FORMAT

(See samples)

Basic data

Your name, phone number, and a complete address should be at the top of your resume. (If you are a university student, you should also show your home address and phone number.)

Separate your education and work experience

In general, list your experience first. If you have recently graduated, list your education first, unless your experience is more important than your education. (For example, if you have just graduated from a teaching school, have some business experience and are applying for a job in business you would list your business experience first.) If you have two or more years of college, you don't need to list high schools.

Reverse chronological order

To a recruiter your last job and your latest schooling are the most important. So put the last first and list the rest going back in time.

Show dates and locations

Put the dates of your employment and education on the left of the page. Put the names of the companies you worked for and the schools you attended a few spaces to the right of the dates. Put the city and state or city and country where you studied or worked to the right of the page.

Avoid sentences and large blocks of type

Your resume will be scanned, not read. Short, concise phrases are much more effective than long-winded sentences. Keep everything easy to find. Avoid paragraphs longer than six lines. Never go ten or more lines in a paragraph. If you have more than six lines of information about one job or school, put it in two or more paragraphs.

RESUME CONTENT

Be factual

In many companies, inaccurate information on a resume or other application material will get you fired as soon as the inaccuracy is discovered. Protect yourself.

Be positive

You are selling your skills and accomplishments in your resume. If you achieved something, say so. Put it in the best possible light. Don't hold back or be modest, no one else will. But don't exaggerate to the point of misrepresentation.

Be brief

Write down the important (and pertinent) things you have done, but do it in as few words as possible. The shorter your resume is, the more carefully it will be examined.

Work experience

Emphasize continued experience in a particular type of function or continued interest in a particular industry. De-emphasize irrelevant positions. Delete positions that you held for less than four months. (Unless you are a very recent college grad or still in school.)

Stress your results

Elaborate on how you contributed to your past employers. Did you increase sales, reduce costs, improve a product, implement a new program? Were you promoted?

**Mention relevant skills and
responsibilities**

Be specific. Slant your past accomplishments toward the type of position that you hope to obtain. Example: Do you hope to supervise people? Then state how many people, performing what function, you have supervised.

Education

Keep it brief if you have more than two years of career experience. Elaborate more if you have less experience. Mention degrees received and any honors or special awards. Note individual courses or research projects that might be relevant for employers. For instance, if you are a liberal arts major, be sure to mention courses in such areas as: accounting, statistics, computer programming, or mathematics.

Job objective?

Leave it out. Even if you are certain of exactly the type of job that you desire, the inclusion of a job objective might eliminate you from consideration for other positions that a recruiter feels are a better match for your qualifications.

Personal data

Keep it very brief. Two lines maximum. A one-word mention of commonly practiced activities such as golf, skiing, sailing, chess, bridge, tennis, etc. can prove to be good way to open up a conversation during an interview. Do not include your age, weight, height, etc.

SHOULD YOU HIRE A RESUME WRITER?

If you write reasonably well, there are some advantages to writing your resume yourself. To write it well, you will have to review your experience and figure out how to explain your accomplishments in clear, brief phrases. This will help you when you explain your work to interviewers.

If your write your resume, everything in it will be in your own words -- it will sound like you. It will say what you want it to say. And you will be much more familiar with the contents. If you are a good writer, know yourself well and have a good idea of what parts of your background employers are looking for, you may be able to write your own resume better than anyone else can. If you write your resume yourself, you should have someone who can be objective (preferably not a close relative) review it with you.

When should you have your resume professionally written?

If you have difficulty writing in Resume Style (which is quite unlike normal written language), if you are unsure of which parts of your background you should emphasize, or if you think your resume would make your case better if it did not follow the standard form outlined here or in a book on resumes, then you should have it professionally written.

There are two reasons even some professional resume writers we know have had their resumes written with the help of fellow professionals. First, when they need the help of someone who can be objective about their background, and second, when they want an experienced sounding board to help focus their thoughts.

If you decide to hire a resume writer

The best way to choose a writer is by reputation -- the recommendation of a friend, a personnel director, your school placement officer or someone else knowledgeable in the field.

You should ask, "If I'm not satisfied with what you write, will you go over it with me and change it?"

You should ask, "How long has the person who will write my resume been writing resumes?"

There is no sure relation between price and quality, except that you are unlikely to get a good writer for less than $50 for an uncomplicated resume and you shouldn't have to pay more than $300 unless your experience is very extensive or complicated. There will be additional charges for printing.

Few resume services will give you a firm price over the phone, simply because some people's resumes are too complicated and take too long to do at any predetermined price. Some services will quote you a price that applies to almost all of their customers. Be sure to do some comparative shopping. Obtain a firm price before you engage their services and find out how expensive minor changes will be.

COVER LETTERS

Always mail a cover letter with your resume. In a cover letter you can show an interest in the company that you can't show in a resume. You can point out one or two skills or accomplishments the company can put to good use.

Make it personal

The more personal you can get, the better. If someone known to the person you are writing has recommended that you contact the company, get permission to include his/her name in the letter. If you have the name of a person to send the letter to, make sure you have the name spelled correctly and address it directly to that person. Be sure to put the person's name and title on both the letter and envelope. This will ensure that your letter will get through to the proper person, even if a new person now occupies this position. But even if you are addressing it to the "Personnel Director" or the "Hiring Partner," send a letter.

Type cover letters in full. Don't try the cheap and easy ways like photocopying the body of your letter and typing in the inside address and salutation. You will give the impression that you are mailing to a multitude of companies and have no particular interest in any one. Have your letters fully typed and signed with a pen.

Phone

Precede or follow your mailing with a phone call.

Bring extra copies of your resume to the interview

If the person interviewing you doesn't have your resume, be prepared. Carry copies of your own. Even if you have already forwarded your resume, be sure to take extra copies to the interview, as someone other than the interviewer(s) might now have the first copy you sent.

Chronological Resume
(Prepared on a Word Processor and Laser Printer.)

WALLACE R. RECTORIAN
412 Maple Court
Seattle, WA 98404
206/555-6584

EXPERIENCE

1984-present   THE CENTER COMPANY, Seattle, WA
Systems Analyst, design systems for the manufacturing unit. Specifically, physical inventory, program specifications, studies of lease buy decisions, selection of hardware the outside contractors and inside users. Wrote On-Site Computer Terminal Operators Manual. Adapted product mix problems to the LASPSP (Logistical Alternative Product Synthesis Program).

As *Industrial Engineer* from February 1984 to February 1986, computerized system design. Evaluated manufacturing operations operator efficiency productivity index and budget allocations. Analyzed material waste and recommended solutions.

ADDITIONAL EXPERIENCE

1980-1984   *Graduate Research Assistant* at New York State Institute of Technology.

1978-1980   *Graduate Teaching Assistant* at Salem State University.

EDUCATION

1982-1984   NEW YORK STATE INSTITUTE OF TECHNOLOGY, Albany, NY
M.S. in Operations Research. GPA: 3.6. Graduate courses included Advanced Location and Queueing Theories, Forecasting, Inventory and Material Flow Systems, Linear and Nonlinear Determination Models, Engineering Economics and Integer Programming.

1980-1982   M.S. in Information and Computer Sciences. GPA: 3.8
Curriculum included Digital Computer Organization & Programming. Information Structure & Process. Mathematical Logic, Computer Systems, Logic Design and Switching Theory.

1976-1980   SALEM STATE UNIVERSITY, Salem, OR
B.A. in Mathematics. GPA: 3.6.

AFFILIATIONS

Member of the American Institute of Computer Programmers, Association for Computing Machinery and the Operations Research Society of America.

PERSONAL

Married, three dependents, able to relocate.

Chronological Resume
(Prepared on a Word Processor and Laser Printer.)

DAMIEN W. PINCKNEY

U.S. Address: Jamaican Address:
15606 Center Street   Oskarrataan Building, Room 1234
Bottineau, ND 58777   Hedonism II
701/555-9320   Negril, Jamaica
                                                    809/555-6634

Experience

1984-present   **HEDONISM II**, Negril, Jamaica
Resident Engineer for this publicly owned resort with main offices in
Kingston. Responsibilities include:

Maintaining electrical generating and distribution equipment.

Supervising an eight-member staff in maintenance of refrigeration equipment, power and light generators, water purification plant, and general
construction machinery.

1982-1984   **NEGRIL BEACH HOTEL**, Negril Beach, Jamaica
Resident Engineer for a privately held resort, assigned total responsibility
for facility generating equipment.

Directed maintenance, operation and repair of diesel generating equipment.

1980-1982   Directed overhaul of turbo generating equipment in two Mid-Western localities
and assisted in overhaul of a turbo generating unit in Mexico.

1975-1980   **CAPITAL CITY ELECTRIC**, Washington, DC
Service Engineer for the power generation service division of this regional
power company, supervised the overhaul, maintenance and repair of large
generators and associated auxiliary equipment.

Education

1972-1975   **FRANKLIN INSTITUTE**, Baltimore, MD
Awarded a degree of Associate of Engineering. Concentration in Mechanical Power Engineering Technology.

Personal   Willing to travel and relocate.
Interested in sailing, scuba diving, deep sea fishing.

References available upon request.

Functional Resume
(Prepared on a Word Processor and Letter-Quality Printer.)

Michelle Hughes
430 Miller's Crossing
Essex Junction, VT 05452
802/555-9354

Solid background in plate making, separations, color matching, background definition, printing, mechanicals, color corrections, and supervision of personnel. A highly motivated manager and effective communicator. Proven ability to:

* **Create Commercial Graphics**
* **Produce Embossing Drawings**
* **Color Separate**
* **Analyze Consumer Acceptance**

* **Meet Graphic Deadlines**
* **Control Quality**
* **Resolve Printing Problems**
* **Expedite Printing Operations**

Qualifications

Printing: Black and white and color. Can judge acceptability of color reproduction by comparing it with original. Can make four or five color corrections on all media. Have long developed ability to restyle already reproduced four-color artwork. Can create perfect tone for black and white match fill-ins for resume cover letters.

Customer Relations: Work with customers to assure specifications are met and customers are satisfied. Can guide work through entire production process and strike a balance between technical printing capabilities and need for customer approval.

Management: Schedule work to meet deadlines. Direct staff in production procedures. Maintain quality control from inception of project through final approval for printing.

Specialties: Make silk screen overlays for a multitude of processes. Velo bind, GBC bind, perfect bind. Have knowledge to prepare posters flyers, and personalized stationery.

Personnel Supervision: Foster an atmosphere that encourages highly talented artists to balance high level creativity with a maximum of production. Meet or beat production deadlines. Am continually instructing new employees, apprentices and students in both artistry and technical operations.

Experience

Professor of Graphic Arts, University of Vermont, Burlington, VT (1977-present).
Assistant Production Manager, Artsign Digraphics, Burlington, VT (1981-present) Part time.

Education

Massachusetts Conservatory of Art, PhD 1977
University of Massachusetts, B.A. 1974

Chronological Resume
(Prepared on an Office-Quality Typewriter.)

Lorraine Avakian
70 Monback Avenue
Oshkosh, WI 54901
Phone: 414/555-4629

Business Experience

1984-1991 **NATIONAL PACKAGING PRODUCTS**, Princeton, WI

1989-1991 **District Sales Manager.** Improved 28-member sales group from a company rank in the bottom thirty percent to the top twenty percent. Complete responsibility for personnel, including recruiting, hiring and training. Developed a comprehensive sales improvement program and advised its implementation in eight additional sales districts.

1986-1988 **Marketing Associate.** Responsible for research, analysis, and presentation of marketing issues related to long-term corporate strategy. Developed marketing perspective for capital investment opportunities and acquisition candidates, which was instrumental in finalizing decisions to make two major acquisitions and to construct a $35 million canning plant.

1984-1986 **Salesperson, Paper Division.** Responsible for a four-county territory in central Wisconsin. Increased sales from $700,000 to over $1,050,000 annually in a 15 month period. Developed six new accounts with incremental sales potential of $800,000. Only internal candidate selected for new marketing program.

AMERICAN PAPER PRODUCTS, INC., Oshkosh, WI
1983-1984 **Sales Trainee.** Completed the intensive six month training program and was promoted to salesperson status. Received the President's Award for superior performance in the sales training program.

HENDUKKAR SPORTING GOODS, INC., Oshkosh, WI
1983 **Assistant Store Manager.** Supervised six employees on the evening shift. Handled accounts receivable.

Education
1977-1982 **BELOIT COLLEGE**, Beloit, WI
Received Bachelor of Science Degree in Business Administration in June 1982. Varsity Volleyball. Financed 50% of educational costs through part-time and co-op program employment.

Personal Background
Able to relocate; Excellent health; Active in community activities.

Chronological Resume
(Prepared on a Word Processor and Laser Printer.)

Melvin Winter
43 Aspen Wall Lane
Wheaton, IL 60512
312/555-6923 (home)
312/555-3000 (work)

RELATED EXPERIENCE
1982-Present GREAT LAKES PUBLISHING COMPANY, Chicago, IL
Operations Supervisor (1986-present)
in the Engineering Division of this major trade publishing house, responsible for maintaining on line computerized customer files, title files, accounts receivable, inventory and sales files.

Organize department activities, establish priorities and train personnel. Provide corporate accounting with monthly reports of sales, earned income from journals, samples, inventory levels/value and sales and tax data. Divisional sales average $3 million annually.

Senior Customer Service Representative (1984-1986)
in the Construction Division. Answered customer service inquiries regarding orders and accounts receivable, issued return and shortage credits and expedited special sales orders for direct mail and sales to trade schools.

Customer Service Representative (1982-1983)
in the International Division. Same duties as for construction division except that sales were to retail stores and universities in Europe.

1980-1982 B. DALTON, BOOKSELLER, Salt Lake City, UT
Assistant Manager of this retail branch of a major domestic book seller, maintained all paperback inventories at necessary levels, deposited receipts daily and created window displays.

EDUCATION
1976-1980 UNIVERSITY OF MAINE, Orono, ME
Awarded a degree of Bachelor of Arts in French Literature.

LANGUAGES
Fluent in French. Able to write in French, German and Spanish.

PERSONAL
Willing to travel and relocate, particularly in Europe.

References available upon request.

General Model for a Cover Letter

```
                                        Your Address
                                        Date


Contact Person Name
Title
Company
Address


Dear Mr./Ms._____:


Immediately explain why your background makes you the best can-
didate for the position that you are applying for. Keep the
first paragraph short and hard-hitting.

Detail what you could contribute to this company. Show how
your qualifications will benefit this firm. Remember to keep
this letter short; few recruiters will read a cover letter
longer than half a page.

Describe your interest in the corporation. Subtly emphasize
your knowledge about this firm (the result of your research ef-
fort) and your familiarity with the industry. It is common
courtesy to act extremely eager to work for any company that
you interview.

In the closing paragraph you should specifically request an in-
terview. Include your phone number and the hours when you can
be reached. Alternatively, you might prefer to mention that
you will follow up with a phone call (to arrange an interview
at a mutually convenient time within the next several days).



                                        Sincerely,

                                        (signature)

                                        Your full name (typed)
```

Cover Letter

49 Chinwick Circle
Houston, TX 77031
October 5, 1993

Ms. Ruth Herman-George
V.P./Director of Personnel
Holly Rock Fire Insurance Group
444 Rolling Cloud Lane, Suite 24
Houston, TX 77035

Dear Ms. Herman-George:

I am a career-oriented individual who can successfully provide technical direction and training to pension analysts in connection with FKLE system.

My major and most recent background is directly involved in the administration of pension and profit sharing plans with TRMZ. Furthermore, my extensive experience both as a Group Pension Pre-Scale Underwriter and as a Pension Underwriter involves data processing knowledge and overall pension administration.

A prime function of mine is decision making with reference to group pension business. You specifically seek an idividual who can recommend changes and/or new procedures of plan administration and maintenance plus assistance in development of pension administration kits for use by the field force at Holly Rock. I feel that I possess the ability to fulfill your need dramatically.

I would welcome the practical opportunity to work directly with general agents and plan trustees in qualifying, revising and requalifying pension and profit sharing plans required by TRMZ. You will note in my resume my background in working with others in both an advisory and shirt-sleeve capacity.

I look forward to hearing from you.

Sincerely,

Henry Washington

Henry Washington

Cover Letter

411 Looksee Avenue
Apt. 449
Medford, MA 02139
March 15, 1993

Mr. Benjamin Deiver
Sales Manager
Yankee Ski Products
456 Pillbox Lane
Denver, CO 80201

Dear Mr. Deiver:

I seek a position as a sales representative with Yankee Ski Products and I offer, in return, thorough industry experience and more than eleven years of solid practical background in sales.

As a sample of sales achievement, I increased my personal monthly gross sales volume to a point where it tripled the combined sales of three other full-time representatives for one ski manufacturer. Also, I have won numerous international and domestic sales awards.

As an experienced sales representative, I have succeeded in improving area or regional sales by employing a combination of aggressiveness, enthusiasm, and persistence, and I have been able to bring out these traits in those whom I have hired and trained in my capacity as National Sales Instructor for two companies.

I feel that your new line of competition skis offers an unbeatable price/performance combination for the serious racer. I am firmly convinced that I can improve your market penetration in the lucrative Upstate New York area at least to a top five position.

I am an avid skier. As such, I am familiar with not only the technical terms involved, but with the types of equipment available and the extent to which it is marketed.

I look forward to hearing from you.

Sincerely,

Christina Harges
Christina Harges

General Model for a Follow-Up Letter

```
                                        Your Address
                                        Date

Contact Person Name
Title
Company
Address

Dear Mr./Ms._____:

Remind the interviewer of the position for which you were in-
terviewed, as well as the date. Thank him/her for the inter-
view.

Confirm your interest in the opening and the organization. Use
specifics to emphasize both that you have researched the firm
in detail and considered how you would fit into the company
and the position.

Like in your cover letter, emphasize one or two of you
strongest qualifications and slant them toward the various
points that the interviewer considered the most important for
the position. Keep the letter brief, a half-page is plenty.

If appropriate, close with a suggestion for further action,
such as a desire to have additional interviews. Mention your
phone number and the hours that you can best be reached. Alter-
natively, you may prefer to mention that you will follow up
with a phone call in several days.


                                        Sincerely yours,

                                        (signature)

                                        Your full name (typed)
```

PART TWO:
OCCUPATION PROFILES

Jobs In Each Industry

JOBS IN EACH INDUSTRY

The following chapter includes descriptions of many of the most common occupations, with an emphasis on those that have especially strong growth outlooks for the 1990's. For each position, you will find a brief description of what the position entails, the background or qualification you would need for entering and advancing in that occupation, the salary expectations for various levels within the occupational category, and a forecast of the job's growth potential for the 1990's.

The occupations listed are as follows:

Accountant/Auditor
Actuary
Administrator
Advertising Worker
Architect
Attorney
Bank Officer/Manager
Biochemist
Blue-Collar Worker Supervisor
Buyer/Merchandise Manager
Chemist
Claims Representative
Commercial Artist
Data Processing Specialist
Dietician/Nutritionist
Draftsperson
Economist
Engineer
Financial Analyst
Food Technologist
Forester
Geographer
Geologist/Geophysicist
Hotel Manager/Assistant Manager
Industrial Designer
Insurance Agent/Broker
Manager
Manaufacturer's Sales Worker
Personnel and Labor Relations Specialist
Physicist
Public Relations Worker

Purchasing Agent
Quality Control Supervisor
Reporter/Editor
Securities and Financial Services
Sales Representative
Statistician
Systems Analyst
Technical Writer/Editor
Underwriter

ACCOUNTANT/AUDITOR

DESCRIPTION:

Accountants prepare and analyze financial reports that furnish important financial information. Four major fields are public, management, and government accounting, and internal auditing. Public accountants have their own businesses or work for accounting firms. Management accountants, also called industrial or private accountants, handle the financial records of their company. Government accountants examine the records of government agencies and audit private businesses and individuals whose dealings are subject to government regulation. Accountants often concentrate on one phase of accounting. For example, many public accountants may specialize in auditing, tax, or estate planning. Others specialize in management consulting and give advice on a variety of matters. Management accountants provide the financial information executives need to make sound business decisions. They may work in areas such as taxation, budgeting, costs, or investments. Internal auditing, a specialization within management accounting, is rapidly growing in importance. Internal auditors examine and ensure efficient and economical operation. Government accountants are often Internal Revenue Service agents or are involved in financial management and budget administration.

About 60 percent of all accountants do management accounting. An additional 25 percent are engaged in public accounting through independent firms. Other accountants work for government, and some teach in colleges and universities. Accountants and auditors are found in all business, industrial, and governmental organizations.

BACKGROUND AND QUALIFICATIONS:

Although many graduates of business schools are successful, most public accounting and business firms require applicants for accountant and internal auditor positions to have at least a BA in Accounting or a closely related field. Many employers prefer those with a Master's degree in Accounting. Most large employers prefer applicants who are familiar with computers and their applications in accounting and internal auditing.

Previous experience in accounting can help an applicant get a job. Many colleges offer students an opportunity to gain experience through summer or part-time internship programs conducted by public accounting firms. Such training is invaluable in gaining permanent employment in the field.

Professional recognition through certification or licensing also is extremely valuable. Anyone working as a certified public accountant (CPA) must hold a certificate issued by a state board of accountancy. All states use the four-part Uniform CPA Exam, prepared by the American Institute of Certified Public Accountants, to establish certification. The CPA exam is very rigorous, and candidates are not required to pass all four parts at once. Most states require applicants to have some public accounting experience for a CPA certificate, and those with BA's often need two years of experience. New trends require the candidate to have a BA plus 30 additional semester hours.

The Institute of Internal Auditors confers the Certified Internal Auditor (CIA) certificate upon graduates from accredited colleges and universities who have completed three years internal auditing and who have passed a four-part exam. The National Association of Accountants (NAA) confers the Certificate in Management Accounting (CMA) upon candidates who pass a series of uniform exams and meet specific educational and professional standards. A growing number of states require both CPA's and licensed public accountants to complete a certain number of hours of continuing education before licenses can be renewed. Increasingly, accountants are studying computer programming so they can adapt accounting procedures to data processing.

Junior public accountants usually start by assisting with auditing work for several clients. They may advance to intermediate positions with greater responsibility in one or two years, and to senior positions within another few years. Those who deal successfully with top industry executives often become supervisors, managers, or partners, or transfer to executive positions in private firms. Beginning management accountants often start as ledger accountants, junior internal auditors, or as trainees for technical accounting positions. They may advance to chief plant accountant, chief cost accountant, budget director, or manager of internal auditing. Some become controllers, treasurers, financial vice-presidents, or corporation presidents.

OUTLOOK:

Employment of accountants and auditors is expected to grow much faster than the average for all occupations through the year 2000 due to the key role these workers play in the management of all types of businesses. Although increased demand will generate many new jobs, most openings win result from the need to replace workers who leave the occupation or retire. While accountants and auditors tend to leave the profession at a lower rate than members of most other occupations, replacement needs will be substantial because the occupation is large. Accountants rarely lose their jobs when other workers are laid off during hard economic times. Financial information must be developed and tax reports prepared regardless of the state of the economy.

ACTUARY

DESCRIPTION:

Actuaries design insurance and pension plans that can be maintained on a sound financial basis. They assemble and analyze statistics to calculate probabilities of death, sickness, injury, disability, unemployment, retirement, and property loss from accident, theft, fire, and other hazards. Actuaries use this information to determine the expected insured loss. The actuary calculates premium rates and determines policy contract provision for each type of insurance offered. Most actuaries specialize in either life and health insurance, or property and liability (casualty) insurance; a growing number specialize in pension plans. About two-thirds of all actuaries work for private insurance companies, the majority in life insurance. Consulting firms and rating bureaus employ about one-fifth of all actuaries. Other actuaries work for private organizations administering independent pension and welfare plans.

BACKGROUND AND EXPERIENCE:

A good educational background for a beginning job in a large life or casualty insurance company is a Bachelor's degree in Mathematics or Statistics; a degree in Actuarial Science is preferred. Courses in accounting, computer science, economics, and insurance also are useful. Of equal importance, however, is the need to pass one or more of the exams offered by professional actuarial societies. Three societies sponsor programs leading to full professional status in the specialty. The Society of Actuaries gives nine actuarial exams for the life and health insurance, and pension fields; The Casualty Actuarial Society gives 10 exams for the property and liability fields; and the American Society of Pension Actuaries gives nine exams covering the pension field. Actuaries are encouraged to complete the entire series of exams as soon as possible; completion generally takes from five to ten years. Actuaries who complete five exams in either the life insurance segment of the pension series, or seven exams in the casualty series are awarded "associate" membership in their society. Those who have passed an entire series receive full membership and the title "Fellow".

Beginning actuaries often rotate among different jobs to learn various actuarial operations and to become familiar with different phases of insurance work. At first, their work may be routine, such as preparing tabulations for actuarial tables or reports. As they gain experience, they may supervise clerks, prepare correspondence and reports, and do research. Advancement to more responsible positions such as assistant, associate, or chief actuary depends largely on job performance and the number of actuarial exams passed. Many actuaries, because of their broad knowledge of insurance and related fields, are selected for administrative positions in other company activities, particularly in underwriting, accounting, or data processing. Many advance to top executive positions.

OUTLOOK:

Employment of actuaries is expected to grow much faster than the average for all occupations through the year 2000. Most job openings, however, are expected to arise each year to replace actuaries who transfer to other occupations, or retire. Job opportunities should be favorable for college graduates who have passed at least two actuarial exams while still in school and have a strong mathematical and statistical background.

ADMINISTRATOR

DESCRIPTION:

Administrators perform a wide variety of office paperwork tasks. These tasks might range from preparing a summary of sales activity to filing and retrieving information. A lower-level administrator might serve primarily as a typist, office machine operator, or secretary, being closely supervised by an office superior. An upper-level administrator might supervise the work of many office workers and be responsible for a broad range of office duties that support an organization's activities.

BACKGROUND AND QUALIFICATIONS:

Because of the broad range of duties and responsibilities of administrators at different levels or within different organizations, the actual job and its requisite background and experience may vary greatly from one firm to the next, and from one position to the next. However, all but the highest managerial levels of administrative work require strong office skills, such as fast and accurate typing and the ability to prepare business correspondence. In larger organizations with more complex office tasks, a college background is becoming an increasingly valuable asset. Also, experience or familiarity with computers, word processors, or data processing equipment greatly improves an applicant's employability and chances for promotion.

OUTLOOK:

Despite the nearly universal use of computer and word processing automation in the office, administrative positions are still expected to offer above average growth. Also, with many new entrants to the job market trying to obtain junior managerial jobs and similar posts, administrative positions are likely to be less competitive than many other types of jobs. Administrators are found in all industries, but especially in banking, insurance, utilities, and other companies with a high volume of paperwork.

ADVERTISING WORKER

DESCRIPTION:

There are several different occupations commonly associated with the field of advertising. Advertising managers direct the advertising program of the business for which they work. They determine the size of the advertising budget, the type of ad and the medium to use, and what advertising agency, if any, to employ. Managers who decide to employ an agency work closely with the advertising agencies to develop advertising programs for client firms and individuals. Copywriters develop the text and headlines to be used in the ads. Media directors negotiate contracts for advertising for advertising space or air time. Production managers and their assistants arrange to have the ad printed for publication, filmed for television, or recorded for radio.

BACKGROUND AND QUALIFICATIONS:

Most employers prefer college graduates. Some employers seek persons with degrees in advertising with heavy emphasis on marketing, business, and journalism; others prefer graduates with a liberal arts background; some employers place little emphasis on the type of degree. Opportunities for advancement in this field generally are excellent for creative, talented, and hard-working people. For example, copywriters and account executives may advance to more responsible work in their specialties, or to managerial jobs if they demonstrate ability in dealing with clients. Some especially capable employees may become partners in an existing agency, or they may establish their own agency.

OUTLOOK:

Employment of advertising managers is expected to increase faster than the average for all occupations through the year 2000 as increasingly intense domestic and foreign competition in products and services offered to consumers requires greater marketing and promotional efforts. In addition to rapid growth, many job openings will occur each year to replace managers who move into the top positions or retire. However, the ample supply of experienced professional and technical personnel and recent college graduates seeking these management positions may result in substantial job competition.

ARCHITECT

DESCRIPTION:

Architects provide a wide variety of professional services to individuals, organizations, corporations, or government agencies planning a building project. Architects are involved in all phases of development of a building or project, from the initial discussion of general ideas through completion of construction. Their duties require a variety of skills, including design, engineering, managerial, and supervisory.

The architect and client first discuss the purposes, requirements, and cost of a project. The architect then prepares schematic drawings that show the scale and the mechanical and structural relationships of the building. If the schematic drawings are accepted, the architect develops a final design showing the floor plans and the structural details of the project.

Architects also specify the building materials and, in some cases, the interior furnishings. In all cases, the architect must ensure that the structure's design and specifications conform to local and state building codes, zoning laws, fire regulations, and other ordinances. After all drawings are completed, the architect assists the client in selecting a contractor and negotiating the construction contract. As construction proceeds, the architect visits the building site from time to time to ensure that the contractor is following the design using the specified materials.

Besides designing structures, architects may also help in selecting building sites, preparing cost and land-use studies, and long-range planning for site development. When working on large projects or for large architectural firms, architects often specialize in one phase of work, such as designing or administering construction contracts. This often requires working with engineers, urban planners, landscape architects, and others.

Most architects work for architectural firms or for builders, real estate firms, or other businesses that have large construction programs. Some work for governmental agencies. Although found in many areas, a large proportion of architects are employed in seven cities: Boston, Chicago, Los Angeles, New York, Philadelphia, San Francisco, and Washington, DC.

BACKGROUND AND QUALIFICATIONS:

Every state requires individuals to be licensed before they may call themselves architects, or contract for providing architectural services. To qualify for the licensing exam, a person must have either a Bachelor of Architecture degree followed by three years of acceptable practical experience in an architect's office, or a Master of Architecture degree followed by two years of experience. As a substitute for formal training, most states accept additional experience (usually 12 years) and successful completion of a qualifying test for admission to the licensing examination. Many architectural school graduates work in the field although they are not licensed. However, a registered architect is required to take legal responsibility for all work. New graduates usually begin as drafters for architectural firms, where they prepare architectural drawings and make models of structures under the direction of a registered architect. After several years of experience, they may advance to Chief or Senior Drafter responsible for all major details of a set of working drawings, and for supervising other drafters. Others may work as designers, construction contract administrators, or specification writers who prepare documents that specify the building materials, their method of installation, the quality of finishes, required tests, and many other related details.

OUTLOOK:

Employment of architects is expected to rise faster than the average for all occupations through the year 2000, although growth in employment will be slower than in recent years; however, demand for architects is highly dependent upon the level of construction, particularly of non-residential structures such as office buildings and shopping centers. Although rapid growth in this area is expected, construction is sensitive to cyclical changes in the economy. During recessions or slow periods for construction, architects will face competition for job openings or clients, and layoffs may occur.

ATTORNEY

DESCRIPTION:

Certain activities are common to nearly every attorney's work. Probably the most fundamental is interpretation of the law. Every attorney, whether representing the defendant in a murder trial, or the plaintiff in a lawsuit, combines an understanding of the relevant laws with knowledge of the facts in the case, to determine how the first affects the second. Based on this determination, the attorney decides what action would best serve the interests of the client.

A significant number specialize in one branch of law, such as corporate, criminal, labor, patent, real estate, tax, admiralty, probate, or international law. Communications lawyers, for example, may represent radio and television stations in their dealings with the Federal Communications Commission in such matters as preparing and filing license renewal applications, employment reports, and other documents required by the FCC on a regular basis. Lawyers representing public utilities before state and federal regulatory agencies handle matters involving utility rates. They develop strategy, arguments, and testimony, prepare cases for presentation, and argue the case. These attorneys also inform clients about changes in regulations and give advice about the legality of certain actions.

A single client may employ a lawyer full time. Known as House Counsel, this lawyer usually advises a company about legal questions that arise from business activities. Such questions might involve patents, governments regulations, a business contract with another company, or a collective bargaining agreement with a union. Some attorneys use their legal background in administrative or managerial positions in various departments of large corporations. A transfer from a corporation's legal department to another department is often viewed as a way to gain administrative experience and rise in the ranks of management. People may also use their legal background as journalists, management consultants, financial analysts, insurance claim adjusters, real estate appraisers, lobbyists, tax collectors, probation officers, and credit investigators.

BACKGROUND AND QUALIFICATIONS:

To practice law in the courts of any state, a person must be admitted to its bar. Applicants for admission to the bar must pass a written examination; however, a few states drop this requirement for graduates from its own law schools. Lawyers who have been admitted to the bar in one state may be admitted in another without taking an examination if they meet the state's standard of good moral character and have a specified period of legal experience. Federal courts and agencies set their own qualifications for those practicing before them. To qualify for the bar examination in most states, an applicant must complete at least three years of college, and graduate from a law school approved by the American Bar Association

OUTLOOK:

Rapid growth in the nation's requirements for lawyers is expected to bring job openings into rough balance with the relatively stable number of law school graduates each year and result in an easing of competition for jobs through the year 2000. During the 1970's, the annual number of law school graduates more than doubled, even outpacing the rapid growth of jobs. Although graduates with superior academic records from well-regarded law schools continued to enjoy excellent opportunities, most graduates encountered increasingly keen competition for jobs. Growth in the yearly number of law school graduates has tapered off during the 1980's, but, nevertheless, the number remains at a level high enough to tax the economy's capacity to absorb them. The number of law school graduates is expected to continue to remain near its present level through the year 2000, allowing employment growth to bring the job market for lawyers back into balance.

Employment of lawyers has grown very rapidly since the early 1970's, and is expected to continue to grow much faster than the average for all occupations through the year 2000. Increased population and growing business activity help sustain the strong demand for attorneys. This demand also will be spurred by growth of legal action in such areas as employee benefits, consumer protection, the environment, and safety, and an anticipated increase in the use of legal services by middle-income groups through legal clinics and prepaid legal service programs.

Turnover of jobs in this occupation is low because its members are well paid and enjoy considerable social status, and a substantial educational investment is required for entry. Nevertheless, most job openings will stem from the need to replace lawyers who transfer to other occupations or retire.

BANK OFFICER/MANAGER

DESCRIPTION:

Because banks offer a broad range of services, a wide choice of careers is available. Loan officers may handle installment, commercial, real estate, or agricultural loans. To evaluate loan applications properly, officers need to be familiar with economics, production, distribution, merchandising, and commercial law, as well as have a knowledge of business operations and financial analysis. Bank officers in trust management must have knowledge of financial planning and investment research for estate and trust administration. Operations officers plan, coordinate, and control the work flow, update systems, and strive for administrative efficiency. Careers in bank operations include electronic data processing manager and other positions involving internal and customer services. A correspondent bank officer is responsible for relations with other banks; a branch manager, for all functions of a branch office; and an international officer, for advising customers with financial dealings abroad. A working knowledge of a foreign country's financial system, trade relations, and economic conditions is beneficial to those interested in international banking. Other career fields for bank officers are auditing, economics, personnel administration, public relations, and operations research.

BACKGROUND AND QUALIFICATIONS:

Bank officers and management positions generally are filled by management trainees, and occasionally by promoting outstanding bank clerks and tellers. A Business Administration degree with concentrations in finance or a liberal arts curriculum, including accounting, economics, commercial law, political science, or statistics, serves as excellent preparation for officer trainee positions. In large banks that have special training programs, promotions may occur more quickly. For a senior officer position, however, an employee usually needs many years of experience. Although experience, ability, and leadership are emphasized for promotion, advancement may be accelerated by special study. The American Bankers Association (ABA) offers courses, publications, and other training aids to officers in every phase of banking. The American Institute of Banking, an arm of the ABA, has long filled the same educational need among bank support personnel.

OUTLOOK:

Employment of financial managers is expected to increase about as fast as the average for all occupations through the year 2000. Expanding automation - such as use of computers for electronic funds transmission and for data and information processing - may make financial managers more productive. However, the growing need for skilled financial management in the face of increasing domestic and foreign competition, changing laws regarding taxes and other financial matters, and greater emphasis on accurate reporting of financial data should spur demand for financial managers. New jobs will also be created by the increasing variety and complexity of services - including financial planning - offered by financial institutions. However, most job openings will result from the need to replace those who transfer to other fields or retire.

BIOCHEMIST

DESCRIPTION:

Biochemists study the chemical composition and behavior of living things. They often study the effects of food, hormones, or drugs on various organisms. The methods and techniques of biochemists are applied in areas such as medicine and agriculture. More than three out of four biochemists work in basic and applied research activities. Some biochemists combine research with teaching in colleges and universities. A few work in industrial production and testing activities. About one-half of all biochemists work for colleges or universities, and about one-fourth for private industry, primarily in companies manufacturing drugs, insecticides, and cosmetics. Some biochemists work for non-profit research institutes and foundations; others for federal, state, and local government agencies. A few self-employed biochemists are consultants to industry and government.

BACKGROUND AND QUALIFICATIONS:

The minimum educational requirement for many beginning jobs as a biochemist, especially in research and teaching, is an advanced degree. A PhD is a virtual necessity for persons who hope to contribute significantly to biochemical research and advance to many management or administrative jobs. A BS in Biochemistry, Biology, or Chemistry may qualify some persons for entry jobs as research assistants or technicians. Graduates with advanced degrees may begin their careers as teachers or researchers in colleges or universities. In private industry, most begin in research jobs, and with experience may advance to positions in which they plan and supervise research.

OUTLOOK:

Employment of biochemists is expected to increase about as fast as the average for all occupations through the year 2000. Most growth will be in private industry, primarily in genetic and biotechnical research and in production - using newly developed biological methods. Efforts to preserve the environment should also result in growth.

Biochemists are less likely to lose their jobs during recessions than those in many other occupations since most are employed on long-term research projects or in agriculture, activities which are not much affected by economic fluctuations.

BLUE-COLLAR WORKER SUPERVISOR

DESCRIPTION:

Supervisors direct the activities of other employees and frequently ensure that millions of dollars worth of equipment and materials are used properly and efficiently. While blue-collar worker supervisors are most commonly known as foremen or forewomen, they also have many other titles. In the textile industry, they are referred to as second hands; on ships, they are known as boatswains, and in the construction industry, they are often called overseers, strawbosses, or gang leaders. Supervisors make work schedules and keep production and employee records. They must use judgement in planning and must allow for unforeseen problems such as absent workers, or machine breakdowns. Teaching employees safe work habits and enforcing safety rules and regulations are among other supervisory responsibilities. Supervisors also may demonstrate timesaving or laborsaving techniques to workers, and train new employees. Worker supervisors tell their subordinates about company plans and policies; recommend good workers for wage increases, awards, or promotions; and deal with poor workers by issuing warnings or recommending that they be fired. In companies where employees belong to labor unions, supervisors meet with union representatives to discuss work problems and grievances. They must know the provisions of labor management contracts and run their operations according to these agreements.

BACKGROUND AND QUALIFICATIONS:

When choosing supervisors, employers generally look for experience, skill and leadership qualities. Most supervisors rise through the ranks; however, a growing number of employers are hiring trainees with a college background. This practice is most prevalent in industries with highly technical production processes, such as the chemical, oil, and electronics industries. Employers generally prefer backgrounds in business administration, industrial relations, mathematics, engineering, or science. The trainees undergo on-the-job training until they are able to accept supervisory responsibilities. Outstanding supervisors may move up to higher management positions. In manufacturing, for example, they may advance to jobs such as department head or plant manager. Some supervisors, particularly in the construction industry, use the experience and skills they gain to go into business for themselves.

OUTLOOK:

Employment of blue-collar worker supervisors is expected to increase more slowly than the average for all occupation through the year 2000. Although rising incomes will stimulate demand for goods such as air-conditioners, home entertainment equipment, personal computers, and automobiles, employment in manufacturing industries will decline, due in part to increasing foreign competition. The production-related occupations in manufacturing, including blue-collar worker supervisors, will be the ones most adversely affected. Offsetting the decline in the number of supervisors in manufacturing, however, will be an increase in jobs in non-manufacturing industries, especially in the trade and service sectors. In addition to the jobs resulting in increased demand for supervisors, many openings will arise from the need to replace workers who leave the occupation. Supervisors have a relatively strong attachment to the occupation, but because the occupation is so large, turnover results in a large number of openings. Because blue-collar worker supervisors are so important to the successful operation of a firm, they are often protected from layoffs during a recession. Supervisors in the construction industry, however, may experience periodic layoffs when construction activity declines.

BUYER/MERCHANDISE MANAGER

DESCRIPTION:

All merchandise sold in a retail store appears in that store on the decision of a buyer. Although all buyers seek to satisfy their stores' customers and sell at a profit, the type and variety of goods they purchase depends on the store where they work. A buyer for a small clothing store, for example, may purchase its complete stock of merchandise. Buyers who work for larger retail businesses often handle a few related lines of goods, such as men's wear, ladies' sportswear, or children's toys, among many others. Some, known as foreign buyers, purchase merchandise outside the United States. Buyers must be familiar with the manufacturers and distributors who handle the merchandise they need. They also must keep informed about changes in existing products and the development of new ones. Merchandise Managers plan and coordinate buying and selling activities for large and medium-sized stores. They divide the budget among buyers, decide how much merchandise to stock, and assign each buyer to purchase certain goods. Merchandise Managers may review buying decisions to ensure that needed categories of goods are in stock, and help buyers to set general pricing guidelines.

Some buyers represent large stores or chains in cities where many manufacturers are located. The duties of these "market representatives" vary by employer; some purchase goods, while others supply information and arrange for store buyers to meet with manufacturer's representatives when they are in the area. New technology has altered the buyers' role in retail chain stores. Cash registers connected to a computer, known as point-of-sale terminals, allow retail chains to maintain centralized, up-to-the-minute inventory records. With these records, a single garden furniture buyer, for example, can purchase lawn chairs and picnic tables for the entire chain.

BACKGROUND AND QUALIFICATIONS:

Because familiarity with the merchandise and with the retailing business itself is such a central element in the buyer's job, prior retailing experience sometimes provides sufficient preparation. More and more, however, employers prefer applicants who have a college degree. Most employers accept college grads in any field of study and train them on the job. In many stores, beginners who are candidates for buying jobs start out in executive training programs. These programs last from six to eight months, and combine classroom instruction in merchandising and purchasing with short rotations in various store jobs. This training introduces the new worker to store operations and policies, and provides the fundamentals of merchandising and management. The trainee's first job is likely to be that of assistant buyer. The duties include supervising sales workers, checking invoices on material received, and keeping account of stock on hand. Assistant buyers gradually assume purchasing responsibilities, depending upon their individual abilities and the size of the department where they work. Training as an assistant buyer usually lasts at least one year. After years of working as a buyer, those who show exceptional ability may advance to merchandise manager. A few find promotion to top executive jobs such as general merchandise manager for a retail store or chain.

OUTLOOK:

Employment of buyers is expected to grow more slowly than the average for all occupations though the year 2000 as more wholesale and retail trade establishments automate and centralize their purchasing departments. Productivity gains resulting from the increased use of computers to control inventory, maintain records, and reorder merchandise will be the principal factor restraining employment growth. Most job openings, therefore, will result from replacement needs, which occur as experienced buyers transfer to other occupations in sales or management, change careers, or stop working altogether. The number of qualified jobseekers will continue to exceed the number of openings because merchandising attracts many college graduates. Prospects are likely to be best for qualified applicants who enjoy the competitive, fast-paced nature of merchandising.

CHEMIST

DESCRIPTION:

Chemists search for and put into practical use new knowledge about substances. Their research has resulted in the development of a tremendous variety of synthetic materials, such as nylon and polyester fabrics. Nearly one-half of all chemists work in research and development. In basic research, chemists investigate the properties and composition of matter and the laws that govern the combination of elements. Basic research often has practical uses. In research and development, new products are created or improved. Nearly one-eighth of all chemists work in production and inspection. In production, chemists prepare instructions (batch sheets) for plant workers that specify the kind and amount of ingredients to use and the exact mixing time for each stage in the process. At each step, samples are tested for quality control to meet industry and government standards. Other chemists work as marketing or sales representative because of their technical knowledge of the products sold. A number of chemists teach in colleges and universities. Some chemists are consultants to private industry and government agencies. Chemists often specialize in one of several subfields of chemistry: analytical chemists determine the structure, composition, and nature of substances, and develop new techniques; organic chemists at one time studied only the chemistry of living things, but their area has been broadened to include all carbon compounds; inorganic chemists study noncarbon compounds; and physical chemists study energy transformations to find new and better energy sources.

BACKGROUND AND QUALIFICATIONS:

A BS with a major in Chemistry or a related discipline is sufficient for many entry-level jobs as a chemist. However, graduate training is required for many research jobs, and most college teaching jobs require a PhD. Beginning chemists with a Master's Degree can usually go into applied research. The PhD is generally required for basic research for teaching in colleges and universities, and for advancement to many administrative positions.

OUTLOOK:

Employment of chemists is expected to grow more slowly than the average for all occupations through the year 2000.

CLAIM REPRESENTATIVE

DESCRIPTION:

The people who investigate insurance claims, negotiate settlements with policy holders, and authorize payments are known as claim representative - a group that includes claim adjusters and claim examiners. When a casualty insurance company receives a claim, the claim adjuster determines whether the policy covers it and the amount of the loss. Adjusters use reports, physical evidence, and testimony of witnesses in investigating a claim. When their company is liable, they negotiate with the claimant and settle the case. Some adjusters work with all lines of insurance. Others specialize in claims from fire, marine loss, automobile damage, workers' compensation loss, or product liability. A growing number of casualty companies employ special adjusters to settle small claims. These workers, generally called inside adjusters or telephone adjusters, contact claimants by telephone or mail and have the policy holder send repair costs, medical bills, and other statements to the company. In life insurance companies, the counterpart of the claim adjuster is the claim examiner, who investigates questionable claims or those exceeding a specified amount. They may check claim applications for completeness and accuracy, interview medical specialists, consult policy files to verify information on a claim, or calculate benefit payments. Generally, examiners are authorized to investigate and approve payment on all claims up to a certain limit; larger claims are referred to a senior examiner.

BACKGROUND AND QUALIFICATIONS:

No specific field of college study is recommended. Although courses in insurance, economics, or other business subjects are helpful, a major in most college fields is adequate preparation. Most large insurance companies provide beginning claim adjusters and examiners with on-the-job training and home study courses. Claim representatives are encouraged to take courses designed to enhance their professional skills. For example, the Insurance Institute of America offers a six semester study program leading to an Associate's Degree in Claims Adjusting, upon successful completion of six exams. A professional Certificate in Insurance Adjusting also is available from the College of Insurance in New York City. The Life Office Management Association (LOMA), in cooperation with the International Claim Association, offers a claims education, program for life and health examiners. The program is part of the LOMA Institute Insurance Education Program leading to the professional designation FLMI (Fellow Life Management Institute) upon successful completion of eight written exams. Beginning adjusters and examiners work on small claims under the supervision of an experienced employee. As they learn more about claim investigation and settlement, they are assigned claims that are either higher in loss value or more complex. Trainees are promoted as they demonstrate competence in handling assignments and as they progress in their course work. Employees who show unusual competence in claims work or outstanding administrative skills may be promoted to department supervisor in a field office, or to a managerial position in the home office. Qualified adjusters and examiners sometimes transfer to other departments, such as underwriting or sales.

OUTLOOK:

Employment of claim representatives is expected to grow faster than the average for all occupations as the increasing volume of insurance sales results in more insurance claims. Shifts in the age distribution of the population will result in a large increase in the number of people who assume career and family responsibilities. People in this group have the greatest need for life and health insurance, and protection for homes, automobiles, and other possessions. A growing demand for insurance coverage for working women is also expected. New or expanding businesses will need protection for new plants and equipment and for insurance covering their employees' health and safety. Opportunities should be particularly good for claim representatives who specialize in complex business insurance such as marine cargo, workers' compensation, and product and pollution liability insurance.

COMMERCIAL ARTIST

DESCRIPTION:

A team of commercial artists with varying skills and specializations often creates the artwork in newspapers and magazines, and on billboards, brochures, and catalogs. This team is supervised by an art director, whose main function is to develop a theme or idea for an ad or advertising campaign. After the art director has determined the main elements of an ad or design, he or she will turn the project over to two specialists for further refinement. The sketch artist, also called a renderer, does a rough drawing of any pictures required. The layout artist, who is concerned with graphics rather than art work, constructs or arranges the illustrations or photographs, plans the typography, and picks colors for the ad. Other commercial artists, usually with less experience, are needed to turn out the finished products. Letterers put together headlines and other words on the ad. Mechanical artists paste up an engraver's guide of the ad. Paste-up artists and other less experienced employees do more routine work, such as cutting mats, assembling booklets, or running errands. Advertising artists create the concepts and artwork for a wide variety of items. These include direct mail advertising, catalogs, counter displays, slides, and filmstrips. They also design or lay out newspapers, magazines, and advertising circulars. Some commercial artists specialize in producing fashion illustrations, greeting cards, or book illustrations, or in making technical drawings for industry.

BACKGROUND AND QUALFICATIONS:

Persons can prepare for a career in commercial art by attending either a 2- or 4-year trade school, community college, college, or university offering a program in commercial art.

OUTLOOK:

The graphic arts fields have a glamorous and exciting image. Because formal entry qualifications are few, many people with a love for drawing and creative ability qualify for entry. As a result, competition for both salaried jobs and freelance work is keen. Freelance work may be hard to come by, especially at first, and many free-lancers earn very little until they acquire experience and establish a good reputation.

DATA PROCESSING SPECIALIST

DESCRIPTION:

The main function of a data processing specialist is to type data from documents such as checks, bills, and invoices quickly and accurately, and enter this information into a computer system. This is done with a variety of typewriter-like equipment. Many specialists use a machine that converts the information they type to magnetic impulses on tapes or disks. The information is then read into the computer from the tape or disk. Some specialists operate on-line terminals of the main computer system that transmit and receive data. Although brands and models of computer terminals and data entry equipment differ somewhat, their operation and keyboards are similar.

Some specialists working from terminals use data from the computer to produce business, scientific, and technical reports. In some offices, specialists also operate computer peripheral equipment such as printers and tape readers, and act as tape librarians.

BACKGROUND AND QUALIFICATIONS:

Employers usually require a high school education and the ability to key data in at a certain speed. Applicants are often tested for speed and accuracy. Some employers prefer applicants with experience or training in the operation of data entry equipment, and console operators are often required to have a college education. In some firms, other clerical workers such as tabulating and bookkeeping machine operators may be transferred to jobs as data processing specialists. Training in the use of data entry and similar keyboard equipment is available in high schools or private business schools.

OUTLOOK:

The employment rate of data processing specialists is expected to decline through the year 2000. Despite this decline, many openings, including part-time ones, will occur each year, due to the need to replace workers who transfer to other occupations or leave the labor force. Related occupations include secretaries, typists, receptionists, and typesetters and compositors.

DIETITIAN/NUTRITIONIST

DESCRIPTION:

Dietitians, sometimes called nutritionists, are professionals trained in applying the principles of nutrition to food selection and meal preparation. They counsel individuals and groups; set up and supervise food service systems for institutions such as hospitals, prisons, and schools; and promote sound eating habits through education and administration. Dietitians also work on education and research. Clinical dietitians, sometimes called therapeutic dietitians, provide nutritional services for patients in hospitals, nursing homes, clinics, or doctors' offices. They assess patients' nutritional needs, develop and implement nutrition programs, and evaluate and report the results. Clinical dietitians confer with doctors and nurses about each patient in order to coordinate nutritional intake with other treatments-medications in particular.

Community dietitians counsel individuals and groups on sound nutrition practices to prevent disease and to promote good health. Employed in such places as home health agencies, health maintenance organizations, and human service agencies that provide group and home-delivered meals, their job is to establish nutritional care plans, and communicate the principles of good nutrition in a way individuals and their families can understand. Research dietitians are usually employed in academic medical centers or educational institutions, although some work in common programs. Using established research methods and analytical techniques, they conduct studies in areas that range from basic science to practical applications. Research dietitians may examine changes in the way the body uses food over the course of a lifetime, for example, or study the interaction of drugs and diet. They may investigate the nutritional needs of persons with particular diseases, behavior modification, as it relates to diet and nutrition, or applied topics such as food service systems and equipment.

BACKGROUND/QUALIFICATIONS:

The basic educational requirement for this field is a bachelor's degree with a major in foods and nutrition or institution management. To qualify for professional credentials as a registered dietitian, the American Dietetic Association (ADA) recommends one of the following educational paths: Completion of a grow-year coordinated undergraduate program which includes 900 to 1,000 hours of clinical experience; completion of a bachelor's degree from an approved program plus an accredited dietetic internship; completion of a bachelor's or master's degree from an approved program and six month's approved work experience.

DRAFTSPERSON

DESCRIPTION:

Drafters prepare detailed drawings based on rough sketches, specifications, and calculations made by scientists, engineers, architects, and designers. Final drawings contain a detailed view of the object from all sides as well as specifications for materials to be used, procedures to be followed, and other information needed to carry out the job. There are two methods by which these drawings are prepared. In the traditional method, drafters sit at drawing boards and use compasses, dividers, protractors, triangles, and other drafting devices to prepare the drawing manually. In the new method, drafters use computer-aided drafting (CAD) systems. They sit at computer work stations and may make the drawing on a videoscreen. In some cases, the design may never be placed on paper. It may be stored electronically and, in some factories, may be used to guide automatic machinery. These systems free drafters from much routine drafting work and permit many variations of a design to be prepared easily. CAD systems allow a design to be viewed from various angles and perspectives not usually available with more traditional drafting methods so that design work can be better, faster, and more thorough. In addition to drafting equipment and CAD systems, drafters use technical handbooks, tables, and calculators in preparing drawings and related specifications.

BACKGROUND/REQUIREMENTS:

It is preferred that applicants have two years of post-high school training in technical institutes, junior and community colleges, or extension divisions of universities. Some persons receive training in the Armed Forces. Training for a career in drafting should include courses in mathematics, physical science, mechanical drawing, and drafting. Courses in shop practices and shop skills are also helpful, since most higher level drafting jobs require knowledge of manufacturing or construction methods. Many technical schools offer courses in structural design, architectural drawing, and engineering or industrial technology. Beginners usually start as junior drafters doing routine work under close supervision. After gaining experience, they do more difficult work with less supervision and may advance to senior drafter or supervisor with appropriate college education, they may become engineers, designers, or architects.

OUTLOOK:

Little change in employment of drafters is expected to occur through the year 2000. Related occupations include architects, engineering technicians, engineers, landscape architects, photogrammetrists, and surveyors.

ECONOMIST

DESCRIPTION:

Economists study the way a society uses scarce resources such as land, labor, raw materials, and machinery to produce goods and services. They analyze the costs and benefits of distributing and using resources in a particular way. Their research might focus on such topics as energy costs, inflation, business cycles, unemployment, tax policy, farm prices, and many other areas. Being able to present economic and statistical concepts in a meaningful way is particularly important for economists whose research is policy directed. Economists who work for business firms may be asked to provide management with information on which decisions such as the marketing or pricing of company products are made; to look at the advisability of adding new lines of merchandise, opening new branches, or diversifying the company's operations; to analyze the effects of changes in the tax laws; or to prepare economic or business forecasts. Business economists working for firms that carry on operations abroad may be asked to prepare forecasts of foreign economic conditions. About three of every economists work in private industry, including manufacturing firms, banks, insurance companies, securities and investment companies, economic research firms and management consulting firms. Some run their own consulting businesses. A number of economists combine a full-time job in government, business or an academic institution with part-time or consulting work in another setting.

BACKGROUND AND QUALIFICATIONS:

A Bachelors degree in Economics is sufficient for many beginning research, administrative, management trainee, and business sales jobs. However, graduate training is increasingly necessary for advancement to more responsible positions as economists. In government research organizations and consulting firms, economists who have Master's degrees can usually qualify for more responsible research and administrative positions. A PhD may be necessary for top positions in some organizations. Experienced business economists may advance to managerial or executive positions in banks, industrial concerns, trade associations, and other orginzations where they formulate practical business and administrative policy.

OUTLOOK:

Employment of economists is expected to grow faster than the average for all occupations through the year 2000. Most job openings, however, will result from the need to replace experienced economists who transfer to other occupations, retire, or leave the labor force for other reasons.

ENGINEER

DESCRIPTION:

Engineers apply the theories and principles of science and mathematics to tactical technical problems. Often, their work is the link between a scientific discovery and its useful application. Engineers design machinery, products, systems, and processes for efficient and economical performance. Engineering is a highly specialized field and the work an engineer does depends greatly upon the industry in which he/she is employed. The following descriptions outline the basic specialties and their respective employment outlooks.

Aerospace Engineer:

Aerospace engineers design, develop, test, and help produce commercial and military aircraft, missiles, spacecraft, and related systems. They play an important role in advancing the state of technology in commercial aviation, defense and space exploration. Aerospace engineers often specialize in an area of work like structural design, navigational guidance and control, instrumentation and communication, or production methods. They also may specialize in one type of aerospace product, such as passenger planes, helicopters, satellites, or rockets.

Outlook:

Employment of aerospace engineers is expected to grow more slowly than average for all occupations through the year 2000. During the 1980's, their employment grew very rapidly. However, because of recent Defense Department expenditure cuts for military aircraft, missiles and other aerospace systems, major growth is not expected.

Chemical Engineer:

Chemical engineers are involved in many phases of the production of chemicals and chemical products. They design equipment and chemical plants as well as determine methods of manufacturing these products. Often, they design and develop chemical processes such as those used to remove chemical contaminants from waste materials. Because the duties of the chemical engineer cut across many fields, these professionals must have knowledge of chemistry, physics, and mechanical and electrical engineering. This branch of engineering is so diversified and complex that chemical engineers frequently specialize in a particular operation such as oxidation or polymerization. Others specialize in a particular area such as pollution control or the production of a specific product like plastics or rubber.

Outlook:

Employment of chemical engineers is expected to grow about as fast as the average for all occupations through the year 2000.

Civil Engineer:

Civil engineers, who work in the oldest branch of the engineering profession, design and supervise the construction of roads, harbors, airports, tunnels, bridges, water supply and sewage systems, and buildings. Major specialties within civil engineering are structural, hydraulic, environmental/ sanitary, transportation, urban planning, and soil mechanics. Many civil engineers are in supervisory or administrative positions ranging from supervisor of a construction site, to city engineer, to top level executive. Others teach in colleges and universities, or work as consultants.

Outlook:

Employment of civil engineers is expected to increase faster than the average for all occupations through the year 2000.

Electrical Engineer:

Electrical engineers design, develop, test and supervise the manufacture of electrical and electronic equipment. Electrical equipment includes power-generating and transmission equipment used by electrical utilities, electric motors, machinery controls, and lighting and wiring in buildings, automobiles, and aircraft. Electronic equipment includes radar, computers, communications equipment, and consumer goods such as television sets and stereos. Electrical engineers also design and operate facilities for generating and distributing electrical power.

Electrical engineers generally specialize in a major area, such as integrated circuits, computers, electrical equipment manufacturing, communications, or power distributing equipment, or in a subdivision of these areas, such as microwave communication or aviation electronic systems. Electrical engineers design new products, specify their uses, and write performance requirements and maintenance schedules.

Outlook:

The outlook for electrical engineers is estimated to be good through the year 2000.

Industrial Engineer:

Industrial engineers determine the most effective ways for an organization to use the basic factors of production--people, machines and materials. They are more concerned with people and methods of business organization than are engineers in other specialties, who generally are concerned more with particular products or processes, such as metals, power or mechanics. To solve organizational, production, and related problems most efficiently, industrial engineers design data processing systems and apply mathematical concepts. They also develop management control systems to aid in financial planning and cost analysis, design production planning and control systems to coordinate activities and control product quality, and design or improve systems for the physical distribution of goods and services. Industrial engineers also conduct plant location surveys, where they look for the best combination of sources of raw materials, transportation, and taxes, and develop wage and salary administration positions and job evaluation programs. Many industrial engineers move into managerial positions because the work is closely related.

Outlook:

Employment opportunities for industrial engineers are expected to be good; their employment is expected to grow faster than the average for all occupations through the year 2000. Most job openings, however, will result from the need to replace industrial engineers who transfer to other occupations or leave the labor force.

Metallurgical Engineer:

Metallurgical engineers develop new types of metals with characteristics that are tailored for specific requirements, such as heat resistance, lightweight strength, or high malleability. They also develop methods to process and convert metals into useful products. Most of these engineers generally work in one of three major branches of metallurgy: extractive or chemical, physical, or mechanical. Extractive metallurgists are concerned with extracting metals from ores, and refining and alloying them to obtain useful materials. Physical metallurgists deal with the nature, structure, and physical properties of metals and their alloys, and with the methods of converting refined metals into final products. Mechanical metallurgists develop methods to work and shape materials, such as casting, forging, rolling, and drawing.

Outlook:

Employment of metallurgical, ceramic, and materials engineers is expected to grow more rapidly than the average for all occupations through the year 2000.

Mining Engineer:

Mining engineers find, extract, and prepare minerals for manufacturing industries to use. They design open pit and underground mines, supervise the construction of mine shafts and tunnels in underground operations, and devise methods for transporting minerals to processing plants. Mining engineers are responsible for the economical and efficient operation of mines and mine safety, including ventilation, water supply, power, communications, and equipment maintenance. Some mining engineers work with geologists and metallurgical engineers to locate and appraise new ore deposits. Others develop new mining equipment or direct mineral processing operations, which involve separating minerals from the dirt, rock, and other materials they are mixed with. Mining engineers frequently specialize in the mining of one specific mineral such as coal or copper. With increased emphasis on protecting the environment, many mining engineers have been working to solve problems related to mined land reclamation, and water and air pollution.

Outlook:

The employment outlook for mining engineers is expected to remain constant through the year 2000, due to expected low growth in demand for coal, metals, and other minerals.

Petroleum Engineer:

Petroleum engineers are mainly involved in exploring and drilling for oil and gas. They work to achieve the maximum profitable recovery of oil and gas from a petroleum reservoir by determining and developing the best and most efficient methods. Since only a small proportion of the oil and gas in a reservoir will flow out under natural forces, petroleum engineers develop and use various artificial recovery methods, such as flooding the oil field with water to force the oil to the surface. Even when using the best recovery methods, about half the oil is still left in the ground. Petroleum engineers' research and development efforts to increase the proportion of oil recovered in each reservoir can make a significant contribution to increasing available energy resources.

Outlook:

Employment of petroleum engineers is expected to grow more slowly than the average for all occupations through the year 2000. With the drop in oil prices, domestic petroleum companies have curtailed exploration, resulting in poor employment opportunities.

BACKGROUND AND QUALIFICATIONS:

A bachelor's degree in engineering from an accredited engineering program is generally acceptable for beginning engineering jobs. College graduates trained in one of the natural sciences or mathematics also may qualify for some beginning jobs. Most engineering degrees may be obtained in branches such as electrical, mechanical, or civil engineering. College graduates with a degree in science or mathematics and experienced engineering technicians may also qualify for some engineering jobs, especially in engineering specialties in high demand. Graduate training is essential for engineering faculty positions but is not required for the majority of entry level engineering jobs. All 50 states require licensing for engineers whose work may affect life, health or property, or who offer their services to the public.

Beginning engineering graduates usually work under the supervision of experienced engineers, and in larger companies, may receive seminar or classroom training. As engineers advance in knowledge, they may become technical specialists, supervisors, or managers or administrators within the field of engineering. Some engineers obtain advanced degrees in business administration to improve their growth opportunities, while others obtain law degrees and become patent attorneys.

FINANCIAL ANALYST

DESCRIPTION:

A financial analyst prepares the financial reports required by the firm to conduct its operations and satisfy tax and regulatory requirements. Financial analysts also oversee the flow of cash and financial instruments and develop information to assess the present and future financial status of the firm.

BACKGROUND AND QUALIFICATIONS:

A bachelor's degree in accounting or finance is suitable academic preparation for a financial manager. An MBA degree in addition to a bachelor's degree in any field is acceptable to many employers.

OUTLOOK:

Employment of financial managers is expected to increase about as fast as the average for occupations through the year 2000.

FOOD TECHNOLOGIST

DESCRIPTION:

A food technologist studies the chemical, physical and biological nature of food to learn how to safely process, preserve, package, distribute, and store it. Some develop new products, while others insure quality standards. They are, like animal scientists, dairy scientists, horticulturists, soil scientists, animal and plant breeders, entomologists, and agriculturalists, classified generally as agricultural scientists by the U.S. Department of Labor.

BACKGROUND AND QUALIFICATIONS:

Educational requirements for the agricultural scientist depend a great deal upon the area and type of work performed. A PhD degree in agricultural science is usually required for college teaching, independent research, and for advancement to many administrative and management jobs. A bachelor's degree is sufficient for some sales, production management, inspection, and other nonresearch jobs, but, in some cases, promotions may be limited. Degrees in some related sciences such as biology, chemistry, or physics or in related engineering specialties also may be acceptable for some agricultural science jobs.

OUTLOOK:

Employment of agricultural scientists is expected to grow about as fast as the average for an occupations through the year 2000.

FORESTER

DESCRIPTION:

Foresters plan and supervise the growing, protection and harvesting of trees. They plot forest areas, approximate the amount of standing timber and future growth, and manage timber sales. Some foresters also protect the trees from fire, harmful insects, and disease. Some foresters also protect wildlife and manage watersheds; develop and supervise campgrounds, parks, and grazing lands; and do research. Foresters in extension work provide information to forest owners and to the general public.

BACKGROUND AND QUALIFICATIONS:

A bachelor's degree in forestry is the minimum educational requirement for professional careers in forestry. In 1986, 55 colleges and universities offered bachelor's or higher degrees in forestry, 47 of these were accredited by the Society of American Foresters.

OUTLOOK:

Employment of foresters and conservation scientists is expected to grow more slowly than the average for all occupations through the year 2000.

GEOGRAPHER

DESCRIPTION:

Geographers study the interrelationship of humans and the environment. Economic geographers deal with the geographic distribution of an area's economic activities. Political geographers are concerned with the relationship of geography to political phenomena. Physical geographers study physical processes in the earth and its atmosphere. Urban geographers study cities and metropolitan areas, while regional geographers specialize in the physical, climatic, economic, political and cultural characteristics of a particular region or area. Medical geographers study the effect of the environment on health.

BACKGROUND AND QUALIFICATIONS:

The minimum educational requirement for entry-level positions is a BA or BS degree in Geography. However, a Masters degree is increasingly required for many entry level positions. Applicants for entry level jobs would find it helpful to have training in a specialty such as cartography, photogrammerty, remote sensing data interpretation, statistical analysis including computer science, or environmental analysis. To advance to a senior research position in private industry and perhaps gain a spot in management, a geographer would probably be required to have an advanced degree.

OUTLOOK:

Average growth is predicted throughout the 1990's.

GEOLOGISTS AND GEOPHYSISICTS

DESCRIPTION:

Geologists study the structure, composition and history of the earth's crust. By examining surface rocks and drilling to recover rock cores, they determine the types and distribution of rocks beneath the earth's surface. They also identify rocks and minerals, conduct geological surveys, draw maps, take measurements, and record data. Geological research helps to determine the structure and history of the earth, and may result in significant advances, such as in the ability to predict earthquakes. An important application of geologists' work is locating oil and other natural and mineral resources. Geologists usually specialize in one or a combination of general areas: earth materials, earth processes, and earth history.

Geophysicists study the composition and physical aspects of the earth and its electric, magnetic and gravitational fields. Geophysicists usually specialize in one of three general phases of the science -- solid earth, fluid earth, and upper atmosphere. Some may also study other planets.

BACKGROUND AND QUALIFICATIONS:

A Bachelor's degree in geology or geophysics is adequate for entry to some lower level geology jobs, but better jobs with good advancement potential usually require at least a master's degree in geology or geophysics. Persons with strong backgrounds in physics, mathematics, or computer science also may qualify for some geophysics jobs. A PhD is essential for most research positions.

OUTLOOK:

Employment of geologists and geophysicists is expected to grow more slowly than the average for all occupations through the year 2000, mainly due to the reduction in energy exploration by oil companies.

HOTEL MANAGER/ASSISTANT MANAGER

DESCRIPTION:

Hotel managers are responsible for operating their establishments profitably and satisfying guests. They determine room rates and credit policy, direct the operation of the food science operation, and manage the housekeeping, accounting, security, and maintenance departments of the hotel. Handling problems and coping with the unexpected are important parts of the job. A small hotel or motel requires only a limited staff, and the manager may have to fill various front office duties, such as taking reservations or assigning rooms. When management is combined with ownership, these activities may expand to include all aspects of the business. General managers of large hotels usually have several assistants or department heads who manage various part of the operation. Because hotel restaurant and cocktail lounges are important to the success of the entire establishment, they are almost always operated by managers with experience in the restaurant field. Other areas that are usually handled separately include advertising, rental of banquet and meeting facilities, marketing and sales, personnel and accounting. Large hotel and motel chains often centralize some activities, such as purchasing and advertising, so that individual hotels in the chain may not need managers for these departments. Managers who work for chains may be assigned to organize a newly-built or purchased hotel, or to reorganize an existing hotel or motel that is not operating successfully.

BACKGROUND AND QUALIFICATIONS:

Experience is the most important consideration in selecting hotel managers. However, employers are increasingly emphasizing college education. A BA in Hotel/Restaurant Administration provides particularly strong preparation for a career in hotel management. Most hotels promote employees who have proven their ability, usually front office clerks, to assistant manager, and eventually to general manager. Hotel and motel chains may offer better employment opportunities because employees can transfer to another hotel or motel in the chain, or to the central office if an opening occurs.

OUTLOOK:

Employment of salaried hotel managers is expected to grow much faster than the average for all occupations through the year 2000 as more large hotels and motels are built.

INDUSTRIAL DESIGNER

DESCRIPTION:

Industrial designers combine artistic talent with a knowledge of marketing, materials, and methods of production to improve the appearance and functional design of products so that they compete favorably with similar goods on the market. Although most industrial designers are engaged in product design, others are involved in different facets of design. To create favorable public images for companies and for government service, some designers develop trademarks or symbols that appear on the firm's products, advertising, brochures, and stationery. Some design containers and packages that both protect and promote their contents. Others prepare small display exhibits or the entire layout for industrial fairs. Some design the interior layout of special purpose commercial buildings such as restaurants and supermarkets.

Corporate designers usually work only on products made by their employer. This may involve filling the day-to-day design needs of the company, or long-range planning of new products. Independent consultants who serve more than one industrial firm often plan and design a great variety of products. Most designers work for large manufacturing companies designing either consumer or industrial products, or for design consulting firms. Others do freelance work, or are on the staffs of architectural and interior design firms.

BACKGROUND AND QUALIFICATIONS:

The normal requirement for entering this field of work involves completing a course of study in industrial design at an art school, university, or technical college. Most large manufacturing firms hire only industrial designers who have a Bachelor's degree in the field. Beginning industrial designers frequently do simple assignments. As they gain experience, they may work on their own, and many become supervisors with major responsibility for the design of a product or group of products. Those who have an established reputation and the necessary funds may start their own consulting firms.

OUTLOOK:

Employment in design occupations is expected to grow faster than the average for all occupations through the year 2000. Continued emphasis on product quality and safety, on design of new products for businesses and offices, and on high-technology products in medicine and transportation should expand the demand for industrial designers.

INSURANCE AGENT/BROKER

DESCRIPTION:

Agents and brokers usually sell one or more of the three basic types of insurance: life, casualty, and health. Underwriters offer various policies that, besides providing health benefits, may also provide retirement income, funds for education, or other benefits. Casualty insurance agents sell policies that protect individual policyholders from financial losses resulting from automobile accidents, fire, or theft. They also sell industrial or commercial lines, such as workers' compensation, products liability, or medical malpractice insurance. Health insurance policies offer protection against the high costs of hospital and medical care, or loss of income due to illness or injury. Many agents also offer securities, such as mutual fund shares or variable annuities.

An insurance agent may be either an insurance company employee or an independent who is authorized to represent one or more insurance companies. Brokers are not under exclusive contract with any single company, instead, they place policies directly with the company that best meets a company's needs.

Insurance agents spend most of their time discussing insurance needs with prospective and existing clients. Some time must be spent in office work to prepare reports, maintain records, plan insurance programs that are tailored to prospects' needs, and draw up lists of prospective customers. Specialists in group policies may help an employer's accountant set up a system of payroll deductions for employees covered by the policy.

BACKGROUND AND QUALIFICATIONS:

All insurance agents and most insurance brokers must obtain a license in the state where they plan to sell insurance. In most states, licenses are issued only to applicants who pass written examinations covering insurance fundamentals and the state insurance laws. Agents who plan to sell mutual fund shares and other securities also must be licensed by the state. New agents usually receive training at the agencies where they will work, and frequently at the insurance company's home office. Beginners sometimes attend company-sponsored classes to prepare for the examination. Others study on their own and accompany experienced sales workers when they call on prospective clients.

OUTLOOK:

Employment of insurance agents and brokers is expected to grow about as fast as the average for all occupations through the year 2000. Turnover is high because many beginners are able to establish a sufficiently large clientele in this highly competitive business. Most individuals and businesses consider insurance a necessity, regardless of economic conditions. Therefore, agents are not likely to face unemployment because of a recession.

MANAGER

DESCRIPTION:

Managers supervise employees and are accountable for the overall success of the operation which they direct. The scope and nature of a manager's responsibilities depend greatly upon the position and the size of his or her organization.

A department manager at a retail store, for example, may actually spend most of his or her time waiting on customers, and his or her managerial duties may be limited to scheduling employees' work shifts to properly staff the department, or to training new employees in such simple tasks as operating the check-out terminal, processing credit card purchases, and displaying merchandise.

A branch manager, even in a small store or service operation, might have considerably broader duties and responsibilities. He or she might, in addition to supervising and training employees, be responsible for hiring and firing decisions. He or she might have a limited ability to purchase items, and might have some control over a local advertising budget. He or she might also deal with local suppliers of goods and services. Some organizations, however, prefer to delegate rather limited responsibility to branch managers, and instead rely upon a strong network of regional managers who travel from branch to branch, making key operating decisions.

Factories or service firms with extensive processing requirements employ operations and production managers. While these managers typically supervise many people, their primary responsibility is the overall success of the operation, which may be dependent upon equipment, raw material, purchased goods, or outside vendors. The operations manager at a bank, for example, remains heavily dependent upon data processing equipment, and usually will have an extensive background in this area. The production manager at a petroleum refinery, for another example, remains heavily dependent upon a large variety of specialized equipment, and will usually have a background in engineering or chemistry.

The general manager is responsible for the overall day-to-day operations of the firm or operating unit. He or she must be acquainted with each part of the operation. In a small store, the general manager may spend most of his or her time performing nonmanagerial tasks such as making purchases, or even waiting on customers. In a large corporation, on the other hand, the general manager (who is often the executive vice president) will spend much of his or her time meeting with key executives in each department to ensure that company operations are being conducted successfully.

BACKGROUND AND QUALIFICATIONS:

The educational background of managers and top executives varies as widely as the nature of their diverse responsibilities. Most general managers and top executives have a bachelor's degree in liberal arts or business administration. Graduate and professional degrees are common. Many managers in administrative, marketing, financial, and manufacturing activities have a master's degree in business administration. Larger firms usually have some form of management training program, usually open to recent college graduates. While such programs are usually competitive, they generally offer an excellent opportunity to quickly familiarize oneself with many different aspects of a firm's business. Also, such programs are often open to a broad range of candidates, including both candidates with a BS in business administration, and liberal arts graduates as well.

OUTLOOK:

Employment of general managers and top executives is expected to grow about as fast as the average for all occupations through the year 2000.

MANUFACTURERS' SALES WORKERS

DESCRIPTION:

Most manufacturers employ sales workers to market their products to other businesses, mainly to other producers, wholesalers, and retailers. Manufacturers also sell directly to institutions such as schools, hospitals, and libraries. The sales workers who represent a manufacturer to prospective buyers are usually called manufacturers' representatives, although the job title may vary by product line.

Manufacturers' sales workers visit prospective buyers to inform them about the products they sell, analyze the buyer's needs, suggest how their products can meet these needs, and take orders. Sales workers visit firms in their territory, using an approach adapted to their line of merchandise. Sometimes sales workers promote their company's products at trade shows and conferences.

Manufacturers' sales workers spend most of their time visiting prospective customers. They also prepare reports on sales prospects or customers' credit ratings, plan their work schedules, draw up lists of prospects, contact the firm to schedule appointments, handle correspondence, and study literature about their products.

BACKGROUND AND QUALIFICATIONS:

Although a college degree is increasingly desirable for a job as a manufacturer's sales worker, many employers hire individuals without a degree who have previous sales experience. Most entrants to this occupation, even those with college degrees, transfer from other occupations, but some are recent graduates. Entrants are older, on the average, than entrants to other occupations. Sales representatives who have good sales records and leadership ability may advance to sales supervisor, branch manager, or district manager. Those with managerial ability eventually may advance to sales manager or other executive positions; many top executives in industry started as sales representatives. Some people eventually go into business for themselves as independent representatives, while others find opportunities in advertising and marketing research.

OUTLOOK:

Little or no change in employment is expected in the occupation through the year 2000. Increased reliance on electronic ordering systems and a trend toward increased utilization of wholesale distribution channels will limit future employment growth.

PERSONNEL AND LABOR RELATIONS SPECIALIST

DESCRIPTION:

Personnel and labor relations specialists provide the necessary link between management and employees which helps management make effective use of employees' skills, and helps employees find satisfaction in their jobs and working conditions. Personnel specialists interview, select, and recommend applicants to fill job openings. They handle wage and salary administration, training and career development, and employee benefits. Labor relations specialists usually deal in union-management relations, and people who specialize in this field work primarily in unionized businesses and government agencies. They help management officials prepare for collective bargaining sessions, participate in contract negotiations with the union, and handle day-to-day matters of labor relations agreements.

In a small company, personnel work consists mostly of interviewing and hiring, and one person usually handles all phases. By contrast, a large organization needs an entire staff, which might include recruiters, interviewers, counselors, job analysts, wage and salary analysts, education and training specialists, as well as technical and clerical workers. Personnel work often begins with the personnel recruiter or employment interviewer who travels around the country, often to college campuses, in the search for promising job applicants. These specialists talk to applicants, and then select and recommend those who appear qualified to fill vacancies. They often administer tests to applicants and interpret the results. Job analysts and salary and wage administrators examine detailed information on jobs, including job qualifications and worker characteristics, in order to prepare manuals and other materials for these courses, and look into new methods of training. They also counsel employees participating in training opportunities, which may include on-the-job, apprentice, supervisory, or management training.

Employee benefits supervisors and other personnel specialists handle the employer's benefits programs, which often include health insurance, life insurance, disability insurance, and pension plans. These specialists also coordinate a wide range of employee services, including cafeterias and snack bars, health rooms, recreational facilities, newsletters and communications, and counseling for worker-related personal problems. Counseling employees who are reaching retirement age is a particularly important part of the job. Labor relations specialists give advice on labor management relations. Nearly three out of four work in private industry, for manufacturers, banks, insurance companies, airlines, department stores, and virtually every other business concern.

BACKGROUND AND QUALIFICATIONS:

The educational backgrounds of personnel training, and labor relations specialists and managers vary considerably due to the diversity of duties and level of responsibility. While some employers look for graduates with degrees in Personnel Administration or Industrial and Labor Relations, others prefer graduates with a general business background. Still others feel that a well-rounded liberal arts education is the best preparation. A college degree in Personnel Administration, Political Science, or Public Administration can be an asset in looking for personnel work with a government agency. Graduate study in industrial or labor relations is often required for work in labor relations. Although a law degree is often required for entry-level jobs, most of the people who are responsible for contract negotiations are lawyers, and a combination of industrial relations courses and a law degree is becoming highly desirable. New personnel specialists usually enter formal or on-the-job training programs to learn how to classify jobs, interview applicants, or administer employee benefits. Next, new workers are assigned to specific areas in the employee relations department to gain experience. Later, they may advance within their own company, transfer to another employer, or move from personnel to labor relations work. Workers in the middle ranks of a large organization often transfer to a top job in a smaller company. Employees with exceptional ability may be promoted to executive positions, such as director of personnel or director of labor relations.

OUTLOOK:

The number of jobs in this field is projected to increase through the year 2000, although most job openings will be due to replacement needs. The job market is likely to remain competitive in view of the abundant supply of college graduates and experienced workers with suitable qualifications.

PHYSICIST

DESCRIPTION:

Through systematic observation and experimentation, physicists describe the structure of the universe and the interaction of matter and energy in fundamental terms. Physicists develop theories that describe the fundamental forces and laws of nature. The majority of physicists work in research and development. Some do basic research to increase scientific knowledge. Some engineering-oriented physicists do applied research and help develop new products. Many physicists teach and do research in colleges and universities. A small number work in inspection, quality control and other production-related jobs in industry, while others do consulting work.

Most physicists specialize in one or more branches of the science. A growing number of physicists are specializing in fields that combine physics and a related science. Furthermore, the practical applications of a physicist's work have become increasingly merged with engineering. Private industry employs more than one half of all physicists, primarily in companies manufacturing chemicals, electrical equipment, and aircraft and missiles. Many others work in hospitals, commercial laboratories, and independent research organizations.

BACKGROUND AND QUALIFICATIONS:

Graduate training in physics or a closely related field is almost essential for most entry-level jobs in physics, and for advancement into all types of work. A PhD is normally required for faculty status at colleges and universities, and for industrial or government jobs administering research and development programs. Those with a Master's Degree qualify for many research jobs in private industry and in the Federal Government. In colleges and universities, some teach and assist in research while studying for their PhD degrees. Those with a BA may qualify for some applied research and development positions in private industry and in government, and some holding Bachelor's degrees are employed as research assistants in colleges and universities while studying for advanced degrees. Many also work in engineering and other scientific fields. Physicists often begin their careers performing routine laboratory tasks. After gaining some experience, they are assigned more complex tasks and may advance to work as project leaders or research directors. Some work in top management jobs. Physicists who develop new products sometimes form their own companies or join new firms to exploit their own ideas.

OUTLOOK:

Physicists with a PhD should experience good employment opportunities by the late 1990s. The employment of physicists is expected to improve as retirements increase. Related industries: chemistry, geology, and geophysics.

PUBLIC RELATIONS WORKER

DESCRIPTION:

Public relations workers aid businesses, government, universities, and other organizations build and maintain a positive public image. They apply their talents and skills in a variety of different areas, including press, community, or consumer relations, political campaigning, interest-group representation, fund-raising, or employee recruitment. Public relations is more than telling the employer's story, however. Understanding the attitudes and concerns of customers, employees, and various other public groups, and effectively communicating this information to management to help formulate policy is an important part of the job.

Public relations staffs in very large firms may number 200 or more, but in most firms the staff is much smaller. The director of public relations, who is often a vice-president of the company, may develop overall plans and policies with a top management executive. In addition, large public relations departments employ writers, research workers, and other specialists who prepare material for the different media, stockholders, and other groups the company wishes to reach.

Manufacturing firms, public utilities, transportation companies, insurance companies, and trade and professional associations employ many public relations workers. A sizeable number work for government agencies, schools, colleges, museums, and other educational, religious, human service and other organizations. The rapidly expanding health field also offers opportunities for public relations work. A number of workers are employed by public relations consulting firms which furnish services to clients for a fee. Others work for advertising agencies.

BACKGROUND AND QUALIFICATIONS:

A college education combined with public relations experience is excellent preparation for public relations work. Although most beginners in the field have a college degree in communications, public relations, or journalism, some employers prefer a background in a field related to the firm's business. Other firms want college graduates who have worked for the news media. In fact, many editors, reporters, and workers in closely related fields enter public relations work. Some companies, particularly those with large public relations staffs, have formal training programs for new workers. In other firms, new employers work under the guidance of experienced staff members.

Promotion to supervisory jobs may come as workers demonstrate their ability to handle more demanding and creative assignments. Some experienced public relations workers start their own consulting firms. The Public Relations Society accredits public relations officers who have at least five years of experience in the field and have passed a comprehensive six-hour examination.

OUTLOOK:

Employment of public relations workers is expected to increase much faster than the average for all occupations through the year 2000.

PURCHASING AGENT

DESCRIPTION:

Purchasing agents, also called industrial buyers, obtain goods and services of the quality required at the lowest possible cost, and see that adequate supplies are always available. Agents who work for manufacturing maintenance and repair supplies; those working for government agencies may purchase such items as office supplies, furniture, business machines, or vehicles, to name some.

Purchasing agents usually specialize in one or more specific groups of commodities. Agents are assigned to sections, headed by assistant purchasing managers, who are responsible for a group of related commodities. In smaller organizations, purchasing agents generally are assigned certain categories of goods. About half of all purchasing agents work for manufacturing firms.

BACKGROUND AND QUALIFICATIONS:

Most large organizations now require a college degree, and many prefer applicants who have an MBA degree. Familiarity with the computer and its uses is desirable in understanding the systems aspect of the purchasing profession. Following the initial training period, junior purchasing agents usually are given the responsibility of purchasing standard and catalog items. As they gain experience and develop expertise in their assigned areas, they may be promoted to purchasing agent and then senior purchasing agent. Continuing education is essential for purchasing agents who want to advance their careers. Purchasing agents are encouraged to participate in frequent seminars offered by Professional societies, and to take courses in the field at local colleges and universities.

The recognized mark of experience and professional competence is the designation certified purchasing manager (CPM). This designation is conferred by the National Association of Purchasing Management, Inc. upon candidates who have passed four examinations and who meet educational and professional experience requirements.

OUTLOOK:

Employment of purchasing agents and managers is expected to increase more slowly than the average for all occupations during the 1990's. Computerization of purchasing coupled with an increased reliance on a smaller number of suppliers should boost the productivity of purchasing personnel.

QUALITY CONTROL SUPERVISOR

DESCRIPTION:

A quality control supervisor may either be involved in the spot checking of items being manufactured or processed or in assuring that the proper processes are being followed. A quality control system involves selection and training of personnel, product design, the establishment of specifications, procedures and tests, the design and maintenance of facilities and equipment, the selection of materials, and recordkeeping. In an effective quality control system, all these aspects are evaluated on a regular basis, and modified and improved when appropriate.

BACKGROUND AND QUALIFICATIONS:

While some quality control positions involved with the supervision of the production of simpler items might require little background besides on-the-job training, many require a specialized degree in engineering, chemistry, or biology. While all manufacturing firms require some degree of quality control, this is especially important in the chemistry, food and drug industries. Some drug manufacturers for example, may assign one out of six production workers to quality assurance functions alone

OUTLOOK:

Varies greatly, depending upon the industry.

REPORTER/EDITOR

DESCRIPTION:

Newspaper reporters gather information on current events and use it to write stories for daily or weekly newspapers. Large dailies frequently assign teams of reporters to investigate social, economic, or political conditions, and reporters are often assigned to beats, such as police stations, courthouses, or governmental agencies, to gather news originating inthese places. General assignment reporters write local news stories on a wide range of topics, from public meetings to human interest stories.

Reporters with a specialized background or interest in a particular area write, interpret, and analyze the news in fields such as medicine, politics, foreign affairs, sports, fashion, art, theater, consumer affairs, travel, finance, social events, science, education, business, labor, religion, and other areas. Critics review literary, artistic, and musical works and performances while editorial writers present viewpoints on topics of interest. Reporters on small newspapers cover all aspects of local news, and may also take photographs, write headlines, lay out pages, and write editorials. On some small weeklies, they may also solicit advertisements, sell subscriptions, and perform general office work. Reporters must be highly motivated, and are expected to work long hours.

BACKGROUND AND QUALIFICATIONS:

Most newspapers will only consider applicants with a degree in journalism, which includes training in the liberal arts in addition to professional training in journalism. Others prefer applicants who have a bachelor's degree in one of the liberal arts and a master's degree in journalism. Experience as a part-time "stringer" is very helpful in finding full time employment as a reporter. Most beginning reporters start on weekly or small daily newspapers, with a small number of outstanding journalism graduates finding work with large daily newspapers, although this is a rare exception. Large dailies generally look for at least three years of reporting experience, acquired on smaller newspapers.

Beginning reporters are assigned duties such as reporting on civic and community meetings, summarizing speeches, writing obituaries, interviewing important community leaders or visitors, and covering police, government, or courthouse proceedings. As they gain experience, they may report on more important events, cover an assigned beat, or specialize in a particular field. Newspaper reporters may advance to large daily newspapers or state and national newswire services. However, competition for such positions is fierce, and news executives are flooded with applications from highly qualified reporters every year. Some experienced reporters become columnists, correspondents, editorial writers, editors, or top executives; these people represent the top of the field, and competition for these positions is extremely keen. Other reporters transfer to related fields, such as public relations, writing for magazines, or preparing copy for radio or television news programs.

OUTLOOK:

Employment of reporters and correspondents is expected to grow through the year 2000, primarily due to the anticipated increase in the number of small-town and suburban daily and weekly newspapers.

SECURITIES AND FINANCIAL SERVICES SALES REPRESENTATIVES

DESCRIPTION:

Securities Sales Representatives:

Most investors, whether they are individuals with a few hundred dollars or large institutions with millions to invest, use securities sales representatives when buying or selling stocks, bonds, shares in mutual funds, or other financial products. Securities sales representatives also provide many related services for their customers. Depending on a customer's knowledge of the market, the representative may explain the meaning of stock market terms and trading practices, offer financial counseling, devise an individual financial portfolio including securities, corporate and municipal bonds, life insurance, annuities, and other investments, and offer advice on the purchase or sale of particular securities.

Financial Services Sales Representative:

Financial services sales representatives call on various businesses to solicit applications for loans and new deposit accounts for banks or savings and loan associations. They also locate and contact prospective customers to present their bank's financial services and to ascertain the customer's banking needs. At most small and medium-sized banks, branch managers and commercial loan officers are responsible for marketing the bank's financial services. As banks offer more and increasingly complex financial services, for example, securities brokerage and financial planning - the job of financial services sales representatives - will assume greater importance.

BACKGROUND AND QUALIFICATIONS:

A college education is becoming increasingly important, as securities sales representatives must be well informed about economic conditions and trends. Although employers seldom require specialized academic training, courses in business administration, economics, and finance are helpful. Securities sales representatives must meet state licensing requirements, which generally include passing an examination and, in some cases, furnishing a personal bond. In addition, sales representatives must register as representatives of their firm according to the regulations of the securities exchanges where they do business or the National Association of Securities Dealers, Inc. (NASD). Before beginners can qualify as registered representatives, they must pass the General Securities Registered Representative Examination. Banks and other credit institutions prefer to hire college graduates for financial services sales jobs. A business administration degree with a specialization in finance or a liberal arts degree including courses in accounting, economics, and marketing serves as excellent preparation for this job. Financial services sales representatives learn through on-the-job training under the supervision of bank officers. Outstanding performance can lead to promotion to managerial positions.

OUTLOOK:

The demand for securities sales representatives fluctuates as the economy expands and contracts. Employment of securities sales representatives is expected to expand as economic growth, rising personal incomes, and greater inherited wealth increase the funds available for investment. Employment of financial services sales representatives is also expected to increase through the year 2000, as banks and credit institutions expand the financial services they offer, and issue more loans for personal and commercial use.

STATISTICIAN

DESCRIPTION:

Statisticians devise, carry out, and interpret the numerical results of surveys and experiments. In doing so, they apply their knowledge of statistical methods to a particular subject area, such as economics, human behavior, the natural sciences, or engineering. They may use statistical techniques to predict population growth or economic conditions, develop quality control tests for manufactured products, or help business managers and government officials make decisions and evaluate the results of new programs. Over half of all statisticians are in private industry, primarily in manufacturing, finance, and insurance firms.

BACKGROUND AND QUALIFICATIONS:

A bachelor's degree in statistics or mathematics is the minimum educational requirement for many beginning jobs in statistics. For other entry-level jobs in the field, however, a BA with a major in an applied field of study such as economics or a natural science, and a minor in statistics is preferable. A graduate degree in mathematics or statistics is essential for college and university teaching. Most mathematics statisticians have at least a BA in mathematics and an advanced degree in statistics. Beginning statisticians who have a BA often spend their time performing routine work under the supervision of an experienced statistician. Through experience, they may advance to positions of greater technical and supervisory responsibility. However, opportunities for promotion are best for those with advanced degrees.

OUTLOOK:

Employment opportunities for persons who combine training in statistics with knowledge of computer science or a field of application - such as biology, economics or engineering - are generally expected to be favorable through the year 2000.

SYSTEMS ANALYST

DESCRIPTION:

Systems analysts plan efficient methods of processing data and handling the results. Analysts use various techniques, such as cost accounting, sampling, and mathematical model building to analyze a problem and devise a new system. The problems that systems analysts solve range from monitoring nuclear fission in a powerplant to forecasting sales for an appliance manufacturing firm. Because the work is so varied and complex, Analysts usually specialize in either business or scientific and engineering applications. Most systems analysts work in manufacturing firms, banks, insurance companies, and data processing service organizations. In addition, large numbers work for wholesale and retail businesses and government agencies.

BACKGROUND AND QUALIFICATIONS:

College graduates are almost always sought for the position of systems analyst. For some of the more complex positions, persons with graduate degrees are preferred. Employers usually seek analysts with a background in accounting, business management, or economics for work in a business environment, while a background in the physical sciences, mathematics, or engineering is preferred for work in scientifically oriented organizations. A growing number of employers seek applicants who have a degree in Computer Science, Information Systems, or Data Processing. Regardless of the college major, employers seek those who are familiar with programming languages.

In order to advance, systems analysts must continue their technical education. Technological advances come so rapidly in the computer field that continuous study is necessary to keep computer skills up to date. Training usually takes the form of one and two-week courses offered by employers and software vendors. Additional training may come from professional development seminars offered by professional computing societies. An indication of experience and professional competence is the Certificate in Data Processing (CDP). This designation is conferred by the Institute for Certification of Computer Professionals, and is Granted to candidates who have five years experience and have passed a five-part examination.

OUTLOOK:

The demand for systems analysts is expected to rise through the year 2000, as advances in technology lead to new applications for computers. Factory and office automation, advances in telecommunications technology, and scientific research are just a few areas where use of computers will expand.

TECHNICAL WRITER/EDITOR

DESCRIPTION:

Technical writers and technical editors research, write, and edit technical materials, and also may produce publications and audiovisual materials. To ensure that their work is accurate, Technical Writers must be expert in the subject area in which they are writing. Editors are also responsible for the accuracy of material on which they work. Some organizations use job titles other than technical writer/editor, such as staff writer, publications engineer, communications specialist, publications engineer, communications specialist, industrial writer, industrial materials developer, and others.Technical writers set out either to instruct or inform, and in many instances they do both. They prepare manuals, catalogs, parts lists, and instructional materials needed by sales representatives who sell machinery or scientific equipment and by the technicians who install, maintain, and service it. Technical writers are often part of a team, working closely with scientists, engineers, accountants, and others. Technical editors take the material Technical writers produce and further polish it for final publication and use. Many writers and editors work for large firms in the electronics, aviation, aerospace, ordinance, chemical, pharmaceutical, and computer manufacturing industries. Firms in the energy, communications, and computer software fields also employ many technical writers, and research laboratories employ significant numbers.

BACKGROUND AND QUALIFICATIONS:

Employers seek people whose educational background, work experience, and personal pursuits indicate they possess both writing skills and appropriate scientific knowledge. Knowledge of graphics and other aspects of publication production may be helpful in landing a job in the field. An understanding of current trends in communication technology is an asset, and familiarity with computer operations and terminology is increasingly important. Many employers prefer candidates with a degree in science or engineering, plus a minor in English, journalism, or technical communications. Other employers emphasize writing ability and look for candidates whose major field of study was journalism, English, or the liberal arts. Depending on their line of business, these employees almost always require course work or practical experience in a specific subject as well, computer science, for example.

People with a solid background in science or engineering are at an advantage in competing for such jobs. Those with BA's or MA's in Technical Writing are often preferred over candidates with little or no technical background. Beginning technical writers often assist experienced writers by doing library research work and preparing drafts of reports. Experienced technical writers in companies with large writing staffs may eventually move to the job of technical editor, or shift to an administrative position in the publication or technical information departments. The top job is usually that of publications manager (and other titles), who normally supervises an of the people directly involved in producing the company's technical documents. The manager supervises not only the technical writers and editors, but also staff members responsible for illustrations, photography, reproduction, and distribution.

OUTLOOK:

Through the year 2000, the outlook for writing and editing jobs is expected to continue to be keenly competitive. With the increasing complexity of industrial and scientific equipment, more users will depend on the technical writer's ability to prepare precise but simple explanations and instructions.

UNDERWRITER

DESCRIPTION:

Underwriters appraise and select the risks their company will insure. Underwriters decide whether their insurance company will accept risks after analyzing information in insurance applications, reports from loss control consultants, medical reports, and actuarial studies. Most Underwriters specialize in one of the three major categories of insurance: life, casualty, and health. They further specialize in group or individual policies.

BACKGROUND AND QUALIFICATIONS:

For beginning underwriters, most large insurance companies seek college graduates with degrees in liberal arts or business administration. Underwriter trainees begin by evaluating routine applicants under the close supervision of an experienced risk appraiser. Continuing education is a necessity if the underwriter expects to advance to senior level positions. Insurance companies generally place great emphasis on completion of one or more of the many recognized independent study programs. Many companies pay tuition and the cost of books for those who successfully complete underwriting courses; some offer salary increases as an additional incentive. Independent study programs are available through the American Institute of Property and Liability Underwriters, the Health Insurance Association of America, and the Life Office Management Association.

As underwriters gain experience, they can qualify as a "Fellow" of the Academy of Life Underwriters by passing a series of examinations and completing a research paper on a topic in the field. Exams are given by the Institute of Home Office Underwriters and the Home Office Life Underwriters Association. The designation of "Fellow" is recognized as a mark of achievement in the underwriting field. Experienced underwriters who complete a course of study may advance to chief underwriter or underwriting manager. Some underwriting managers are promoted to senior managerial positions after several years.

OUTLOOK:

Employment of underwriters is expected to rise faster than the average for all occupations through the year 2000 as insurance sales continue to expand. Most job openings, however, are expected to result from the need to replace underwriters who transfer to other occupations or stop working altogether.

PART THREE:
WHERE THE JOBS ARE

Primary Twin Cities Employers

For more information on professional employment opportunities in the accounting and auditing industries, contact the following professional and trade associations, as listed beginning on page 251:

AMERICAN INSTITUTE OF CERTIFIED PUBLIC ACCOUNTANTS
THE EDP AUDITORS ASSOCIATION
INSTITUTE OF INTERNAL AUDITORS
INSTITUTE OF INTERNAL AUDITORS/TWIN CITIES CHAPTER
NATIONAL ASSOCIATION OF ACCOUNTANTS
NATIONAL SOCIETY OF PUBLIC ACCOUNTANTS

COOPERS & LYBRAND
1000 TCF Tower
Minneapolis MN 55402
612/370-9300
Contact Ann S. Nehring, Personnel Manager. A management consulting and accounting firm offering a wide range of professional services in health care, manufacturing, higher education and financial services. Common positions include: Accountant. Principal educational backgrounds sought include: Accounting. Internships offered. Corporate headquarters location: New York, NY.

ERNST & YOUNG
1400 Pillsbury Center
Minneapolis MN 55402
612/343-1000
Contact Frank Flett, Recruiter. One of the world's largest management consulting and accounting firms, offering services in such areas as strategic management, operations management, information technology management, and marketing management.

GRANT THORNTON
500 Pillsbury Center
Minneapolis MN 55402
612/332-0001. Contact Roger Richters, Personnel Director. Provides a comprehensive scope of consulting and accounting services as well as strategic and tactical planning assistance to a diverse clientele.

KPMG PEAT MARWICK
90 South 7th Street
Minneapolis MN 55402-3900
612/341-2222
Contact Alice Richter, Recruiting Partner. Local office of worldwide Big 6 accounting firm, specializing in audit/accountant/tax and management consulting services. Common positions include: Accountant; Tax Services Specialist; Management Consultant. Principal educational backgrounds sought: Accounting. Company benefits include: medical, dental, and life insurance; pension plan; disability coverage. Corporate headquarters location: New York, NY. Operations at this facility include: service.

SCHECHTER, DOKKEN, KANTER
100 Washington Square
Suite 1650
Minneapolis MN 55401
612/332-5500
Contact Hiring. Regional office of the worldwide management consulting and accounting firm.

ADVERTISING, MARKETING, PUBLIC RELATIONS

For more information on professional employment opportunities in advertising, contact the following professional and trade associations, as listed beginning on page 251:

AMERICAN ADVERTISING FEDERATION
AMERICAN ASSOCIATION OF ADVERTISING AGENCIES
AMERICAN MARKETING ASSOCIATION
BUSINESS-PROFESSIONAL ADVERTISING ASSOCIATION
PUBLIC RELATIONS SOCIETY OF AMERICA
TELEVISION BUREAU OF ADVERTISING

ASSOCIATES & LARRANAGA, INC.
10601 Red Circle Drive
Minnetonka MN 55343
612/933-1446
Contact Bob Larranaga, President. A leading Minneapolis-area advertising company. Common positions include: Accountant; Advertising Worker. Principal educational backgrounds sought: Art/Design; Business Administration; Communications; Finance. Company benefits include: medical insurance; pension plan; life insurance; tuition assistance; disability coverage; profit sharing. Corporate headquarters location.

AUSTIN/LYMAN ADVERTISING
10 South 5th, Suite 330
Minneapolis MN 55402
612/332-1557
Contact Ike Austin, President. A leading Minneapolis advertising agency.

BAXTER ADVERTISING
600 S. Highway 169
Suite 1950
Minneapolis MN 55426
612/593-2500
Contact Terry Keegan, Vice President. A major Minneapolis advertising firm. Common positions include: Advertising Worker. Principal educational backgrounds sought: Art/Design; Communications; Marketing; Writing. Company benefits include: medical and dental insurance; profit sharing. Corporate headquarters location. Operations at this facility include: service.

CAMPBELL-MITHUN ESTY
222 South 9th Street
Minneapolis MN 55402
612/347-1000
Contact Bob Seper, Director of Human Resources. An area advertising agency.

CARLSON MARKETING GROUP
P.O. Box 59159
Carlson Parkway
Minneapolis MN 55459-8262
612/540-5589
Contact Sue Moe, Director of Human Resources. One of the nation's leading marketing firms engaged in the following operations: incentive travel, meetings, motivation and training programs, consumer promotion programs and trading stamps.

CARMICHAEL-LYNCH ADVERTISING
800 Hennepin Avenue
Minneapolis MN 55403
612/334-6000
Contact Personnel Administrator. An area advertising agency. Common positions include: Accountant; Advertising Worker; Marketing Specialist; Public Relations Worker; Writer; Art Director. Principal educational backgrounds sought: Accounting; Art/Design; Business Administration; Communications; Marketing; Journalism. Company benefits include: medical insurance; life insurance; tuition assistance; disability coverage; employee discounts. Corporate headquarters operations include: regional headquarters; divisional headquarters; administration.

COHEN, OKERLUND, SMITH ADVERTISING AND MARKETING INC.
1219 Marquette Avenue South
Suite 100
Minneapolis MN 55403
612/339-1387
Contact Steve Seidl, President. A leading area advertising and marketing firm.

COLEMAN & CHRISTISON INC.
545 Fort Road
St. Paul MN 55102
612/227-9391
Contact Nancy Stein, Office Manager. A major St. Paul advertising agency.

COLLE & McVOY ADVERTISING AGENCY, INC.
7900 International Drive
Minneapolis MN 55425
612/851-2500
Contact Bob Hettlinger, Human Resources Director. One of Minneapolis' leading advertising agencies.

DAMART ADVERTISING
7700 France Avenue South
Minneapolis MN 55435
612/830-2286
Contact Account Supervisor. A leading Minneapolis yellow pages advertising agency. Common positions include: Advertising Worker; Account Executive; Assistant Account Executive. Principal educational backgrounds sought: Marketing; Advertising; Communications. Training programs offered. Company benefits include: medical insurance; dental insurance; pension plan; life insurance; tuition assistance; disability coverage; daycare assistance; employee discounts; savings plan. Corporate headquarters location. Parent company: National Car Rental. Operations at this facility include: Worldwide headquaters; research/development; administration; service; sales.

DATA RESEARCH INC.
4635 Nicols Road
Suite 100
Eagan MN 55122
612/452-8267
Contact Jolene Dasto, Marketing Director. A telemarketing company providing full outbound telemarketing services. Common positions include: Customer Service Representative; Telemarketing Representative. Training programs offered. Company benefits include: medical insurance; pension plan; life insurance. Corporate headquarters location.

THE DUFFY DESIGN GROUP
311 First Avenue North
Minneapolis MN 55401
612/339-3247
Contact Joe Duffy, President. A major area advertising agency.

FABER SHERVEY ADVERTISING
160 West 79th Street
Minneapolis MN 55420
612/881-5111
Contact Paul Shervey, President. A major Minneapolis advertising firm. Common positions include: Copywriter; Art Director; Public Relations Writer; Sales Representative; Technical Writer/Editor. Principal educational backgrounds sought: Art/Design; Communications; Marketing. Company benefits include: medical insurance; pension plan; life insurance; profit sharing. Corporate headquarters location. Operations at this facility include: service; sales.

FALLON McELLIGOTT RICE
701 Fourth Avenue South
Suite 1500
Minneapolis MN 55415
612/332-2445
Contact Joe Papotola, Office Manager. A major area advertising firm.

FERRIS MARKETING, INC.
18305 Minnetonka Boulevard
Wayzata MN 55391
612/475-3979
Contact June Ferris, Vice President. A leading area advertising firm.

FUNARI ADVERTISING
7900 West 78th Street
Suite 100
Edina MN 55439
612/944-5050
Contact Personnel. A major area advertising firm.

THE GRUBB-CLELAND CORPORATION
500 WCCO Building
Minneapolis MN 55402
612/338-0567
Contact Rodney Grubb, President. A leading Minnesota advertising agency.

HAGGLUND & ASSOCIATES
121 West Franklin Avenue
Minneapolis MN 55404
612/874-7300
Contact George Hagglund, President. A leading area advertising company.

HARRIS & WEST ADVERTISING
701 4th Avenue South
Suite 1330
Minneapolis MN 55415
612/333-4614
Contact Tammie Gaustad, Vice-President/Operations. A major area advertising/public relations firm specializing in consumer/retail, agribusiness, hi-tech business to business and medical marketing communications.

THE HAWORTH GROUP INC.
6117 Blue Circle Drive
Minnetonka MN 55343
612/935-4454
Contact Dale Haworth, Chairman. A leading area advertising firm. Common positions include: Accountant; Advertising Worker. Principal educational backgrounds sought: Business Administration; Communications; Computer Science; Liberal Arts; Marketing. Training programs offered. Company benefits include: medical insurance; dental insurance; life insurance; tuition assistance; disability coverage; profit sharing. Corporate headquarters location. Operations at this facility include: administration; service; sales.

KAMSTRA COMMUNICATIONS INC.
370 Selby Avenue
St. Paul MN 55102
612/228-1419
Contact Dean Buresh, President. A major St. Paul advertising agency.

KERKER AND ASSOCIATES, INC.
1000 Southgate Office Plaza
Minneapolis MN 55437
612/835-7922
Contact Vice President/Controller. A major Minneapolis advertising firm. Common positions include: Advertising Worker; Marketing Specialist; Public Relations Worker; Copy Writer; Art Director. Principal educational backgrounds sought: Art/Design; Business Administration; Liberal Arts; Marketing. Previous advertising agency experience required. Corporate headquarters location.

MARTIN WILLIAMS ADVERTISING INC.
10 South Fifth Street
Suite 1100
Minneapolis MN 55402
612/340-0800
Contact Executive Secretary. A major Minneapolis/St. Paul advertising agency. Common positions include: Marketing Specialist. Principal educational backgrounds sought: Communications; Marketing. Training programs offered. Internships offered. Company benefits include: medical insurance; dental insurance; life insurance; tuition assistance; disability coverage; daycare assistance; profit sharing. Corporate headquarters location. Operations at this facility include: regional headquarters.

McCRACKEN BROOKS COMMUNICATIONS, INC.
8400 Normandale Lake Boulevard
Suite 375
Minneapolis MN 55437
612/921-8400
Contact John P. Harmon, Vice President, Controllor. A full service national sales promotion, marketing and advertising agency. Common positions include: Accountant; Administrator; Advertising Worker; Buyer; Sales/Account Executive; Copywriter; Art Director. Educational backgrounds sought: Communications; Marketing. Internships available. Company benefits include: medical insurance; dental insurance; pension plan; life insurance; disability coverage; profit sharing; savings plan. Corporate headquarters location. Operations at this facility include: regional headquarters; divisional headquarters; research; administration; sales.

McMANUS ADVERTISING COMPANY
100 North 6th Street
Suite 955C
Minneapolis MN 55403
612/341-3990
Contact Personnel Department. A major area advertising agency.

MORE DIRECT INC.
1825 Chicago Avenue South
Minneapolis MN 55404
612/872-1616
Contact Ken Henderson, President. A major Minneapolis advertising agency.

PEDERSON, HERZOG, AND NEE INC.
P.O. Box 32007
Minneapolis MN 55432
612/333-1234
Contact Kay Bonner, Creative Director. A major area advertising agency.

PRIDE, BARBER & WHALEY
43 Main Street SE
Suite 506
Minneapolis MN 55414
612/378-2045
Contact Bob Pride, President. A leading Minneapolis advertising agency.

RADA RECRUITMENT COMMUNICATIONS
8300 Norman Center Drive
Suite 220
Minneapolis MN 55437
612/831-3442
Contact Marianne Kulka, Director of Minneapolis Division. A major national recruitment advertising agency. Common positions include: Customer Service Representative; Sales Representative. Company benefits include: medical, dental and life insurance; tuition assistance; profit sharing. Parent company; Grey Advertising. Corporate headquarters location: Chicago, IL. Operations at this facility include: service; sales. New York Stock Exchange.

JOHN RISDALL AND ASSOCIATES
2475 15th Street NW
Suite E
New Brighton MN 55112
612/631-1098
Contact John Risdall, President. A major area advertising firm.

GORDON ROBINSON AND ASSOCIATES INC.
7701 Normandale Road
Suite 110
Edina MN 55435
612/831-4666
Contact Melissa Albachton, Personnel Manager. A major area advertising firm.

RUHR/PARAGON INC.
1221 Nicollet Mall
Minneapolis MN 55403
612/332-4565
Contact Catherine A. Marchio, Manager of Human Resources. A major Minneapolis advertising agency. Common positions include: Advertising Worker; Commercial Artist; Marketing Specialist. Principal educational backgrounds sought: Art/Design; Business Administration; Communications; Liberal Arts; Marketing. Internships offered. Company benefits include: medical insurance; dental insurance; life insurance; tuition assistance; disability coverage; profit sharing. Corporate headquarters location.

SAATCHI & SAATCHI ADVERTISING
8300 Norman Center Drive, #280
Minneapolis MN 55437
612/893-1700
Contact Darcy Sorlien, Office Manager. A leading Minneapolis advertising agency. Common positions include: Advertising Worker. Company benefits include: medical, dental, and life insurance; pension plan; disability coverage; profit sharing. Corporate headquarters location: New York, NY. Operations at this facility include: regional headquarters.

TELEPHONE MARKETING PROGRAMS/MINNEAPOLIS INC.
6600 France Avenue South
Suite 460
Edina MN 55435
612/922-2300
Contact Shannon Atwill, Agency Manager. A major area advertising firm specializing in the placement of National Yellow Pages. Common positions include: Advertising Worker. Principal educational backgrounds sought: Business Administration; Communications. Corporate headquarters location: New York, NY. Parent company: Telephone Marketing Programs, Inc. Operations at this facility include: research/development; service; sales.

TRADEMARK COMMUNICATIONS, INC.
7601 Washington Avenue South
Edina MN 55439
612/941-6818
Contact Dave Maiser, President. A leading advertiser.

TUNKS COMMUNICATION GROUP
5801 Duluth Street, Suite 100
Golden Valley MN 55422
612/540-0060
Contact Fred Tunks, President. A leading advertising firm.

WILSON LEARNING CORPORATION
7500 Flying Cloud Drive
Eden Prairie MN 55344
612/944-2880
Contact June Gilbert, Personnel Administrator. A management, consulting and public relations services firm. Common positions include: Accountant; Computer Programmer; Customer Service Representative; Financial Analyst; Personnel Specialist; Sales Representative. Principal educational backgrounds sought: Accounting; Business Administration; Finance; Liberal Arts; Training & Development; Humanities. Company benefits include: medical, dental, and life insurance; tuition assistance; disability coverage; employee discounts; savings plan. Parent company is John Wiley & Sons. Corporate and divisional headquarters location. Operations at this facility include: research/development; administration; manufacturing; service; sales.

AMUSEMENT, ARTS, AND ENTERTAINMENT

For more information on professional employment opportunities in the arts and entertainment industries, contact the following professional and trade associations, as listed beginning on page 251:

AMERICAN FEDERATION OF TELEVISION AND RADIO ARTISTS
AMERICAN ASSOCIATION OF ZOOLOGICAL PARKS & AQUARIUMS
AMERICAN FEDERATION OF MUSICIANS
AMERICAN FEDERATION OF TELEVISON AND RADIO ARTISTS
NATIONAL ENDOWMENT FOR THE ARTS
THEATRE COMMUNICATIONS GROUP

GUTHRIE THEATER
725 Vineland Place
Minneapolis MN 55403
612/347-1100
Contact Personnel. An internationally acclaimed theater, featuring a resident professional repertory company that presents ensemble productions of classical and modern drama.

INTERNATIONAL BROADCASTING CORPORATION
5101 EDS Center
Minneapolis MN 55402
612/333-5100
Conact Personnel. A leading entertainment company engaged in the operation of the Ice Capades theatrical skating production.

MINNEAPOLIS INSTITUTE OF ARTS
2400 Third Avenue South
Minneapolis MN 55404
612/870-3090
Contact Debra Duffy, Director of Personnel. A leading regional museum. Divisions of the museum include a publications department, among others.

MINNESOTA TIMBERWOLVES
Target Center
600 1st Avenue
Minneapolis MN 55403
612/337-3865
Contact Len Komoroski, Vice-President/Corporate Sales. Operates a professional National Basketball Association basketball club.

MINNESOTA TWINS
501 Chicago Avenue
Minneapolis MN 55415
612/375-1366
Contact Accounting Department. Operates a major league baseball franchise.

MINNESOTA VIKINGS
9520 Viking Drive
Eden Prairie MN 55344
612/828-6500
Contact Personnel Department. Operates an National Football League team.

ST. PAUL ATHLETIC CLUB
340 Cedar Street
St. Paul MN 55101
612/222-3661
Contact Dan Kennedy, General Manager. A full service athletic facility.

SCIENCE MUSEUM OF MINNESOTA
30 East 10th Street
St. Paul MN 55101
612/221-9488
Contact Director of Human Resources. The Science Museum of Minnesota (SMM) is a private, nonprofit educational and research institution organized to collect, study, and preserve objects of scientific significance and to interpret the objects, discoveries, and insights of science for the general public through its exhibits and education programs. SMM has exhibits in anthropology, biology, geography, paleontology, technology, cultural history, and natural history. Additionally the museum houses a collection of over 1.5 million scientific objects and an Omnitheater that produces and distributes OMNIMAX films shown around the world. Departments include finance, public programs and visitor services, exhibits, graphics, development (fundraising), community relations, and science. Common positions include: Exhibit Fabricator; Graphic Designer, Curator, Geographer, Marketing Specialist; Public Relations Worker; Writer/Editor; Fundraiser; Interpreter. Principal educational backgrounds sought: Accounting; Anthropology; Art/Design; Biology; Communications; Finance; Geography; Liberal Arts; Marketing; Mathematics; Paleontology; Physics. Advanced degree in the Natural Sciences required for curatorial positions. Company benefits (for full time salaried positions only) include: medical, dental, and life insurance; pension plan; employee discounts; tax deferred savings plan.

WALKER ART CENTER
Vineland Place
Minneapolis MN 55403
612/375-7617
Contact Wendy Lane, Personnel Manager. An internationally renowned museum of contemporary art with an active exhibition program and an extensive collection of 20th Century art as well as education, film, and performing arts programs. Located across the street from the 7 1/2 acre Minneapolis Sculpture Garden. Common positions include: Accountant; Administrator; Buyer; Graphic Artist; Customer Service Representative; Department Manager; General Manager; Marketing Specialist; Personnel and Labor Relations Specialist; Public Relations Specialist; Purchasing Agent; Reporter/Editor; Sales Representative; Curator; Program Director; Exhibition Technician; Secretary. Principal educational backgrounds sought: Accounting; Art/Design; Business Administration; Communications; Liberal Arts; Marketing; Art History; Art Education; Arts Administration. Training programs offered; Internships offered. Company benefits include: medical insurance; dental insurance; pension plan; life insurance; disability coverage; employee discounts; vacation; employee assistance program. Corporate headquarters location.

APPAREL AND TEXTILES

For more information on professional employment opportunities in the apparel and textile industries, contact the following professional and trade associations, as listed beginning on page 251:

AMERICAN APPAREL MANUFACTURERS ASSOCIATION
AMERICAN TEXTILE MANUFACTURERS INSTITUTE
NORTHERN TEXTILE ASSOCIATION
TEXTILE RESEARCH INSTITUTE

AERO DRAPERY CORPORATION
5601 Smetana Drive, Suite 100
Minnetonka MN 55343
612/935-3343
Contact Gail Meany, Director of Personnel. A large manufacturer of assorted curtains and drapes.

AMERICAN LINEN SUPPLY CO.
47 South 9th Street
Minneapolis MN 55402
612/371-4200
Contact Bob Tabolich, Personnel Director. A linen supply company.

BUTWIN SPORTSWEAR
3401 Spring Street NE
Minneapolis MN 55413
612/331-3300
Contact Ray Doenges, Office Manager. Manufacturers of athletic outerwear and other apparel.

S.B. FOOT TANNING CO.
Bench Street
Red Wing MN 55066
612/388-4731
Contact Jerry Dietzman, Personnel Manager. A leather tanning and finishing company. Common positions include: Accountant; Blue-Collar Worker Supervisor; Customer Service Representative; Industrial Engineer; Industrial Manager; Purchasing Agent. Principal educational backgrounds sought: Business Administration; Chemistry; Liberal Arts. Training programs offered; Internships offered. Company benefits include: medical and life insurance; pension plan; tuition assistance; disability coverage. Corporate headquarters location. Parent company: Red Wing Shoe Company. Operations at this facility include: manufacturing; research/development; administration; service; sales.

MUNSINGWEAR, INC.
724 North First Street
Minneapolis MN 55401
612/340-4743
Contact Charles Campbell, President. A well-known manufacturer of women's, children's, and infants' underwear.

RED WING SHOE COMPANY
314 Main Street
Red Wing MN 55066
612/388-8211
Contact Rich Chalmers, Personnel Director. A major area manufacturer of men's footwear.

BANKING/SAVINGS AND LOAN

For more information on professional employment opportunities in the banking industry, contact the following professional and trade associations, as listed beginning on page 251:

AMERICAN BANKERS ASSOCIATION
BANK ADMINISTRATION INSTITUTE
BANK ADMINISTRATION INSTITUTE/MINNEAPOLIS CHAPTER
INDEPENDENT BANKERS ASSOCIATION OF AMERICA

INDEPENDENT BANKERS ASSOCIATION OF AMERICA/
SAUK CENTER OFFICE
INSTITUTE OF FINANCIAL EDUCATION
MINNESOTA BANKING ASSOCIATION
NATIONAL COUNCIL OF SAVINGS INSTITUTIONS

AMERICAN NATIONAL BANK & TRUST CO./ST. PAUL
101 East 5th Street
St. Paul MN 55101
612/298-6000
Contact Mrs. Terry Saber, Director of Personnel. A full service banking institution.

BREMER FINANCIAL CORP.
445 Minnesota Street
Suite 2000
St. Paul MN 55101-2107
612/227-7621
Contact Personnel. A bank holding company.

DROVERS FIRST AMERICAN BANK
633 South Concord Street
South St. Paul MN 55075
612/451-6822
Contact Personnel. A St. Paul area banking institution.

FIRST BANK SYSTEM
First Bank Place East
120 S. 6th Street
Minneapolis MN 55402
612/370-4085
Contact Ken Smith, Manager of College Recruitment. A bank holding company. Corporate headquarters location. Operations include: administration. New York Stock Exchange. Common positions include: Accountant; Administrator; Bank Officer/Manager; Financial Analyst; Insurance Agent/Broker. Principal educational backgrounds sought: Business Administration; Economics; Finance; Liberal Arts. Company benefits include: medical insurance; dental insurance; pension plan; life insurance; tuition assistance; disability coverage; employee discounts; savings plan.

FIRST NATIONAL BANK OF ST. PAUL
332 Minnesota Street
St. Paul MN 55101
612/291-5000
Contact Kathy Dudley, Human Resource Manager. An area banking institution.

FIRST TRUST
180 East Fifth Street
Suite 200
St. Paul MN 55101
612/223-7944
Contact Director of Personnel. A full service bank.

FIRSTAR BANK OF MINNESOTA, NA
6500 Nicollet Avenue
South Richfield MN 55423
612/866-0031
Contact Personnel. An area banking institution.

FIRSTAR METROBANK
601 Marquette Avenue
Minneapolis MN 55402
612/340-5500
Contact Personnel. A major Twin Cities financial institution.

FIRSTAR ROSEVILLE BANK
2100 Snelling Avenue North
Roseville MN 55113
612/631-1300
Contact Personnel. A leading financial services institution.

FIRSTAR SHELARD BANK
400 South Highway 169
St. Louis Park MN 55426
612/546-6811
Contact Personnel. A major St. Louis Park banking institution.

FIRSTAR STILLWATER BANK
213 E. Chestnut Street
P.O. Box 198
Stillwater MN 55802
612/439-4411
Contact Personnel. A major Stillwater financial institution.

INVESTORS SAVINGS CORP.
1817 Plymouth Road South
Minnetonka MN 55343
612/542-8000
Contact Personnel. A holding company for a major savings and loan institution.

LIBERTY STATE BANK
P.O. Box 64075
St. Paul MN 55164
612/646-8681
Contact Personnel. A leading St. Paul bank.

MARQUETTE BANK OF MINNEAPOLIS
6th & Marquette
Minneapolis MN 55480
612/341-5600
Contact William McKnight, Vice President of Human Resources. A major full-service banking institution.

MIDWAY NATIONAL BANK OF ST. PAUL
1578 University Avenue
St. Paul MN 55104
612/646-2661
Contact Personnel. A major St. Paul area banking institution.

MIDWEST FEDERAL SAVINGS & LOAN ASSOCIATION OF MINNEAPOLIS
801 Nicollet Mall
Minneapolis MN 55402
612/372-6364
Contact Ms. Terry Bailey, Staffing Administrator. Engaged in savings, checking, commercial banking, and lending (offered by subsidiary corporations). Common positions include: Accountant; Bank Officer/Manager; Computer Programmer; Credit Analyst; Customer Service Representative; Financial Analyst; Assistant Manager; Branch Manager; Department Manager; Personnel Specialist; Purchasing Agent; Sales Representative; Systems Analyst. Principal educational backgrounds sought: Accounting; Business Administration; Communications; Computer Science; Economics; Finance; Marketing; Mathematics. Company benefits include: medical, dental, and life insurance; pension plan; tuition assistance; disability coverage; 401K plan; employee discounts; flex compensation. Corporate headquarters, regional, and divisional headquarters location. Operations at this facility include: administration; service; sales.

NATIONAL CITY BANK OF MINNEAPOLIS
75 South 5th Street
Minneapolis MN 55402
612/340-3131
Contact Personnel Department. A major area banking institution.

NORWEST BANK
7900 Xerxes Avenue South
Bloomington MN 55431
Contact Personnel Department. A leading Minneapolis-area banking institution.

PARK NATIONAL BANK OF ST. LOUIS PARK
5353 Wayzata Boulevard
St. Louis Park MN 55416
612/544-3544
Contact Personnel. A leading suburban financial institution.

SCCU/STATE CAPITAL CREDIT UNION
95 Sherbourne Avenue
St. Paul MN 55103
612/291-3700
Contact Personnel Department. A major credit corporation providing banking services.

TCF BANK F.S.B.
801 Marquette Avenue
Minneapolis MN 55402
612/370-7000
Contact Director of Human Resources. A full service bank.

BOOK AND MAGAZINE PUBLISHING

For more information on professional employment opportunities in the publishing industry, contact the following professional and trade associations, as listed beginning on page 251:

AMERICAN BOOKSELLERS ASSOCIATION
ASSOCIATION OF AMERICAN PUBLISHERS
MAGAZINE PUBLISHERS ASSOCIATION
WRITERS GUILD OF AMERICA, EAST INC.
WRITERS GUILD OF AMERICA, WEST INC.

ABDO & DAUGHTERS
P.O. Box 36036
Minneapolis MN 55439
612/944-5522
Contact Jill Hansen, Personnel Director. A major area publisher of children's books.

ARCHITECTURE TECHNOLOGY CORPORATION
P.O. Box 24344
Minneapolis MN 55424
612/935-2035
Contact Ken Thurber, President. A major area publishing and consulting firm.

AUGSBURG PUBLISHING HOUSE
P.O. Box 1209, 426 South 5th Street
Minneapolis MN 55440
612/330-3300
Contact Judy Thorkelson, Personnel Director. A publisher of a wide range of religious reading material.

BURGESS INTERNATIONAL
7110 Ohms Lane
Edina MN 55439
612/831-1344
Contact Marge Gronseth, Personnel Director. Area publishers of college textbooks, laboratory manuals, and non-fiction general interest trade books.

CALLAN PUBLISHING
6465 Wayzata Boulevard
Minneapolis MN 55426
612/541-9000
Contact Diane Ditter, Personnel Director. Publisher of trade periodicals.

MILLER PUBLISHING CO.
P.O. Box 2400
Minnetonka MN 55343
612/931-0211
Contact Al Oppedal, Editorial. Publishers of leading agricultural trade magazines. A subsidiary of Capital Cities, Inc./ABC.

BROADCASTING

For more information on professional employment opportunities in broadcasting , contact the following professional and trade associations, as listed beginning on page 251:

BROADCAST EDUCATION ASSOCIATION
CABLE TELEVISION ASSOCIATION
INTERNATIONAL RADIO AND TV SOCIETY
NATIONAL ASSOCIATION OF BROADCASTERS
NATIONAL ASSOCIATION OF BUSINESS AND EDUCATIONAL RADIO
TELEVISION BUREAU OF ADVERTISING

WOMEN IN RADIO AND TV, INC.
WOMEN IN RADIO AND TV, INC./NORTH STAR CHAPTER

HUBBARD BROADCASTING INC.
3415 University Avenue
St. Paul MN 55114
612/646-5555
Contact Personnel. An area radio and television broadcasting company. Common positions include: Accountant; Attorney; Computer Programmer; Credit Manager; Electrical Engineer; General Manager; Operations/ Production Manager; Purchasing Agent; Reporter/Editor; Sales Representative. Principal educational backgrounds sought: Accounting; Communications; Journalism. Company benefits include: medical insurance; pension plan; life insurance; disability coverage; profit sharing.

MIDWEST COMMUNICATIONS
90 South 11th Street
Minneapolis MN 55403
612/330-2400
Contact Steve Blum, Personnel Director. A major television broadcasting company, operating the station WCCO-TV.

MULTI-TECH SYSTEMS
2205 Woodale Drive
Mounds View MN 55112
612/785-3500
Contact Personnel. Manufacturers of modems and telephone and telegraph multiplex equipment.

NORTHWEST TELEPRODUCTIONS
4455 West 77th Street
Minneapolis MN 55435
612/835-4455
Contact Bob Haak, Operations Supervisor. A videotape production service.

CHARITABLE, NON-PROFIT, HUMANITARIAN

For more information on professional employment opportunities with charitable, non-profit, or humanitarian organizations, contact the following professional association, as listed beginning on page 251:

NATIONAL ASSOCIATION OF SOCIAL WORKERS

LEAGUE OF WOMEN VOTERS OF MINNESOTA
550 Rice Street
St. Paul MN 55103
612/224-5445
Contact Sally Sawyer, Director. Regional office of the national voter education organization. Publishers of voting and related political materials.

AMHERST H. WILDER FOUNDATION
919 LaFond Avenue
St. Paul MN 55104
612/642-4000
Contact Jenny Danielson, Human Resources Administrator. A non-profit human services foundation.

CHEMICAL AND RELATED: PRODUCTION, PROCESSING, DISPOSAL/ENVIRONMENTAL SERVICES

For more information on professional employment opportunities in the chemical industry, contact the following professional and trade associations, as listed beginning on page 251:

AMERICAN CHEMICAL SOCIETY
AMERICAN INSTITUTE OF CHEMICAL ENGINEERING
AMERICAN INSTITUTE OF CHEMICAL ENGINEERING/TWIN CITIES CHAPTER
AMERICAN INSTITUTE OF CHEMISTS
ASSOCIATION OF STATE & INTERSTATE WATER POLUTION CONTROL ADMINISTRATORS
MINNESOTA WATER POLLUTION CONTROL ASSOCIATION
WATER POLLUTION CONTROL FEDERATION

AERATION INDUSTRIES INTERNATIONAL
P.O. Box 59144
Minneapolis MN 55459
612/448-6789
Contact Personnel Department. World leader in restoring lakes, rivers, and harbors as well as wastewater treatment and agriculture.

ASHLAND CHEMICAL COMPANY/INDUSTRIAL CHEMICALS
P.O. Box 319
Shakopee MN 55379
612/445-7214
Contact Forest Colston, District Manager. A subsidiary of Ashland Oil Company, involved in the production of industrial chemicals and solvents.

ECOLAB INC.
370 Wabasha, Ecolab Center
St. Paul MN 55102
612/293-2233
Contact G.D. Gieske, V.P./Corporate Human Resources. Area producers of a variety of cleaning products.

H.B. FULLER COMPANY
1200 West County Road East
Arden Hills MN 55112
Contact Leo Johnson, Manager of Employee Planning. Manufacturer of adhesives, sealants, coatings, paints, sanitation chemicals and other specialty chemical products. Primary customers are industrial users of adhesives and related products. Common positions include: Accountant; Attorney; Chemist; Computer Programmer; Customer Service Representative; Chemical Engineer; Sales Representative; Industrial Manager. Principal educational backgrounds sought: Accounting; Chemistry; Engineering; Finance. Training programs offered; Internships offered. Company benefits include: medical insurance; dental insurance; life insurance; pension plan; tuition assistance; disability coverage; daycare assistance; profit sharing; savings plan. Corporate headquarters location. Nationwide locations.

HAWKINS CHEMICAL, INC.
3100 East Hennepin Avenue
Minneapolis MN 55413
612/331-6910
Contact Personnel. A distributor of industrial chemicals.

LONDON FOG INCORPORATED
505 Brimhall Avenue, P.O. Box 406
Long Lake MN 55356
612/473-5366
Contact Bob Bonnett, President. Manufacture and sell foggers, insecticides, and dispersal machines

COLLEGES AND UNIVERSITIES

For more information on professional employment opportunities in education, contact the following professional and trade associations, as listed beginning on page 251:

AMERICAN ASSOCIATION OF SCHOOL ADMINISTRATORS
ASSOCIATION OF AMERICAN UNIVERSITIES
MINNESOTA ASSOCIATION OF SCHOOL ADMINISTRATORS

MANKATO STATE UNIVERSITY
P.O. Box 8400
Mankato MN 56001
507/389-2015
Contact Human Resources. A major state university.

MOORHEAD STATE UNIVERSITY
Moorhead MN 56560
218/236-6011
Contact Personnel Department. A major state university.

ST. CLOUD STATE UNIVERSITY
720 4th Avenue South
Administration Building 204
St. Cloud MN 56301
612/255-3203
Contact Personnel Director. A major four-year state university.

UNIVERSITY OF MINNESOTA/MORRIS
600 East 4th and College
Morris MN 56267
612/589-2211
Contact Personnel Department. A major university.

UNIVERSITY OF MINNESOTA/TWIN CITIES CAMPUS
Room 2, Morrill Hall
100 Church Street SE
Minneapolis MN 55455
612/625-5000
Contact Personnel Department. A major university.

UNIVERSITY OF ST. THOMAS
2115 Summit Avenue
St. Paul MN 55105
612/647-5404
Contact Human Resources, Personnel Department. A major area college.

WINONA STATE UNIVERSITY
P.O. Box 5838
Winona MN 55987-5838
507/457-5000
Contact Personnel. A well known state university.

COMMUNICATIONS: EQUIPMENT & SERVICES

For more information on professional employment opportunities in the communications industry, contact the following professional and trade associations, as listed beginning on page 251:

COMMUNICATIONS WORKERS OF AMERICA
UNITED STATES TELEPHONE ASSOCIATION
UNITED STATES TELEPHONE ASSOCIATION/NORTH STAR
      CHAPTER

ADC TELECOMMUNICATIONS
4900 West 78th Street
Minneapolis MN 55435
612/835-6800
Contact Personnel. An area telecommunications company.

BLACKBOURN INC.
7550 Corporate Way
Eden Prairie MN 55344
612/949-2155
Contact Marnie Mikulay, Human Resources Manager. A manufacturer of communications packaging systems. Common positions include: Accountant; Blue-Collar Worker Supervisor; Industrial Engineer; Operations/Production Manager; Sales Representative. Principal educational backgrounds sought: Accounting; Business Administration; Communications; Engineering. Company benefits include: medical, dental, and life insurance; tuition assistance; disability coverage; profit sharing; savings plan. Corporate headquarters location. Operations at this facility include: manufacturing; administration; sales.

CENTEL COMMUNICATIONS SYSTEMS
6101 Baker Road
Suite 209
Minnetonka MN 55345
612/933-5331
Contact Personnel Department. A national leader in business communication system sales. Common positions include: Branch Manager; Sales Representative; Telephone Technician. Training programs available. Company benefits include: medical insurance; dental insurance; pension plan; life insurance; tuition assistance; profit sharing. Corporate headquarters location: Rolling Meadows, IL. Operations include: service; sales. New York Stock Exchange.

CONTINENTAL TELEPHONE OF MINNESOTA (CONTEL)
P.O. Box 507770
St. Paul MN 55150
612/681-2500
Contact John Oldendorf, Human Resources Supervisor. A major area telephone communications company.

ITT FINANCIAL CORP.
1696 Suburban Avenue
St. Paul MN 55106
612/772-2017
Contact Personnel Department. A major area corporation involved in telephone systems. Multiple area locations. Engaged primarily in the business of Telecommunication and Electronics; Engineered Products; Consumer Products and Services; Natural Resources; and Insurance and Finance. Company maintains manufacturing or sales operations in approximately 100 countries. Corporate headquarters located in New York. International. New York Stock Exchange.

NCR NETWORK PRODUCTS DIVISION
2700 Snelling Avenue North
St. Paul MN 55113
612/638-7369
Contact Kay Reissner, Recruitment and College Relations. Develops and manufactures communications processing systems. Divisional headquarters located in St. Paul, MN. Common positions include: Computer Programmer; Electrical Engineer; Industrial Engineer; Mechanical Engineer; Financial Analyst; Operations/Production Manager; Personnel and Labor Relations Specialist; Quality Control Supervisor; Systems Analyst; Technical Writer/Editor. Principal educational backgrounds sought: Accounting; Business Administration; Computer Science; Engineering; Finance; Mathematics; Physics. Company benefits include: medical insurance; dental insurance; pension plan; life insurance; tuition assistance; disability coverage; profit sharing; savings plan. Corporate headquarters location. Parent company: NCR Corporation.

NORTHERN TELECOM, INC.
Mail Station M-103
P.O. Box 1222
Minneapolis MN 55440
612/932-8000
Contact Personnel Department. A major manufacturer of computers and telephones. Common positions include: Accountant; Blue-Collar Worker Supervisor; Buyer; Computer Programmer; Electrical Engineer; Industrial Engineer; Mechanical Engineer; Financial Analyst; Department Manager; Operations/Production Manager; Personnel & Labor Relations Specialist; Quality Control Supervisor. Principal educational backgrounds sought: Accounting; Business Admiministration; Computer Science; Engineering;

Finance; Marketing. Training programs offered. Company benefits include: medical, dental, and life insurance; tuition assistance; disability coverage; employee discounts; savings plan. Corporate headquarters location: Nashville, TN. Parent company: Canada. Operations at this facility include: manufacturing; administration; service.

U.S. WEST COMMUNICATIONS, INC.
150 South Fifth Street
Suite 2880
Minneapolis MN 55402
612/663-4161
Contact Director of Personnel. A local provider of telephone and related communications services.

COMPUTERS: HARDWARE, SOFTWARE, AND SERVICES

For more information on professional employment opportunities in the computer industry, contact the following professional and trade associations, as listed beginning on page 251:

ADAPSO/THE COMPUTER SOFTWARE AND SERVICES
        INDUSTRY ASSOCIATION
ASSOCIATION FOR COMPUTER SCIENCE
ASSOCIATION FOR COMPUTING MACHINERY
ASSOCIATION FOR COMPUTING MACHINERY/
        TWIN CITIES CHAPTER
IEEE COMPUTER SOCIETY
IEEE COMPUTER SOCIETY/ST. PAUL CHAPTER
SEMICONDUCTOR INDUSTRY ASSOCIATION

AMERIDATA SYSTEMS, INC.
10200 51st Avenue North
Minneapolis MN 55442
612/557-2500
Contact David Schallenkamp, Personnel Director. A major distributor of computer systems. Employs 120.

ANALYSTS INTERNATIONAL CORPORATION
7615 Metro Boulevard
Minneapolis MN 55439-3050
612/835-2330
Contact Department J-200. A computer programming and analytic services firm. Common positions include: Computer Programmer; Systems Analyst. Principal educational backgrounds sought: Computer Science. Company benefits include: medical insurance; dental insurance; tuition assistance;

profit sharing; employee discounts. Corporate headquarters location. Operations at this facility include: divisional headquarters.

CIPRICO, INC.
2955 Xenium Lane
Plymouth MN 55441
612/559-2034
Contact Personnel Department. A leading designer and manufacturer of intelligent disk and tape controller boards.

CONTROL DATA CORPORATION
8100 34th Avenue
S. Minneapolis MN 55425
612/853-8100
Contact Personnel. Produces computer systems, services and data storage equipment. Corporate headquarters location.

CRAY RESEARCH INC. SOFTWARE DEVELOPMENT
665 Lone Oak Drive
Eagan MN 55121
612/452-6650
Contact Personnel Department. A producer of large-scale scientific computers with local, regional and national branches.

DECISION SYSTEMS INC.
75 South 5th Street
Minneapolis MN 55402
612/338-2585
Contact Personnel. Company develops software for leasing companies.

DICOMED CORPORATION
1701 E. 79th Street
Minneapolis MN 55425
612/854-7522
Contact Personnel. Manufacturers of high-performance computer graphics products used in information communications.

DUN AND BRADSTREET SOFTWARE SERVICE/
ADVANCED MANUFACTURING INTERNATIONAL
3400 Yankee Drive
Eagan MN 55122
612/681-7000
Contact Allen Vaughn, Personnel Director. Developers of manufacturing applications software. Common positions include: Computer Programmer; Customer Service Representative; Systems Analyst. Principal educational backgrounds sought: Business Administration; Computer Science; Engineering. Training programs offered. Company benefits include: medical insurance; dental insurance; life insurance; tuition assistance; disability

coverage; savings plan. Corporate headquarters location: Atlanta, GA. Parent company: Dun & Bradstreet Software Services. Operations at this facility include: research/development.

EGGHEAD DISCOUNT SOFTWARE
2395 Fairview Avenue North
Roseville MN 55113
612/631-3795
Contact Personnel Department. Nation's leading software reseller. Engaged in computer software retail sales.

KALVAR CORPORATION
15 South 9th Street
Minneapolis MN 55402
612/375-1171
Contact Personnel Department. A major computer programming firm.

LAWSON ASSOCIATES
1300 Godward Street NE
Minneapolis MN 55413
612/379-2633
Contact Personnel. A leading computer software company.

MECC/MINNESOTA EDUCATIONAL COMPUTING CORP.
6160 Summit Drive North
Minneapolis MN 55430
612/569-1500
Contact Personnel. Company develops software, specifically for educational computing systems.

METAPHOR COMPUTER SYSTEMS
11000 West 78th Street
Eden Prairie MN 55344
612/941-6000
Contact Personnel Department. Decision-making professionals providing fully intergrated data interpretation systems and applications for Fortune 500 Companies. Common positions include: Administrator; Computer Programmer; Department Manager; General Manager; Operations Manager; Sales Representative; Systems Analyst. Principal educational backgrounds sought include: Business Administration; Chemistry; Computer Science; Engineering; Marketing. Company benefits include: medical insurance; dental insurance; life insurance; tuition assistance; disability coverage; daycare assistance; 401K. Corporate headquarters location: Mountain View, CA.

MICRO-SOTA SOFTWARE, INC.
3549 Lake Elmo Avenue
Lake Elmo MN 55042
612/779-9444
Contact Ron Vagley, President. An area software producer.

MINNESOTA SUPER COMPUTER CENTER INC.
1200 Washington Avenue South
Minneapolis MN 55415
612/626-1888
Contact Personnel Department. A major computer center involved in computer simulation, affiliated with the University of Minnesota.

MOORE DATA MANAGEMENT SERVICES
2117 West River Road
Minneapolis MN 55411
612/588-7200
Contact Human Resources Manager. A primary provider of on-line computer services and printed products to Fortune 500 companies and the real estate industry.

NATIONAL COMPUTER SYSTEMS INC.
4401 West 76th Street
Edina MN 55435
612/830-7600
Contact Victor Bettendorf, Human Resources Manager. A manufacturer of electronic computing equipment.

NETWORK SYSTEMS CORPORATION
7600 Boone Avenue North
Minneapolis MN 55428
612/424-4888
Contact Carol Christiansen, Personnel Director. One of the nation's leading data telecommunications firms, specializing in the local networking of mainframe computers and subsystems. Employs over 1,000.

NORTHGATE COMPUTER SYSTEMS
1 Northgate Parkway
Edin Prairie MN 55344
612/943-8181
Contact Personnel. Manufacturers of personal computers.

RIMAGE CORPORATION
P.O. Box 1726
Minnetonk MN 55345
612/934-5432
Contact Personnel. Producers of computer duplication equipment.

SCICOM DATA SERVICES
10101 Bren Road East
Minnetonka MN 55343
612/933-4200
Contact John Honzl, Vice President of Finance. A major information services company.

TECHNALYSIS CORPORATION
6700 France Avenue S
Edina MN 55435
612/925-5900
Contact Personnel. A custom computer programming services company.

UNISYS CORPORATION
1305 Corporate Center Drive
Eagan MN 55121
612/456-2222
Contact Personnel Department. Provides advanced computer-based information systems, networks, and related services.

CONSTRUCTION: SERVICES, MATERIALS & RELATED

For more information on professional employment opportunities in the construction industry, contact the following professional and trade associations, as listed beginning on page 251:

**BUILDING OFFICIALS AND CODE ADMINISTRATORS
        INTERNATIONAL, INC.
CONSTRUCTION INDUSTRY MANUFACTURERS ASSOCIATION
INTERNATIONAL CONFERENCE OF BUILDING OFFICIALS
MINNESOTA ASSOCIATION OF HOME BUILDERS
NATIONAL ASSOCIATION OF HOME BUILDERS**

API INC.
2366 Rose Place
St. Paul MN 55113-2511
612/636-4320
Contact Lauren Rachley, Personnel. A major St. Paul wholesaler of insulation products.

ADOLFSON AND PETERSON INC.
Box 9377
6701 West 23rd Street
St. Louis Park MN 55426
Contact Personnel. A major construction company.

ARCON CONSTRUCTION COMPANY
903 East Forest
Mora MN 55051
612/679-2244
Contact Alan Sjoberg, Controller/Secretary. A contracting firm specializing in highway and street construction.

BOR-SON CONSTRUCTION INC.
2001 Killebrew Drive, Suite 400,
Bloomington MN 55425
612/854-8444
Contact Personnel Department. A regional construction firm.

DAN J. BRUTGER INC.
P.O. Box 399
St. Cloud MN 56302
612/252-6262
Contact Dianne Wysoski, Corporate Administrator. A general contractor specializing in the construction of large residential units.

CATERPILLAR PAVING PRODUCTS
P.O. Box 1362
Minneapolis MN 55440
612/425-4100
Contact Bill Jetson, Manager of Personnel. A major manufacturer of road construction equipment.

EGAN AND SONS COMPANY
7100 Medicine Lake Road
Minneapolis MN 55427
612/544-4131
Contact Shirley Stein, Personnel Manager. Mechanical and electrical contractors, with activities in commercial and industrial projects.

GAF BUILDING MATERIALS CORP.
50 Lowry Avenue North
Minneapolis MN 55411
612/529-9121
Contact Jean M. Walley, Human Resources Manager. Produces roofing materials. Regional facility. Common positions include: Accountant; Blue-Collar Worker Supervisor; Buyer; Customer Service Representative; Industrial Engineer; Industrial Manager; Personnel and Labor Relations Specialist; Quality Control Supervisor. Principal educational backgrounds sought: Accounting; Business Administration; Engineering; Finance; Company benefits include: medical insurance; dental insurance; life insurance; pension plan; tuition assistance; disability coverage. Corporate

headquarters location: Wayne, NJ. Parent company: GAF Corporations. Operations at this facility include: manufacturing; administration; sales.

HANS HAGEN HOMES
2353 North Rice Street
St. Paul MN 55113
612/483-0801
Contact Marie Reese, Personnel. A major construction company specializing in town-houses and one-family dwellings.

HARDRIVES INC./MAPLE GROVE
9724 10th Avenue North
Plymouth MN 55441
612/542-9060
Contact Scott Sinjem, Secretary/Treasurer. A manufacturer of paving mixes and associated material.

JESCO INC.
7175 Cahill Road
Edina MN 55439
612/944-7700
Contact Dave Olson, Controller. A concrete and masonry sub-contractor.

AL JOHNSON CONSTRUCTION CO.
3209 West 76th Street
Edina MN 55435
612/831-8151
Contact Personnel. A major Twin Cities area construction company.

KNUTSON CONSTRUCTION CO.
5301 East River Road
Minneapolis MN 55421-1095
612/572-5757
Contact Personnel. A major construction company.

KRAUS-ANDERSON INC.
523 South 8th Street
Minneapolis MN 55404
612/332-1241
Contact Andy Duda, Assistant Vice President of Personnel. An area contractor specializing in the construction of industrial buildings and warehouses.

LAMPERT LUMBER COMPANY
36 South Snelling Avenue
St. Paul MN 55105
612/698-3804
Contact Human Resources - TNJB. A premier home and building materials retailer headquartered in St. Paul. Company has over 40 stores in Minnesota, South Dakota, North Dakota, and Nebraska. Common positions include: Accountant; Advertising Worker; Buyer; Computer Programmer; Credit Manager; Customer Service Representative; Draftsperson (store locations); Department Manager (store locations); Management Trainee (store locations); Marketing Specialist; Personnel and Labor Relations Specialist; Sales Representative (store location). Systems Analyst. Principal educational backgrounds sought include: Accounting; Art/Design; Business Administration; Communications; Computer Science; Finance; Marketing; Forest Products. Training programs and internships available. Company benefits include: medical insurance; dental insurance; pension plan; life insurance; disability coverage; employee discounts. Corporate headquarters location.

GUSTAVE A. LARSON CO.
14005 13th Avenue North
Plymouth MN 55441
612/546-9508
Contact Randy Green, Manager. A major wholesaler of heating and air conditioning systems. Common positions include: Administrator; Mechanical Engineer; Sales Representative. Principal educational backgrounds sought: Business Administration; Engineering; Marketing. Company benefits include: medical, dental, and life insurance; pension plan; tuition assistance; disability coverage; employee discounts; savings plan. Corporate headquarters location: St. Louis, MO. Operations at this facility include: sales.

PAUL A. LAURENCE COMPANY
P.O. Box 1267
Minneapolis MN 55440
612/546-6911
Contact Gordon Moore, Hiring. A major area heavy construction firm.

LESTERS BUILDING SYSTEMS
P.O. Box 37
Lester Prairie MN 55354
612/395-2531
Contact Gary Rahmann, Director of Personnel. An area contractor specializing in the construction of prefabricated wooden buildings.

McGOUGH CONSTRUCTION COMPANY
2737 North Fairview Avenue
St. Paul MN 55113
612/633-5050
Contact Lorraine Hansen, Personnel Director. Contractor specializing in industrial buildings and warehouses.

MILES HOME COMPANY
P.O. Box 9495
4700 Nathan Lane
Minneapolis MN 55440-9495
612/553-8300
Contact Bob Trill, Payroll Officer. A builder of pre-cut homes.

MILLER CONSTRUCTION
P.O. Box 1228
St. Cloud MN 56302
612/251-4109
Contact Personnel Department. A major contracting construction company.

M.A. MORTENSON CO.
P.O. Box 710
Minneapolis MN 55400
612/522-2100
Contact Personnel. A major industrial construction company. Projects include institutional buildings, power plants, and commercial and office buildings.

OUR OWN HARDWARE CO.
P.O. Box 720
Minneapolis MN 55440
612/890-2700
Contact Personnel. A wholesale supplier of hardware, housewares, building materials and lumber products.

PARK CONSTRUCTION COMPANY
7900 Beech Street East
Minneapolis MN 55432
612/786-9800
Contact Personnel Manager. A major area contractor specializing in the construction of bridges and tunnels.

PROGRESSIVE CONTRACTORS
Box 407
8736 Zachery Lane
Osseo MN 55369
612/425-4515
Contact Greg Olsen, Vice President/Office Manager. An area contractor specializing in highway and street construction.

RYAN CONSTRUCTION CO. OF MINNESOTA
700 International Center
900 2nd Avenue South
Minneapolis MN 55402
612/339-9847
Contact Personnel. A major Minneapolis construction company.

ST. PAUL LINOLEUM & CARPET COMPANY, INC.
1505 University Avenue
St. Paul MN 55104
612/645-4601
Contact Clemment J. Commers, President. A floor covering contractor and acoustical products distributor.

J.L. SHIELY COMPANY
1101 North Snelling Avenue
St. Paul MN 55108
612/646-8601
Contact Dianne Minnick, Manager of Human Resources. A producer of Aggregate materials. Common positions include: Accountant; Computer Programmer; Credit Manager; Customer Service Representative; Industrial Engineer; Mechanical Engineer; Operations/Production Manager; Personnel & Labor Relations Specialist; Purchasing Agent. Principal educational backgrounds sought: Accounting; Business; Engineering. Company benefits include: medical, dental, and life insurance; pension plan; tuition assistance; disability coverage; savings plan. Corporate headquarters location: Denver, CO. Parent company: EEC Construction Materials America, Inc. Operations at this facility include: administration; service; sales.

THOMPSON ENTERPRISES
12201 Minnetonka Boulevard
Minnetonka MN 55343
612/933-2521
Contact Steve Tittelkow, Director of Personnel. A plumbing and lighting firm involved in the retail and construction industries.

THE TRANE COMPANY/
COMMERCIAL SYSTEMS GROUP
5916 Pleasant Avenue
Minneapolis MN 55419
612/861-7232
Contact Larry Koenig, Controller. A major distributor of air-conditioning and heating systems to commercial clients.

UNITED HARDWARE DISTRIBUTING CO.
5005 North Nathan Lane
Plymouth MN 55442
612/559-1800
Contact Personnel. A leading hardware distributor.

WRIGHT PRODUCTS INCORPORATED
2515 Wabash Avenue
St. Paul MN 55114
612/642-2800
Contact Jane Grapevine, Personnel Department. An area manufacturer of hardware, doors, and windows.

WYATT READY MIX
8502 Central Avenue NE
Blaine MN 55434
612/784-3512
Contact Personnel Department. A local, regional, and national producer of ready mix concrete.

DEFENSE

FMC CORPORATION/NAVAL SYSTEMS DIVISION
Box 59043
Minneapolis MN 55459
Contact Manager of Staffing. Producers of shipboard missile launching equipment and gun mounts; also operates machine shop, heat treating, welding, plating, and foundry facilities. Common positions include: Accountant; Computer Programmer; Electrical Engineer; Industrial Engineer; Mechanical Engineer. Principal educational backgrounds sought: Accounting; Computer Science; Engineering. Limited internships offered. Company benefits include: medical, dental, and life insurance; pension plan; tuition assistance; disability coverage; savings plan. Corporate headquarters location: Chicago, IL. Parent company: FMC. Operations at this facility include: divisional headquarters; manufacturing; research/development. New York Stock Exchange.

ELECTRONICS

For more information on professional employment opportunities in the electrical and electronic industries, contact the following professional and trade associations, as listed beginning on page 251:

AMERICAN ELECTROPLATERS AND SURFACE FINISHERS SOCIETY
AMERICAN ELECTROPLATERS & SURFACE FINISHERS SOCIETY/
    UPPER MIDWEST BRANCH
ELECTROCHEMICAL SOCIETY
ELECTROCHEMICAL SOCIETY/TWIN CITIES CHAPTER
ELECTRONIC INDUSTRIES ASSOCIATION
ELECTRONICS TECHNICIANS ASSOCIATION
INSTITUTE OF ELECTRICAL AND ELECTRONICS ENGINEERS
INTERNATIONAL BROTHERHOOD OF ELECTRICAL WORKERS
INTERNATIONAL BROTHERHOOD OF ELECTRICAL WORKERS/
    LOCAL 160
INTERNATIONAL SOCIETY OF CERTIFIED ELECTRONICS
    TECHNICIANS
MINNESOTA ELECTRONIC SALES
    AND SERVICES ASSOCIATION
NATIONAL ELECTRICAL MANUFACTURERS ASSOCIATION
NATIONAL ELECTRONICS SALES AND SERVICES ASSOCIATION

ADC TELECOMMUNICATIONS
4900 West 78th Street
Minneapolis MN 55435
612/835-6800
Contact Human Resources. A diversified manufacturer of electromechanical and electronic products for the computer, telecommunication and related industries.

ADVANCE CIRCUITS
15102 Minnetonka Industrial Road
Minnetonka MN 55345
612/935-3311
Contact Personnel Department. An area manufacturer of electronic circuit boards.

ADVANCED FLEX, INC.
15115 Minnetonka Industrial Road
Minnetonka MN 55345
612/930-4800
Contact Personnel. Manufacturers of circuit boards.

ALTRON INCORPORATED
6700 Industry Avenue Northwest
Anoka MN 55303
612/427-7735
Contact Personnel Department. A firm involved in circuit board assembly and wiring and harnessing.

ARGOSY ELECTRONICS
10300 West 70th Street
Eden Prairie MN 55344
612/942-9232
Contact Personnel. A leading Minnesota electronics firm.

AULT INCORPORATED
7300 Boone Avenue North
Minneapolis MN 55411
Mailed inquiries only
Contact Linda O. Shockley, Human Resources Director. A leading designer, manufacturer and marketer of power conversion products for the OEM market. Common positions include; Accountant; Buyer; Electrical Engineer; Industrial Engineer; Operations/Production Unit Manager. Principal educational backgrounds sought: Business Administration; Engineering. Company benefits include: medical insurance; dental insurance; life insurance; tuition assistance; disability coverage; profit sharing; savings plan. Corporate headquarters location. Operations at this facility include: manufacturing. American Stock Exchange.

BMC INDUSTRIES, INC.
Two Appletree Square
Suite 400
Minneapolis MN 55425
612/851-6000
Contact Personnel. BMC designs, manufactures and markets precision etched, electroformed components, and specialty printed circuits and ophthalmic lenses.

CPT CORPORATION
8100 Mitchell Road
Eden Prairie MN 55344
612/937-8000
Contact Human Resources. Manufactures electronic computing equipment and office automation equipment. Common positions include: Administrator; Computer Programmer; Customer Service Representative; Electrical Engineer; Technical Writer/Editor. Principal educational backgrounds sought: Accounting; Business Administration; Computer Science; Engineering. Company benefits include: medical insurance; dental insurance; life insurance; tuition assistance; employee discounts. Corporate headquarters location.

DOTRONIX INC.
160 First Street S.E.
New Brighton MN 55112
612/633-1742
Contact Personnel. Producers of cathode ray tube displays.

EPERTUS TECHNOLOGIES
7275 Flying Cloud Drive
Eden Prairie MN 55344
612/828-0300
Contact Kevin Websters, Vice President/Personnel. Manufacturers of electronic computing equipment.

FSI INTERNATIONAL
322 Lake Hazeltine Drive
Chaska MN 55318-1096
612/448-5440
Contact Michael Lorinser, Employee Relations Manager. Engaged in the development, manufacture and sale of semiconductor processing equipment. Common positions include: Customer Service Representative; Electrical Engineer; Mechanical Engineer; Sales Representative; Semiconductor Process Engineer. Principal educational backgrounds sought: Chemistry; Engineering. Company benefits include: medical insurance; pension plan; life insurance; tuition assistance; disability coverage; profit sharing. Corporate headquarters location. Operations at this facility include: manufacturing; research/development; administration; service; sales.

GOPHER ELECTRONICS COMPANY
222 East Little Canada Road
St. Paul MN 55117
612/483-3322
Contact Controller. An area distributor of electronic equipment.

HEI INC.
1495 Steiger Lake Lane
P.O. Box 5000
Victoria MN 55386
612/443-2500
Contact Personnel Department. A growing high tech electronics firm.

HOFFMAN ENGINEERING COMPANY
900 Ehlen Drive
Anoka MN 55303
612/421-2240
Contact Personnel Department. A prominent local, regional, and national manufacturer of electrical electronic enclosures and corrosion inhibiting products.

HONEYWELL INC.
Honeywell Plaza
MN12-2109
Minneapolis MN 55408
612/870-2596
Contact Personnel Director. A major international electronic products corporation serving customer needs for automation and control through five businesses: Space and Aviation, Industrial, Homes and Buildings, and International, which handles administration, marketing, distribution, and services for the other four divisions worldwide. Over 62,000 employees internationally. Company benefits include: Accountant; Administrator; Attorney; Computer Programmer; Credit Manager; Customer Service Representative; Dietician; Financial Analyst; Personnel and Labor Relations Specialist. Principal educational backgrounds sought include: Accounting; Business Administration; Computer Science; Finance. Training programs and internships available. Company benefits include: medical insurance; dental insurance; pension plan; life insurance; tuition assistance; disability coverage; daycare assistance; profit sharing; employee discounts; savings plan. Operations at this facility include: administration; service. New York Stock Exchange.

KATUN CORPORATION
10951 Bush Lake Road
Bloomington MN 55438
612/941-9505
Contact Personnel. Producers of copying equipment and supplies.

MTS SYSTEMS CORPORATION
14000 Technology Drive
Eden Prairie MN 55344
612/937-4000
Contact Bruce Hebeisen, Personnel Director. Maker of electronic instruments, hydraulic devices, mechanical testing and analysis instruments.

MICOM CIRCUITS
475 8th Avenue NW
New Brighton MN 55112
612/636-5616
Contact Personnel. Manufacture printed circuit boards.

MICRO COMPONENT TECHNOLOGY INC.
3850 North Victoria
Shoreview MN 55126
612/482-5100
Contact Ms. Jo Ebertowski, Personnel Director. Manufacturers of instruments for the measuring and testing of electricity and electrical signals.

MONITERM CORP.
5740 Green Circle
Minnetonka MN 55343
612/935-4151
Contact Personnel. Produces high resolution CRT displays.

NORTRONICS COMPANY INC.
145 3rd Street South
Dassel MN 55325
612/275-3325
Contact Human Resource Coordinator. A producer of magnetic recording heads for the information processing industry. Common positions include: Accountant; Computer Programmer; Credit Manager; Customer Service Representative; Draftsperson; Ceramics Engineer; Electrical Engineer; Industrial Engineer; Mechanical Engineer; Metallurgical Engineer; Industrial Manager; Department Manager; General Manager; Operations/Production Manager; Purchasing Agent; Quality Control Supervisor; Sales Representative; Systems Analyst; Technical Writer/Editor. Principal educational backgrounds sought: Accounting; Business Administration; Chemistry; Economics; Engineering; Finance; Marketing; Mathematics; Physics. Company benefits include: medical, dental and life insurance; tuition assistance; disability coverage; profit sharing; savings plan; stock purchase plan. Corporate headquarters location: Eden Prairie, MN. Parent company: Applied Magnetics Corporation. Operations at this facility include: manufacturing; research/development; administration; sales. New York Stock Exchange.

SCHOTT CORPORATION
1000 Parkers Lake Road
Wayzata MN 55391
612/475-1173
Contact Personnel. Manufacturers of transformers and power equipment.

TELEX COMMUNICATIONS INC.
9600 Aldrich Avenue South
Minneapolis MN 55420
612/884-4051
Contact Kathy Curran, Personnel Director. An electronic components manufacturer specializing in intercom systems and other related communications products.

TELEX COMMUNICATIONS/GLENCOE
1720 East 14th Street
Glencoe MN 55336
612/864-3177
Contact Ms. Graupmann, Personnel. An electronic components manufacturer specializing in such products as intercom systems and other communications related products.

TURTLE MOUNTAIN CORPORATION
380 Oak Grove Parkway
Vadnais Heights MN 55127
612/481-1427
Contact Personnel. Electronic subcontractors.

VTC INCORPORATED
2800 East Old Shakapee Road
Bloomington MN 55425
612/853-5100
Contact Human Resources. A corporation engaged in the production of semiconductors.

ENGINEERING AND ARCHITECTURE

For more information on professional employment opportunities in engineering and architecture, contact the following professional and trade associations, as listed beginning on page 251:

AMERICAN INSTITUTE OF ARCHITECTS
AMERICAN INSTITUTE OF ARCHITECTS/MINNEAPOLIS CHAPTER
AMERICAN SOCIETY OF CIVIL ENGINEERS
AMERICAN SOCIETY FOR ENGINEERING EDUCATION
AMERICAN SOCIETY OF HEATING, REFRIGERATING, AND
    AIR CONDITIONING ENGINEERS
AMERICAN SOCIETY OF LANDSCAPE ARCHITECTS
AMERICAN SOCIETY OF NAVAL ENGINEERS
AMERICAN SOCIETY OF PLUMBING ENGINEERS
AMERICAN SOCIETY OF SAFETY ENGINEERS
ILLUMINATING ENGINEERING SOCIETY OF NORTH AMERICA
INSTITUTE OF INDUSTRIAL ENGINEERS
NATIONAL ACADEMY OF ENGINEERING
NATIONAL SOCIETY OF PROFESSIONAL ENGINEERS
SOCIETY OF FIRE PROTECTION ENGINEERS
UNITED ENGINEERING TRUSTEES

COM-TAL MACHINE & ENGINEERING INC.
1239 Wolters Boulevard
Vadnais Heights MN 55110
612/483-2611
Contact Personnel. A machine and engineering company.

ELLERBE BECKET
One Appletree Square
Minneapolis MN 55425
612/853-2028
Contact Julienne Sprint, Director of Human Resources. An architectural/engineering firm engaged in the design of industrial, commercial, educational, and medical buildings nationwide. Common positions include: Accountant; Architect; Computer Programmer; Draftsperson; Civil Engineer; Electrical Engineer; Mechanical Engineer; Marketing Specialist. Principal educational backgrounds sought: Accounting; Engineering; Marketing. Internships offered. Company benefits include: medical insurance; dental insurance; life insurance; tuition assistance; disability coverage; daycare assistance; profit sharing; savings plan. Corporate headquarters location. Operations include: Divisional headquarters; administration; sales.

FLUIDYNE ENGINEERING CORPORATION
5900 Olson Memorial Highway
Golden Valley MN 55422
612/544-2721
Contact Personnel. An engineering corporation.

HAMMEL GREEN & ABRAHAMSON, INC.
1201 Harmon Place
Minneapolis MN 55403
612/332-3944
Contact Sandy Parsley, Personnel Director. A leading architectural engineering firm.

LULL ENGINEERING COMPANY
3045 Highway 13
St. Paul MN 55121-1699
612/454-4300
Contact Bob Braatz, Personnel Manager. A St. Paul engineering and manufacturing company.

POSSIS CORPORATION
825 Rhode Island Avenue South
Minneapolis MN 55426
612/545-1471
Contact Betty Anastasia, Personnel Manager. A contract engineering and CAD/CAM service bureau.

TWIN CITY TESTING CORPORATION
662 Cromwell Avenue
St. Paul MN 55114
Contact Human Resources. Twin City Testing provides consulting engineering and chemistry services from 28 offices in 9 Midwest States.

Common positions include: Chemist; Civil Engineer; Geologist. Principal educational backgrounds sought: Chemistry; Engineering; Geology. Internships offered. Company benefits include: medical, dental, and life insurance; tuition assistance; disability coverage; savings plan. Corporate headquarters location. Parent company: Huntington International Holdings. Operations at this facility include: administration; service; sales. New York Stock Exchange.

FABRICATED AND PRIMARY METALS

For more information on professional employment opportunities in the fabricated and primary metals industries, contact the following professional and trade associations, as listed beginning on page 251:

AMERICAN CASTE METALS ASSOCIATION
AMERICAN POWDER METALLURGY INSTITUTE
ASSOCIATION OF IRON AND STEEL ENGINEERS
NATIONAL ASSOCIATION OF METAL FINISHERS

A & B TOOL AND GAGE CORPORATION
2025 105th Avenue
Blaine MN 55434
612/784-5330
Contact Daniel M. Bjorn, President. A corporation engaged in the making of metal stampings, tools, dies, jigs, fixtures, special machinery, and machine work.

AMERICAN NATIONAL CAN CO./ST. PAUL
755 North Prior
St. Paul MN 55104
612/645-0771
Contact Richard Kiessling, Personnel Manager. A major manufacturer of metal cans.

BROWN-MINNEAPOLIS TANK COMPANY
P.O. Box 64670
St. Paul MN 55164
612/454-6750
Contact Wayne Romsos, Director of Human Resources. A fabricated plate work company.

EDGECOMB METALS COMPANY
401 NE Harding Street
Minneapolis MN 55413
612/331-4000
Contact Personnel. Distributors of stainless steel and other metals to industrial clients.

HOFFMAN, INC.
900 Bob Ehlen Drive
Anoka MN 55303
612/422-2566
Contact Mike Bauman, Corporate Human Resources Specialist. Manufacturers of non-current wire devices and electric/electronic enclosures. Common positions include: Accountant; Attorney; Buyer; Computer Programmer; Draftsperson; Mechanical Engineer; Metallurgical Engineer; General Manager; Marketing Specialist; Personnel and Labor Relations Specialist; Systems Analyst; Technical Writer/Editor; Transportation & Traffic Specialist. Principal educational backgrounds sought: Accounting; Business Administration; Communications; Computer Science; Engineering. Company benefits include: medical insurance; dental insurance; pension plan; life insurance; tuition assistance; disability coverage; profit sharing; employee discounts; savings plan. Corporate, regional, divisional headquarters location. Operations at this facility include: manufacturing; research and development; administration; service; sales.

FORESTER BOATS
180 Industrial Boulevard East
Faux Rapids MN 56379
612/252-4304
Contact Personnel Department. A local, national, and regional firm involved in aluminum and steel fabricating, as well as constructing pontoon boats.

HITCHCOCK INDUSTRIES INC.
8701 Harriet Avenue South
Minneapolis MN 55420
612/887-7800
Contact Anita Balkan, Salaried Employment & Compensation. Manufacturer of aluminum and magnesium castings for aerospace and industry. Common positions include: Mechanical Engineer; Metallurgical Engineer. Principal educational backgrounds sought: Engineering. Company benefits include: medical, dental and life insurance; pension plan; tuition assistance; disability coverage; employee discounts; savings plan. Corporate headquarters location. Operations at this facility include: manufacturing.

J & M METAL FABRICATING INCORPORATED
9303 Science Center Drive
New Hope MN 55428
612/533-0629
Contact Personnel Department. An area supplier of machine shop subcontract work.

LEE STAMPINGS
1750 West 96th Street
Bloomington MN 55431
612/888-8831
Contact Martha Richardson, Office Manager. A leading Minneapolis area metal stampings company.

METAL-MATIC INC.
629 2nd Street South East
Minneapolis MN 55414
612/378-0411
Contact Personnel. A major manufacturer of steel tubing. Common positions include: Accountant; Computer Programmer; Draftsperson; Systems Analyst. Company benefits include: medical, dental, and life insurance; tuition assistance; disability coverage; profit sharing. Corporate headquarters location. Operations at this facility include: manufacturing; administration; sales.

MINNESOTA REBAR/DIV. OF PHOENIX STEEL INC.
1025 33rd Avenue S.E.
Minneapolis MN 55414
612/623-0302
Contact Mr. G.E. Zieger, General Manager. Minnesota Rebar is the largest reinforcing bar fabricator in the upper midwest. Fabricates reinforcing steel for a variety of reinforced concrete structures including highway and bridge construction; water treatment, paper and electrical power plants; sports facilities; hydro dams and locks; and commercial, industrial and educational buildings. Common positions include: Accountant; Customer Service Representative; Draftsperson; Civil Engineer. Principal educational backgrounds sought: Engineering; Drafting. Company benefits include: medical insurance; dental insurance; life insurance; tuition assistance; disability coverage; profit sharing; savings plan. Corporate headquarters location: Eau Claire, WI. Parent company: Phoenix Steel Inc. Operations at this facility include: divisional headquarters; manufacturing; sales.

PAPER, CALMENSON & CO.
P.O. Box 64432
St. Paul MN 55164-0432
612/631-1111
Contact Carmella Busch, Human Resources Administrator. Manufacturers of fabricated steel for industrial use. Common positions include: Accountant;

Blue-Collar Worker Supervisor; Customer Service Representative; Draftsperson; Personnel and Labor Relations Specialist; Sales Representative. Training programs offered. Company benefits include: medical insurance; dental insurance; pension plan; life insurance; tuition assistance; disability coverage; savings plan. Corporate headquarters location. Operations at this facility include: manufacturing; administration; service; sales. Equal Opportunity Employer.

TOOL PRODUCTS
5100 Boone Avenue North
New Hope MN 55428
612/536-5520
Contact Kim Burnes, Human Resources Director. A nationwide leader in the die cast industry. Common positions include: Accountant; Blue-Collar Worker Supervisor; Buyer; Customer Service Representative; Draftsperson; Industrial Engineer; Mechanical Engineer; Department Manager; Personnel & Labor Relations Specialist; Quality Control Supervisor; Sales Representative; CNC Machining Specialist. Principal educational backgrounds sought: Accounting; Business Administration; Computer Science; Engineering; Marketing; Mathematics; CNC Machining. Company benefits include: medical, dental, and life insurance; pension plan; tuition assistance; disability coverage; savings plan; vacation; holiday; 401K plan. Corporate headquarters location: St. Louis Park, MN. Parent company: Quadion. Operations at this facility include: manufacturing; research/development; administration; sales.

VINCENT METALS/A DIVISION OF RIO ALGOM, INC.
P.O. Box 360
Minneapolis MN 55440
Contact Mr. D.P. Wilson, Personnel Manager. A major distributor of ferrous and non-ferrous metals. Common positions include: Accountant; Administrator; Blue-Collar Worker Supervisor; Buyer; Computer Programmer; Credit Manager; Customer Service Representative; Metallurgical Engineer; Financial Analyst; Branch Manager; Department Manager; Management Trainee; Operations/Production Manager; Personnel and Labor Relations Specialist; Marketing Specialist; Purchasing Agent; Sales Representative; Systems Analyst; Transportation & Traffic Specialist. Principal educational backgrounds sought: Accounting; Business Administration; Communications; Computer Science; Finance; Liberal Arts; Marketing. Company benefits include: medical insurance; dental insurance; pension plan; life insurance; tuition assistance; disability coverage; profit sharing; savings plan; workout room; tennis courts; swimming pool. Corporate, regional, divisional headquarters location. Operations at this facility include: administration; sales; service. Operations vary at 15 other locations.

WATEROUS COMPANY
300 John E. Carroll Avenue
South St. Paul MN 55075
612/450-5000
Contact Rich Ryan, Personnel Director. A major iron foundry.

WHEELING CORRUGATING COMPANY
P.O. Box 581009
Minneapolis MN 55458-1009
612/789-7233
Contact Jim Lanerd, Operations Manager. A subsidiary of Wheeling-Pittsburgh Steel Corporation, a major manufacturer of steel and steel products. Corporate headquarters location: Pittsburgh, PA.

FINANCIAL SERVICES

For more information on professional employment opportunities in financial services, contact the following professional and trade associations, as listed beginning on page 251:

AMERICAN FINANCIAL SERVICES ASSOCIATION
AMERICAN MANAGEMENT ASSOCIATION
AMERICAN MANAGEMENT ASSOCIATION/MINNEAPOLIS
    CHAPTER
AMERICAN SOCIETY OF APPRAISERS
AMERICAN SOCIETY OF APPRAISERS/TWIN CITIES CHAPTER
ASSOCIATION OF MANAGEMENT CONSULTING FIRMS
FEDERATION OF TAX ADMINISTRATORS
FINANCIAL ANALYSTS FEDERATION
FINANCIAL EXECUTIVES INSTITUTE
INSTITUTE OF FINANCIAL EDUCATION
INSTITUTE OF FINANCIAL EDUCATION/MINNESOTA CHAPTER 50
INSTITUTE OF MANAGEMENT CONSULTANTS
MINNESOTA CONSUMER FINANCE CONFERENCE
NATIONAL ASSOCIATION OF BUSINESS ECONOMISTS
NATIONAL ASSOCIATION OF CREDIT MANAGEMENT
NATIONAL ASSOCIATION OF CREDIT MANAGEMENT/NORTH
    CENTRAL CHAPTER
NATIONAL ASSOCIATION OF REAL ESTATE INVESTMENT TRUST
NATIONAL CORPORATE CASH MANAGEMENT ASSOCIATION
SECURITIES INDUSTRY ASSOCIATION
TWIN CITIES CASH MANAGEMENT ASSOCIATION

ALLISON-WILLIAMS COMPANY
333 South 7th Street,
Minneapolis MN 55402
612/333-3475
Contact June Johnson, Office Manager. A financial services firm engaged in the sale of municipal bonds, corporate bonds and private placement. Employs 45.

CRAIG-HALLUM, INC.
701 4th Avenue South, 10th Floor
Minneapolis MN 55415
612/332-1212
Contact Mark Hengesteg, Executive V.P./Sales. A leading Minneapolis investment banking company.

DAIN BOSWORTH, INC.
100 Dain Tower, 21st Floor
Minneapolis MN 55402
612/371-2711
Contact Mary Melbo, Personnel. A major financial consulting and securities firm. Common positions include: Financial Analyst; Operations/Production Manager; Stock Broker. Principal educational backgrounds sought: Accounting; Business Administration; Economics; Finance. Company benefits include: medical, dental, and life insurance; pension plan; tuition assistance; disability coverage; profit sharing; employee discounts. Corporate headquarters location. Parent company: Inter-Regional Financial Group. Operations at this facility include: regional headquarters; divisional headquarters; research/development; administration; service; sales. New York Stock Exchange and American Stock Exchange.

FIDELITY ACCEPTANCE CORPORATION
330 2nd Ave. S.
Towle Building
Suite 790
Minneapolis MN 55401
612/338-5479
Contact Ivan Fercho, Secretary. A financial services company engaged in loan financing.

GMAC/RESIDENTIAL FUNDING CORPORATION
8400 Normandale Lake Boulevard
Suite 600
Minneapolis MN 55437
612/832-7000
Contact Janine Mack, Employment Assistant. A leader in the secondary mortgage market. Common positions include: Accountant; Computer Programmer; Customer Service Representative; Financial Analyst; Department Manager; Personnel and Labor Relations Specialist; Systems

Analyst; Underwriter. Principal educational backgrounds sought: Business Administration; Economics; Finance. Internships offered. Company benefits include: medical insurance; dental insurance; pension plan; life insurance; tuition assistance; disability coverage; savings plan; 401K. Corporate headquarters location. Parent company: GMAC Mortgage Corporation. Operations at this facility include: regional headquarters; divisional headquarters; administration; service; sales.

GREEN TREE ACCEPTANCE, INC.
500 Landmark Towers
St. Paul MN 55102
612/293-3400
Contact Personnel. A financing company for mobile manufactured homes.

ROBERT HALF OF MINNESOTA, INC.
2800 Norwest Center
Minneapolis MN 55402
612/339-9001
Contact Paul Gentzkow, General Manager. The world's largest professional research firm specializing in finance, accounting, data processing and banking. Common positions include: Accountant; Bank Officer/Manager; Computer Programmer; Credit Manager; Systems Analyst. Principal educational backgrounds sought: Accounting; Business Administration; Computer Science; Finance. Corporate headquarters location: San Fransisco, CA. Parent companny: Robert Half International. Operations at this facility include: regional headquarters. National O.T.C.

THE HAY GROUP
TCF Tower #1350
Minneapolis MN 55402
612/339-0555
Contact William E. Lough II, Vice-President/General Manager. A management consulting firm that provides services ranging from total compensation planning to strategic management, business culture, employee surveys, and outplacement. Common positions include: Management Consultant. Company benefits include: medical insurance; dental insurance; pension plan; life insurance; tuition assistance; disability coverage. Corporate headquarters location: Philadelphia, PA. Operations at this facility: field office.

HEWITT ASSOCIATES
45 South 7th Street, Suite 2100
Minneapolis MN 55402
612/339-7501
For professional hiring information, contact home office at 100 Half Day Road, Lincolnshire IL 60015. Hewitt Associates is an international firm of consultants and actuaries specializing in the design, financing,

communication, and administration of employee benefit and compensation programs.

IDS FINANCIAL SERVICES
P.O. Box 534
Minneapolis MN 55440
612/372-3131
Contact Personnel Department. A diversified financial services firm doing business through a variety of operations, including, among others, IDS Life Insurance Co., a life and disability income insurance firm; IDS Mutual, Inc., IDS New Dimensions Fund, Inc., IDS Progressive Fund, Inc., IDS Selective Fund, Inc., and IDS Stock Fund, a group of open-end diversified mutual fund companies. Company employs 3,600.

ITT CONSUMER FINANCIAL CORPORATION
605 Highway 169 North
Minneapolis MN 55441
612/540-0800
Contact Gail Merritt, Personnel. A leading provider of consumer and commercial loans, doing business as a subsidiary of ITT Corporation.

INTER-REGIONAL FINANCIAL GROUP
100 Dain Tower
Minneapolis MN 55402
612/371-7750
Contact Personnel. One of Minneapolis' leading security brokerage and investment banking companies.

McGLADREY & PULLEN
1300 Midwest Plaza East
800 Marquette Avenue
Minneapolis MN 55402
612/332-4300
Contact Paul Annett, Principal. Local office of a national management and consulting firm. Common positions include: Accountant; Civil Engineer; Electrical Engineer; Mechanical Engineer; Department Manager; General Manager; Marketing Specialist; Personnel and Labor Relations Specialist; Sales Representative. Principal educational backgrounds sought: Accounting; Business Administration; Chemistry; Engineering; Liberal Arts; Marketing. Company benefits include: medical insurance; dental insurance; life insurance; disability coverage; profit sharing. Operations at this facility include: regional headquarters.

MILLER & SCHROEDER

7900 Xerxes Avenue
Suite 2300
Minneapolis MN 55431
612/831-1500
Contact Carol Anderson, Personnel Director. A financial services firm engaged in the underwriting and sale of municipal bonds. Employs 250.

MINNESOTA MUTUAL COMPANIES

400 North Roberts
St. Paul MN 55101
612/298-3448
Contact Gary H. Schwartz, Director of Human Resources. A five billion dollar, national financial services organization headquartered in Minnesota. Employee sales and customer service representative positions located in major metropolitan areas. Common positions include: Customer Service Representative; Sales Representative. Principal educational backgrounds sought: Business Administration; Economics. Company benefits include: medical, dental, and life insurance; pension plan; tuition assistance. Corporate headquarters location. New York Stock Exchange (MMLIC).

MINNESOTA TITLE FINANCIAL CORPORATION

400 2nd Avenue South
Minneapolis MN 55401
612/371-1111
Contact Cheryl Jones, Personnel Director. A prominent Minneapolis-based financial services firm.

NORWEST MORTGAGE INC.

Midwest Plaza
Suite 1200 East Tower
800 Marquette Avenue South
Minneapolis MN 55402
612/343-3400
Contact Kathy Peterson, Personnel Representative. A mortgage banking company.

PIPER JAFFRAY

P.O. Box 28
Minneapolis MN 55440
612/342-6000
Contact Personnel Recruiting. An investment banking and securities firm. Common positions include: Accountant; Administrator; Advertising Worker; Financial Analyst; Personnel and Labor Relations Specialist; Sales Representative; Underwriter. Principal educational backgrounds sought: Accounting; Business Administration; Communications; Finance; Mathematics. Training programs offered; Internships offered. Company benefits include: medical insurance; dental insurance; pension plan; life

insurance; tuition assistance; disability coverage; daycare assistance; profit sharing; employee discounts; savings plan. Corporate headquarters location.

CH ROBINSON CO.
8100 Mitchell Road, Suite 200
Eden Prairie MN 55344
612/937-8500
Contact Personnel. An agricultural brokerage and financing company.

TOWERS, PERRIN, FORSTER, AND CROSBY
8300 Norman Center Drive, Suite 600
Bloomington MN 55437-1097
612/897-3300
Contact Kathy Halverson, Personnel Director. Regional office of an international consulting organization specializing in total compensation, actuarial and communications consulting services.

TRAVELERS EXPRESS COMPANY
1550 Utica Avenue South
Minneapolis MN 55416
612/591-3000
Contact Gary Busch, Personnel Director. Regional office for the well-known financial products company.

FOOD AND BEVERAGE RELATED: PROCESSING AND DISTRIBUTION

For more information on professional employment opportunities in the food and beverage industries, contact the following professional and trade associations, as listed beginning on page 251:

AMERICAN ASSOCIATION OF CEREAL CHEMISTS
AMERICAN SOCIETY OF AGRICULTURAL ENGINEERS
AMERICAN SOCIETY OF BRWEING CHEMISTS
DAIRY COUNCIL OF MINNESOTA
DAIRY AND FOOD INDUSTRIES SUPPLY ASSOCIATION
NATIONAL AGRICULTURAL CHEMICALS ASSOCIATION
NATIONAL DAIRY COUNCIL
UNITED FOOD AND COMMERCIAL INTERNATIONAL UNION
UNITED FOOD AND COMMERCIAL WORKERS UNION/LOCAL 653

ADM GRAIN COMPANY
P.O. Box 15166
Commerce Station
Minneapolis MN 55415
612/371-3400
Contact Harold Hackelman, Personnel. A major area grain firm operating as a subsidiary of Archer Daniels Company, a national food processing company.

ADM MILLING COMPANY
3501 Hiawatha Avenue
Minneapolis MN 55406
612/729-8381
Contact Manager. A major area flour mill doing business as a subsidiary of Archer Daniels Company, a national food processing company.

CARTER-DAY INDUSTRIES
500 73rd Avenue, NE
Minneapolis MN 55432
612/571-1000
Contact Personnel Department. A company engaged in the engineering, designing, and manufacturing to size of seed grains and plastic pellets for the agricultural processing and petro chemical industries.

CENEX/LAND O'LAKES
P.O. Box 64089
St. Paul MN 55164-0089
612/451-5151
Contact Human Resources Manager. A producer of agricultural supplies. Principal educational backgrounds sought: Accounting; Business Administration; Computer Science; Liberal Arts; Marketing; Agriculture; Animal Science; Agronomy. Company benefits include: medical, dental, and life insurance; tuition assistance; disability coverage; savings plan. Corporate headquarters location. Operations at this facility include: administration; service; sales.

COCA-COLA/MIDWEST
2750 Eagandale
St. Paul MN 55121
612/454-5460
Contact Personnel Manager. Regional office for the international bottled and canned soft drink company.

CONAGRA P.V. GRAIN COMPANY
730 2nd Avenue South, 14th Floor
Minneapolis MN 55402
612/370-7500
Contact Roberta M. Mellen, Personnel Director. A major grain company. Common positions include: Accountant; Administrator; Financial Analyst; Grain/Commodity Merchandiser. Company benefits include: medical insurance; dental insurance; pension plan; life insurance; tuition assistance; disability coverage; savings plan. Corporate headquarters location. Operations at this facility include: regional headquarters; administration; New York Stock Exchange.

CONTINENTAL BAKING COMPANY
1511 Excelsior Avenue East
Hopkins MN 55343
612/935-3034
Contact Donna Braun, Personnel Manager. A regional distributor of bread and cake products. Common positions include: Route Sales Represenative; Retail Sales Clerk. Principal educational backgrounds sought: Business Administration; Marketing. Company benefits include: medical, dental, and life insurance; pension plan; disability coverage. Corporate headquarters location: St. Louis, MO. Operations at this facility include: sales and distribution.

THE CORNELIUS COMPANY
1 Cornelius Place
Anoka MN 55303
612/421-6120
Contact Human Resources. A local, regional, and national company involved in beverage dispensing and providing food service equipment.

COUNTRY LAKE FOODS
Box 64223
St. Paul MN 55164
612/851-1260
Contact Personnel Department. A leading producer of dairy products. Employs 760.

CREAMETTE COMPANY
428 North 1st Street
Minneapolis MN 55401
612/333-4281
Contact Wayne Johnson, Personnel Director. A major food company operating as a subsidiary of Borden, Inc. Products include macaroni and egg noodles, frozen foods and other food products.

GENERAL MILLS, INC.
P.O. Box 1113
Minneapolis MN 55440
612/540-2311
Contact Dixie Lindsley, Personnel Director. A nationally-known producer of a wide variety of consumer foods, with an emphasis on flour, feeds, cereals, wheat, starches, vitamins and cake mixes.

GOLDEN VALLEY MICROWAVE FOODS, INC.
450 Metro Boulevard
Edina MN 55439
612/835-6900
Contact Personnel Department. A leading processor of microwave foods.

GRIST MILL COMPANY
P.O. Box 430
21340 Hayes Avenue
Lakeville MN 55044
612/469-4981
Contact Kathy Parenteau, Personnel Director. A major area food preparation company.

HARVEST STATES COOPERATIVE
P.O. Box 64594
St. Paul MN 55164
612/646-9433
Contact Allen Anderson, VP/Administration. A major area grain marketing company.

HOBART CORPORATION
1610 Broadway Street NE
Minneapolis MN 55413
612/379-7544
Contact Teresa M. Snorek, Regional Operations Manager. Company sells and services commercial food preparing equipment used in the food service industry and in the food retail (supermarket) industry. Common positions include: Branch Manager; General Manager; Management Trainee; Sales Representative; Service Technician. Company benefits include; medical, dental, and life insurance; pension plan; savings plan. Corporate headquarters location: Troy, OH. Parent company: Premark International. Operations at this facility include: regional headquarters; administration; service; sales. New York Stock Exchange.

INTERNATIONAL DAIRY QUEEN, INC.
P.O. Box 39286
Minneapolis MN 55439-0286
612/830-0200
Contact Personnel. Corporate headquarters location of the well-known retail soft-serve ice cream company.

INTERNATIONAL MULTIFOODS
Multifoods Tower
P.O. Box 2942
Minneapolis MN 55402
612/340-3300
Contact Terri Nelson, Recruiting Representative. A major national processor and distributor of food. Corporate headquarters location. New York Stock Exchange. Common positions include: Accountant; Computer Programmer; Department Manager; General Manager; Operations/Production Manager; Personnel and Labor Relations Specialist; Systems Analyst. Principal educational backgrounds sought: Accounting; Business Administration; Computer Science; Finance. Company benefits include: medical insurance; dental insurance; pension plan; life insurance; tuition assistance; disability coverage; profit sharing; employee discounts; savings plan.

KRAFT/AMERICAN
2864 Eagandale Boulevard
Eagan MN 55121
612/454-6580
Contact Richard Frederick, Manager, Human Resources. A major foodservice distributor. Primary customers include hotels, restaurants, schools, and government institutions. Positions include: Accountant; Blue Collar Worker Supervisor; Buyer; Computer Programmer; Credit Manager; Customer Service Representative; Dietician; Financial Analyst; Department Manager; General Manager; Management Trainee; Operations/Production Manager; Marketing Specialist; Personnel and Labor Relations Specialist; Purchasing Agent; Sales Representative; Systems Analyst; Transportation and Traffic Specialist. Principal educational backgrounds sought include: Accounting; Business Administration; Marketing. Training programs offered. Company benefits include: medical insurance; dental insurance; pension plan; life insurance; tuition assistance; disability coverage; savings plan. Corporate headquarters location: Chicago, IL. Parent company: Philip Morris. Operations include: service; sales.

LAND O'LAKES INC.
P.O. Box 116
Minneapolis MN 55440
612/481-2222
Contact Staffing Director. A nationally known company involved in the processing and distribution of dairy-related food products.

MEI DIVERSIFIED INC.
90 South Sixth Street
Suite 800
Minneapolis MN
612/339-8853
Contact Personnel. Produces snack and health foods, and candy.

MALT-O-MEAL CO.
2600 IDS Tower
80 South 8th Street
Minneapolis MN 55402
612/338-8551
Contact Personnel. Producers of breakfast cereals.

MARIGOLD FOODS
2929 University S.E.
Minneapolis MN 55414
612/331-3775
Contact Betsy Rausch, Human Resources Director. A producer of ice cream and related products. Common positions include: Accountant; Computer Programmer; Operations/Production Manager; Personnel and Labor Relations Specialist. Principal educational backgrounds sought: Accounting; Business Administration; Computer Science; Liberal Arts; Marketing. Training programs offered. Company benefits include: medical insurance; dental insurance; pension plan; life insurance; tuition assistance; disability coverage. Corporate headquarters location. Parent company: Wessanen Inc. Operations at this facility include: divisional headquarters; manufacturing; administration; sales.

McGARVEY COFFEE, INC.
5725 Highway 7
Minneapolis MN 55416
612/929-0461
Contact Personnel Department. A major Minneapolis coffee producer.

McGLYNN BAKERIES INC.
7752 Mitchell Road
Eden Prairie MN 55344
612/937-9404
Contact Personnel Office. A large regional bakery. Common positions include: Industrial Engineer; Food Technologist. Company benefits include: medical insurance; profit sharing; employee discounts. Corporate headquarters location. Operations at this facility include: manufacturing; research/development; administration; sales.

METZ BAKING COMPANY
2745 Long Lake Road
P.O. Box 130340
Roseville MN 55113
612/636-8400
Contact Office Manager. An area bakery specializing in the wholesale production of bread and rolls. Common positions include: Accountant; Industrial Engineer; General Manager; Sales Representative. Principal educational backgrounds sought: Accounting; Business Administration; Mathematics. Company benefits include: medical, dental, and life insurance; pension plan; disability coverage. Corporate headquarters location: Sioux City, IA. Operations at this facility include: manufacturing; service; sales.

MICHAEL FOODS INC.
5353 Wayzata Boulevard
Suite 324
Minneapolis MN 55416
612/546-1500
Contact Barb Ness, Personnel Director. A producer of dairy, potato and egg products.

MID AMERICA DAIRYMEN INC.
1313 Northstar Drive
Zumbrota MN 55992
507/732-5124
Contact Bob Hawley, Personnel Director. An area producer of cheddar cheese. Common positions include: Accountant; Blue-Collar Worker Supervisor; Mechanical Engineer; Manager; Department Manager; Management Trainee; Operations/Production Manager; Personnel & Labor Relations Specialist; Quality Control Supervisor. Principal educational backgrounds sought: Accounting; Engineering; Mathematics. Company benefits include: medical, dental, and life insurance; pension plan; disability coverage; savings plan. Corporate headquarters location: Springfield, MO. Operations at this facility include: manufacturing.

NORTH STAR UNIVERSAL INC.
5353 Wayzata Boulevard
Suite 610
Minneapolis MN 55416
612/546-7500
Contact Personnel. Producers of dairy products, groceries and related products.

OLD DUTCH FOODS
2375 Terminal Road
P.O. Box 64627
St. Paul MN 55164
612/633-8810
Contact Personnel Office. A well-known food preparation company.

PEPSI-COLA COMPANY/
CENTRAL DIVISION
1300 East Cliff Road
Burnsville MN 55337
612/890-8940
Contact Nick deNicola, Area Employee Relations Manager. Regional office for the international bottled and canned soft drink corporation. Common positions include: Accountant; Biochemist; Blue-Collar Worker Supervisor; Computer Programmer; Credit Manager; Industrial Engineer; Mechanical Engineer; Financial Analyst; Industrial Manager; Branch Manager; Department Manager; Management Trainee; Operations/Production Manager; Marketing Specialist; Personnel & Labor Relations Specialist; Quality Control Supervisor; Sales Representative; Transportation & Traffic Specialist. Principal educational backgrounds sought: Accounting; Business Administration; Communications; Engineering; Finance; Industrial Relations; Liberal Arts; Marketing. Company benefits include: medical, dental, and life insurance; pension plan; tuition assistance; disability; employee discounts; savings plan. Corporate headquarters location: Somers, NY. Operations at this facility include: regional headquarters; manufacturing; administration; service; sales. Parent company: Pepsico. New York Stock Exchange.

PHILLIPS BEVERAGE CO.
2345 Kennedy Street NE
Minneapolis MN 55413
612/331-6230
Contact Personnel. Specializing in wine and distilled beverages, beer and other fermented malt liquors.

PILLSBURY COMPANY
Mail Station 38R5
200 South 6th Street
Minneapolis MN 55402-1464
612/330-2305
Contact Mr. Develle Turner, Staffing Supervisor. Manufactures and markets food products for consumer, industrial, and international markets. Corporate headquarters location. Common positions include: Accountant; Computer Programmer. Principal educational backgrounds sought: Accounting.

PILLSBURY/GREEN GIANT
101 West 8th Street
Glencoe MN 55336
612/864-3151
Contact Vince Venne, Human Resources Manager. A nationally recognized canned vegetables company. Common positions include: Mechanical Engineer; Operations/Production; Manager. Principal educational backgrounds sought: Engineering; Operations. Company benefits include: medical, dental, and life insurance; pension plan; tuition assistance; disability coverage; profit sharing; employee discounts; savings plan. Corporate headquarters location: London. Parent company: Grand Metropolitan. Operations at this facility include: manufacturing.

PURINA MILLS
3901 Hiawatha Avenue South
Minneapolis MN 55406
612/722-9581
Contact Mr. Nile Walter, Area Controller. A major area grain mill specializing in the production of livestock feeds.

RALSTON PURINA COMPANY
1380 Corporate Center Curve
Suite 108
Eagan MN 55121
612/688-2760
Contact Sheila Barsness, Operations Coordinator. Area sales office of the well known producer of food for people and animals. For sales positions, contact Mike Page, Regional Sales Manager. Corporate headquarters location: St. Louis, MO. Common positions at this facility include: Administrator; Customer Service Representative; Branch Manager; Sales Representative. Principal educational backgrounds sought: Marketing. Company benefits include: medical insurance; dental insurance; pension plan; life insurance; tuition assistance; disability coverage; savings plan. Operations at this facility: regional headquarters.

SANDOZ NUTRITION CORPORATION
5320 West 23rd Street
P.O. Box 370
Minneapolis MN 55440
612/925-2100
Contact Walt Rohmann, Personnel. A leading food production and distribution company. Makers of Ovaltine as well as many other well-known brands.

J. SCHMIDT BREWING COMPANY
882 West 7th Street
St. Paul MN 55102
612/290-8227
Contact Human Resources. A local, regional, and national processor of malt beverages.

TASTY BAKERY
97 East 12th Street
St. Paul MN 55101
612/224-3891
Contact Lyle Host, Personnel Director. A major area baking company.

WEINSTEIN INTERNATIONAL CORPORATION
5738 Olson Memorial Highway
Minneapolis MN 55422
612/546-4471
Contact Doug Hagen, Controller. A division of American Foods Group, Weinstein is a major area wholesaler of frozen foods.

FOOD/TRADE

APPLEBAUMS FOOD MARKETS/RAINBOW FOODS
1515 Excelsior Avenue East
Hopkins MN 55343
612/931-1100
Contact Eileen Langeslay, Personnel Director. A major area chain of retail grocery stores.

BYERLY'S INC.
7171 France Avenue South
Edina MN 55435
612/831-3601
Contact Personnel Department. Corporate office of a grocery store company that operates seven stores in the Minneapolis-St. Paul region.

COUNTRY CLUB MARKETS
3000 France Avenue South
St. Louis MN 55416
612/920-9337
Contact Personnel. A major supermarket chain. Employs 1300.

HOLIDAY COMPANIES
4567 West 80th Street
Bloominton MN 55437
612/830-8700
Contact Robert S. Nye, Human Resources Department. Owner and operator of a group of grocery and convenience stores throughout the Upper Midwest. Common positions include: Computer Programmer; Management Trainee; Secretarial. Principal educational backgrounds sought: Computer Science; Liberal Arts; Business; Supermarket Management. Company benefits include: medical insurance; dental insurance; life insurance; tuition assistance; disability coverage; profit sharing; employee discounts. Corporate headquarters location. Operations at this facility include: administration.

JERRY'S ENTERPRISES
5101 Vernon Avenue South
Edina MN 55436
612/929-2685
Contact W.W. O'Brien, Controller. A major area grocery store chain.

KNOWLAN'S SUPER MARKETS
281 Maria Avenue
St. Paul MN 55106
612/774-9621
Contact Marie Aarthun, President. Corporate offices for a major St. Paul chain of retail grocery stores.

LUND'S INC.
1450 West Lake Street
Minneapolis MN 55408
612/825-4433
Contact Jeff Oden, Operations Director. A major area retail grocery store chain.

NASH FINCH COMPANY
3381 Gorham Avenue
St. Louis Park MN 55426
612/929-0371
Contact Duane Wanner, Personnel Administration. Wholesalers of a general line of groceries.

SUPER VALU STORES
11840 Valley View Road
Eden Prairie MN 55344
612/828-4000
Contact Mike Overline, Director of Personnel. A well known grocery wholesaler and retail support company.

TOM THUMB FOOD MARKETS, INC.
110 East 17th Street
Hastings MN 55033
612/437-9023
Contact Joseph Adrew, Personnel Director. A major area grocery and convenience store chain. Common positions include: Management Trainee. Principal educational backgrounds sought: Accounting; Business Administration; Economics; Finance; Marketing. Company benefits include: medical, dental, and life insurance; disability coverage; profit sharing. Corporate headquarters location. Operations at this facility include: regional headquarters; administration; service; sales.

GENERAL MERCHANDISE

For more information on professional employment opportunities in the retail industry, contact the following professional association, as listed beginning on page 251:

NATIONAL RETAIL MERCHANTS ASSOCIATION

BEST BUY COMPANY
4400 West 78th Street
Bloomington MN 55435
612/896-2300
Contact Human Resources Department. The corporate office for a retail radio and TV company.

BEST PRODUCTS
13513 Richdale Drive
District Office,
Minnetonka MN 55343
612/546-4561
Contact Personnel Department. A regional catalogue showroom and mail order company.

CALSTAR INCORPORATED
6470 Sycamore Court
Maple Grove MN 55369
Contact Marylyn Benson, Administrative Assistant. A direct mail marketer of rare stamps and coins. Common positions include: Accountant; Administrator; Blue-Collar Worker Supervisor; Credit Manager; Customer Service Representative; Financial Analyst; Industrial Manager; Department Manager; General Manager; Operations/Production Manager; Marketing Specialist; Quality Control Supervisor; Sales Representative; Systems Analyst; Technical Writer/Editor. Principal educational backgrounds sought:

Accounting; Art/Design; Communications; Computer Science; Economics; Finance; Marketing. Operations at this facility include: regional and divisional headquarters; research/development; administration; service; sales.

CARSON PIRIE SCOTT
600 Nicollet Mall
Minneapolis MN 55402
612/347-7611
Contact Human Resources. A major retail department store.

DAYTON-HUDSON CORP.
777 Nicollet Mall
Minneapolis MN 55402
612/370-6948
Contact Personnel. Owners and operators of one of the nation's largest retail department stores.

FINGERHUT CORPORATION
4400 Baker Road
Minnetonka MN 55343
612/932-3100
Contact Employment Representative. A major national mail order house.

FRITZ COMPANY
1912 Hastings Avenue
Newport MN 55055
612/459-9751
Contact Personnel. An area wholesaler.

GABBERTS INC.
3501 West 69th Street
Edina MN 55435
612/927-1500
Contact Cathy Graham, Personnel Director. A major area retail furniture store.

GENERAL OFFICE PRODUCTS CO.
4521 Highway 7
St. Louis Park MN 55416
612/925-7698
Contact Diane Lambrecht, Human Resources Director. A leading supplier of assorted office supplies and furniture. Common positions include: Accountant; Credit Manager; Customer Service Representative; Operations/Production Manager; Personnel and Labor Relations Specialist; Sales Representative. Principal educational backgrounds sought: Accounting; Art/Design; Business Administration; Computer Science. Company benefits include: medical insurance; dental insurance; pension plan; life insurance; tuition assistance; disability coverage; employee discounts; savings plan.

Corporate headquarters location. Parent company: Josephson Office Products. Operations at this facility include: administration; service; sales.

GOPHER NEWS COMPANY
9000 10th Avenue North
Minneapolis MN 55427
612/546-5300
Contact Personnel Department. A distributor of periodicals, paperback and trade books, audio and video tapes and children's toys.

HOIGAARD'S
3550 South Highway 100
Minneapolis MN 55416
612/929-1351
Contact Gary Chambers, Personnel Director. A retailer of sporting goods.

JCPENNEY COMPANY
P.O. Box 947
Minneapolis MN 55440
612/942-0116
Contact Lois Johnson, Personnel Manager. Area office of the nationally known department store.

JOSTENS
5501 Norman Center Drive
Minneapolis MN 55437
612/830-3300
Contact Human Resources Department. Jostens is a leading provider of products and services for the youth, education, sports award and recognition markets. The primary products of the company include class rings, yearbooks, graduation products, customized sales and service awards, custom-imprinted activewear, student photography packages, sports awards, customized products for university alumni, and computer-based educational products and services. Company headquarters location.

JUSTER BROTHERS INC.
500 Nicollet Mall
Minneapolis MN 55402
612/333-1431
Contact Personnel Department. A retailer of men's and women's clothing and furnishings.

K-TEL INTERNATIONAL (USA), INC.
15535 Medina Road
Plymouth MN 55447
612/559-6800
Contact Manager of Human Resources. Distributors of recorded music products. Common positions include: Accountant. Principal educational

backgrounds sought include: Accounting. Company benefits include: medical, dental, and life insurance; tuition assistance; disability coverage; employee discounts; 401K Retirement Savings Plan. Corporate headquarters location. Parent company: K-Tel International, Inc.

KNOX LUMBER COMPANY
801 Transfer Road
St. Paul MN 55114
612/649-0911
Contact Mary Medved, Personnel Manager. A major retail lumber company. Common positions include: Accountant; Advertising Worker; Buyer; Computer Programmer; Personnel & Labor Relations Specialist; Sales Representative; Technical Writer/Editor; Transportation & Traffic Specialist. Almost all hiring done at entry level. Principal educational backgrounds sought: Accounting; Art/Design; Business Administration; Communications; Computer Science; Liberal Arts; Marketing. Company benefits include: medical insurance; dental insurance; life insurance; tuition assistance; disability coverage; savings plan. Corporate headquarters. Parent company is Payless Cashways. Operations at this facility include: administration; sales.

LANCER STORES INC.
64 W. 66th Street
Richfield MN 55423
612/861-1774
Contact Skip Thomas, Vice President/Personnel. Lancer Stores Inc. (8 stores) is engaged in men's and women's retail apparel. Corporate headquarters location. Common positions include: Management Trainee. Principal educational backgrounds sought: Business Administration; Fashion Merchandising. Company benefits include: medical insurance; life insurance; employee discounts; paid holidays and vacation. Operations at this facility include: administration; service; sales.

LIEBERMAN ENTERPRISES
10801 Red Circle Drive
Minnetonka MN 55343
612/945-3365
Contact Staffing Manager. A wholesale record and tape distributor. Common positions include: Accountant; Administrator; Advertising Worker; Buyer; Commercial Artist; Computer Programmer; Customer Service Representative; Financial Analyst; Branch Manager; Department Manager; Operations/Production Manager; Marketing Specialist; Personnel Specialist; Retail Manager; Sales Representative; Systems Analyst. Principal educational backgrounds sought: Accounting; Art/Design; Business Administration; Communications; Economics; Finance; Marketing. Training programs offered; Internships offered. Company benefits include: medical, dental, and life insurance; tuition assistance; 401K plan; disability coverage; employee

discounts; savings plan; fitness center. Parent company: LIVE. Operations at this facility include: administration; sales. American Stock Exchange.

LIEMANDT'S INC.
119 Roseville Center
Roseville MN 55113
612/636-0951
Contact Bob Robinson, Area Manager. A major Minneapolis retail clothing store. A subsidiary of Hart, Schaffner, and Marx, a national clothing manufacturer and retailer. Common positions include: Accountant; Administrator; Customer Service Representative; Department Manager; General Manager; Sales Representative; Department Manager; General Manager; Sales Representative. Company benefits include: medical, dental, and life insurance; pension plan; disability coverage; profit sharing; employee discounts; savings plan. Corporate headquarters location: Chicago, IL. Parent company is Hartmarx.

MUSICLAND GROUP, INC.
7500 Excelsior Boulevard
Minneapolis MN 55426
612/932-7700
Contact Kathleen Miller, Manager of Employment. Headquarters of the well-known retail specialty music store company.

QVC NETWORK, INC.
1405 Xenium Lane North
Plymouth MN 55441
612/557-5411
Contact Human Resources. Company sells consumer merchandise, including electronic equipment, jewelry, auto accessories and housewares through mail order and cable television. Common positions include: Customer Service Representative; Order Entry Representative. Training programs available. Company benefits include: medical insurance; dental insurance; employee discounts; savings plan. Corporate headquarters location: West Chester, PA. Parent company: QVC Network, Inc. Operations at this facility: service.

REGIS CORPORATION
5000 Normandale Road
Minneapolis MN 55436
612/929-6776
Contact Ernest Halpern, Senior Vice President/Personnel. An area chain of beauty salons.

SCHMITT MUSIC
88 South 10th Street
Minneapolis MN 55403
612/339-4811
Contact Debbie Gacek, Director of Personnel. An area chain of music stores.

SEARS, ROEBUCK & CO.
900 East Lake Street
Minneapolis MN 55407
612/874-2706
Contact Clara Mancino, Personnel Specialist. Area office for the nationally known retail store. Common positions include: Customer Service Representative; Sales Representative; Warehouse Worker; Auto Center Mechanic. Company benefits include: medical and life insurance; disability coverage; pension plan; profit sharing; employee discounts. Corporate headquarters location: Chicago, IL. Operations at this facility include: sales. New York Stock Exchange.

TARGET
33 South Sixth Street
P.O. Box 1392,
Minneapolis MN 55440-1392
612/370-6060
Contact Personnel Department. Offices for the discount retail chain. Company benefits include: medical, dental, and life insurance; pension plan; tuition assistance; disability coverage; profit sharing; employee discounts; savings plan. Corporate headquarters location.

THRIFTY WHITE STORES
8441 Wayzata Boulevard
Minneapolis MN 55426
612/545-2234
Contact Gary Sticka, Director of Human Resources. Retail drug store chain with approximately 60 locations in Minnesota, the Dakotas, Iowa, and Montana. Employee owned. Common positions include: Accountant; Blue-Collar Worker Supervisor; Buyer; Computer Programmer; Customer Service Representative; Department Manager; General Manager; Management Trainee; Operations/Production Manager; Personnel and Labor Relations Specialist; Systems Analyst. Principal educational backgrounds sought: Accounting; Business Administration; Liberal Arts; Retail. Training programs offered; Internships offered. Company benefits include: medical insurance; dental insurance; life insurance; tuition assistance; disability coverage; profit sharing; employee discounts; savings plan. Corporate headquarters location. Operations at this facility include: administration.

TONKA CORPORATION
Interchange N. Building
300 South HIghway 169
Suite 500
St. Louis Park MN 55426
612/525-3500
Contact Personnel. Headquarters of the well-known children's toy manufacturers.

HEALTH CARE AND PHARMACEUTICALS

For more information on professional employment opportunities in the health care and pharmaceuticals industries, contact the following professional and trade associations, as listed beginning on page 251:

AMERICAN ACADEMY OF FAMILY PHYSICIANS/MINNESOTA
    CHAPTER
AMERICAN ACADEMY OF PHYSICIANS ASSISTANTS
AMERICAN ASSOCIATION FOR CLINICAL CHEMISTRY
AMERICAN COLLEGE OF HEALTHCARE EXECUTIVES
AMERICAN DENTAL ASSOCIATION
AMERICAN HEALTH CARE ASSOCIATION
AMERICAN MEDICAL ASSOCIATION
AMERICAN OCCUPATIONAL THERAPY ASSOCIATION
AMERICAN PHARMACEUTICAL ASSOCIATION
AMERICAN PHYSICAL THERAPY ASSOCIATION
AMERICAN SOCIETY FOR BIOCHEMISTRY AND MOLECULAR
    BIOLOGY
AMERICAN SOCIETY OF HOSPITAL PHARMACISTS
AMERICAN VETERINARY MEDICAL ASSOCIATION
CARDIOVASCULAR CREDENTIALING INTERNATIONAL
CARE PROVIDERS OF MINNESOTA
MEDICAL GROUP MANAGEMENT ASSOCIATION
MEDICAL GROUP MANAGEMENT ASSOCIATION/MINNEAPOLIS
MINNEAPOLIS VETERINARY MEDICAL ASSOCIATION
MINNESOTA DENTAL ASSOCIATION
MINNESOTA OCCUPATIONAL THERAPY ASSOCIATION
MINNESOTA STATE PHARMACEUTICAL ASSOCIATION
NATIONAL HEALTH COUNCIL
NATIONAL MEDICAL ASSOCIATION
NATIONAL MEDICAL ASSOCIATION/MINNEAPOLIS-ST. PAUL

ABBOTT NORTHWESTERN HOSPITAL
800 East 28th Street at Chicago Avenue
Minneapolis MN 55407
612/863-4838
Contact Personnel. One of Minneapolis' leading health care facilities.

AMERICAN MEDICAL SYSTEMS
11001 Bren Road East
Minnetonka MN 55343
612/933-4666
Contact Director of Personnel. An area supplier of orthodontic and surgical supplies.

AEQUITRON MEDICAL INC.
14800 28th Avenue North
Minneapolis MN 55447
612/557-9200
Contact Kris Anders, Personnel Administrator. Manufactures medical electronic equipment. Employs 165.

BETHEDSA LUTHERAN HOSPITAL
559 Capital Boulevard
St. Paul MN 55103
612/221-2200
Contact Personnel. A leading St. Paul hospital.

BIO-MEDICS INC.
9600 West 76th Street
Suite K
Eden Prairie MN 55344
612/944-7784
Contact Personnel. Produces blood pumps and blood pump consoles.

CARDIAC PACEMAKERS INC./
SUBSIDIARY OF ELI LILLY & COMPANY
4100 Hamline Avenue North
St. Paul MN 55112
612/638-4290
Contact Katie Pearson, Manager of Human Resources. Develops, manufactures, and sells a wide range of products used in the treatment of cardiac arrhythmias. The company's products are both implantable and external electronic devices and accessories that are sold to hospitals and other healthcare providers worldwide. Common positions at this facility include: Biomedical Engineer; Electrical Engineer; Mechanical Engineer; Financial Analyst; Systems Analyst. Principal educational backgrounds sought: Business Administration; Computer Science; Engineering. Company benefits include: medical insurance; dental insurance; life insurance; tuition assistance; disability coverage; profit sharing; savings plan. Corporate headquarters location. Operations at this facility include: manufacturing; research/development; administration.

CHILDREN'S HOSPITAL OF ST. PAUL
345 N. Smith Avenue
St. Paul MN 55102
612/220-6000
Contact Personnel. A major St. Paul medical facility.

DAHLBERG, INC.
4101 Dahlberg Drive
Golden Valley MN 55422
612/545-3721
Contact Deb Pender, Personnel. A major manufacturer of hearing aids and related items.

DOW BRANDS
5601 East River Road
Fridley MN 55432
612/571-1234
Contact Manager of Human Resources. A manufacturer of personal grooming products.

EMPI INC.
1275 Grey Fox Road
Arden Hills MN 55112
612/636-6600
Contact Personnel. Manufacturers of a tens unit, a muscle stimulator.

FMG TSUMURA
12800 Whitewater Drive
Minnetonka MN 55343
612/945-9400
Contact Jane Lucken, Human Resources Manager. A major producer of home fragrances and personal care products. Common positions include: Accountant; Buyer; Chemist; Computer Programmer; Credit Manager; Customer Service Representative; Department Manager; Marketing Specialist. Principal educational backgrounds sought: Accounting; Business Administration; Chemistry; Computer Science; Marketing. Internships offered. Company benefits include: medical insurance; dental insurance; life insurance; tuition assistance; disability coverage; profit sharing; employee discounts; savings plan. Parent company: Tsumara International, Inc.

GV MEDICAL INC.
3750 Annapolis Lane
Plymouth MN 55447
612/559-4000
Contact Personnel Department. Designs, manufactures, and markets laser-based medical devices for the treatment of heart and blood vessel diseases.

GILLETTE CHILDREN'S HOSPITAL
200 University Avenue
East St. Paul MN 55101
612/291-2848
Contact Personnel. A leading St. Paul hospital.

THE GILLETTE COMPANY
310 East 5th Street
St. Paul MN 55101
612/292-2929
Contact Kathy Larkin, Sr. Employee Relations Representative. A regional office of the well-known razor blade and personal care products company.

GOLDEN VALLEY HEALTH CENTER
4101 Golden Valley Road
Golden Valley MN 55422
612/588-2771
Contact Personnel. A major metro Twin Cities health services company.

HAZELDEN FOUNDATION
P.O. Box 11
Center City MN
612/257-4010
Contact Personnel. An area healthcare facility.

HENNEPIN COUNTY MEDICAL CENTER
701 Park Avenue
Minneapolis MN 55415
612/347-2121
Contact Personnel. A major public hospital.

INCSTAR CORP.
1990 Industrial Boulevard
Stillwater MN 55082
612/439-9710
Contact Personnel. Incstar researches, develops and manufactures medical diagnostic kits.

KALLESTAD DIAGNOSTICS
1000 Lake Hazeltine Drive
Chaska MN 55318
612/448-4848
Contact Human Resources Manager. A manufacturer of medical diagnostic test kits. Operations include: manufacturing; research/development. Corporate headquarters location. Common positions include: Accountant; Biochemist; Chemist; Electrical Engineer; Mechanical Engineer; General Manager; Marketing Specialist; Quality Control Supervisor; Sales Representative; Systems Analyst. Principal educational backgrounds sought:

Chemistry; Engineering. Training programs offered. Company benefits include: medical, dental, and life insurance; pension plan; tuition assistance; disability coverage; employee discounts; savings plan. Operations at this facility include: manufacturing; research/development; administration; service; sales.

KRELITZ INDUSTRIES, INC.
P.O. Box 59095
Minneapolis MN 55459-0095
Contact Human Resources Department. Distributes prescription drugs, proprietary products, health and beauty aids and sundries to drug stores, pharmacies, hospitals and mass merchandisers, medical, surgical and laboratory products to hospitals, clinics, physicians offices, laboratories and nursing homes, general merchandise to drug, food, hardware and home improvement, retailers and computerized management systems for independent, chain and hospital pharmacies.

LAKE REGION MANUFACTURING INC.
340 Lake Hazeltine Drive
Chaska MN 55318
612/448-5111
Contact Personnel. Manufacturers of medical equipment.

LOSSING ORTHOPEDIC
P.O. Box 6224
Minneapolis MN 55406-0224
612/331-3985
Contact Personnel Department. A manufacturer of medical supplies specializing in the production and marketing of back and neck devices.

MAICO HEARING INSTRUMENTS INC.
7375 Bush Lake Road
Minneapolis MN 55439
612/835-4400
Contact Human Resources Manager. A producer of audiometers and hearing aids. Common positions include: Accountant; Administrator; Advertising Worker; Buyer; Credit Manager; Customer Service Representative; Draftsperson; Electrical Engineer; Mechanical Engineer; General Manager; Operations/Production Manager; Marketing Specialist; Personnel and Labor Relations Specialist; Purchasing Agent; Quality Control Supervisor; Sales Representative; Technical Writer/Editor; Assembler. Principal educational backgrounds sought: Accounting; Business Administration; Communications; Engineering; Marketing. Company benefits include: medical insurance; dental insurance; pension plan; life insurance; tuition assistance; disability coverage. Corporate headquarters location. Parent company: Gfeller, US. Operations at this facility include: manufacturing; research/development; administration; service; sales.

MEDICAL GRAPHICS CORPORATION
350 Oak Grove Parkway
St. Paul MN 55127
612/484-4874
Contact Personnel Department. A leading manufacurer of computerized medical testing equipment for the health care industry.

MEDRONIC INC.
7000 Central Avenue, NE
Minneapolis MN 55432
612/574-4000
Contact Tamara Tucker, Human Resources Administrator. One of the nation's leading producers of medical devices. Primary products are cardiac pacemakers. Employs over 4,000.

MENTOR CORPORATION
1601 West River Road North
Minneapolis MN 55411
612/588-4685
Contact Mary Bellin, Personnel Director. Manufacturer and distributor of specialized medical devices and related disposable health care products and surgical implant products, primarily for urology, plastic and general surgery. Employs 350.

METHODIST HOSPITAL
6500 Excelsior Boulevard
St. Louis Park MN 55426
612/932-5056
Contact Personnel. A major suburban hospital.

METROPOLITAN-MT. SINAI MEDICAL CENTER
900 South 8th Street
Minneapolis MN 55404
612/336-6000
Contact Personnel. One of the leading hospitals in the Twin Cities.

MIDWAY HOSPITAL
1700 University Avenue
St. Paul MN 55104
612/641-5500
Contact Personnel. A leading St. Paul hospital.

MINNEAPOLIS CHILDREN'S MEDICAL CENTER
2525 Chicago Avenue
Minneapolis MN 55404
612/863-6227
Contact Personnel. One of Minnesota's leading health care institutions.

MINNTECH CORP.
14605 28th Avenue North
Minneapolis MN 55447
612/553-3300
Contact Personnel. Company develops and manufactures medical devices.

NORTH CENTRAL LABORATORIES INC.
P.O. Box 1417
St. Cloud MN 56302
612/253-1958
Contact Ms. Renae Struck, Human Resources Director. An independent clinical laboratory providing a broad range of testing services to customers in Minnesota, Wisconsin, North Dakota, and South Dakota. Testing services are provided in the areas of clinical chemistry, toxicology, serology, cytology, hematology, immunohemtology, microbiology, parasitology, virology,and urinalysis. Corporate headquarters location: San Juan Capistrano, CA. Parent company: Nichols Insititute. Operations include: testing; service; sales.

NORTHWESTERN DRUG CO.
2001 Kennedy Street N.E.
Minneapolis MN 55440
612/331-6550
Contact Personnel. Wholesaler of pharmaceuticals, drugs, and sundries.

ORTHOMET, INC.
6301 Cecilia Circle
Bloomington MN 55439
612/944-6112
Contact Personnel. Company makes replacements for knees and hips.

PATTERSON DENTAL COMPANY
1100 East 80th Street
Minneapolis MN 55402
612/854-2881
Contact Mary Martins, Director of Human Resources. A wholesaler of dental equipment and supplies.

PERSONNEL DECISIONS, INC.
2000 Plaza VII Tower
45 South 7th Street
Minneapolis MN 55402
612/339-0927
Contact Cathy Nelson, Human Resources Manager. PDI is a nationwide consulting firm of organized psychologists and consultants who specialize in assessment-based development and who have created and implemented innovative programs, services, and products that are tailored to client needs. PDI services and products have proven their effectiveness in the selection and promotion of employees at all levels, the development of managers and

executives, the fostering of a positive group dynamic for the organization as a whole, and outplacement and career transition. Corporate headquarters location.

ST. CLOUD HOSPITAL
1406 North Sixth Avenue
St. Cloud MN 56303
612/255-5650
Contact Diane Salzer, Recruiter. A leading area hospital. Common positions include: Dietician; Nurse; OT/PT. Principal educational background sought: Health Care. Training programs offered; Internships offered. Company benefits include: medical, dental, and life insurance; pension plan; tuition assistance; disability coverage; daycare assistance; employee discounts. Corporate headquarters location. Operations at this facility include: service.

SCI MED LIFE SYSTEMS, INC.
13010 County Road 6
Minneapolis MN 55441
612/559-9504
Contact Personnel. Producers of membrane oxygenators, reservoir bags, heat exchangers, and angioplasty catheters. Employs 230.

SNYDER BROTHERS INC.
7251 Ohms Lane
Edina MN 55439
612/830-9062
Contact Shirley Stensrud, Payroll & Benefits Administrator. A major area chain of drug stores. Common positions at this facility include: Accountant; Buyer. Principal educational backgrounds sought: Accounting; Business Administration; Marketing. Company benefits include: medical insurance; dental insurance; life insurance; tuition assistance; profit sharing; employee discounts. Corporate headquarters location.

SNYDER DRUG STORES
P.O. Box 320
Minneapolis MN 55440
612/935-5441
Contact Rich Oorlog, Vice President, Human Resources. A chain of retail drug stores.

STARKEY LABS
6700 Washington Avenue South
Eden Prairie MN 55344
612/941-6401
Contact Larry Miller, Personnel Director. Supplier of surgical and medical supplies.

UNITED HEALTHCARE CORPORATION
P.O. Box 1459, Route 9440
Minneapolis MN 55440
612/936-1300
Contact Personnel Department. A leading Minneapolis health care facility.

WALMAN OPTICAL COMPANY
801 12th Avenue North
Minneapolis MN 55411
612/520-6028
Contact Personnel Director. A major ophthalmic goods company. Common positions include: Blue-Collar Worker Supervisor; Computer Programmer; Credit Manager; Customer Service Representative; Branch Manager; Department Manager; Operations/Production Manager; Purchasing Agent; Sales Representative; Opticians. Training programs offered. Company benefits include: medical insurance; dental insurance; pension plan; life insurance; disability coverage; profit sharing; employee discounts; savings plan; 401K. Operations at this facility include: manufacturing; administration; service; sales.

HIGHLY DIVERSIFIED

CARLSON COMPANIES, INC.
P.O. Box 59159, Carlson Parkway
Minneapolis MN 55459
612/540-5000
Contact Human Resources Department. A highly diversified corporation doing business through a variety of subsidiary operations, including trading stamps, incentive promotions, food premium programs, real estate, hotels, restaurant operations, and retail and wholesale travel. Employs 50,000.

LIBERTY DIVERSIFIED INDUSTRIES
5600 North Highway 169
New Hope MN 55428
612/536-6680
Contact Dan Petrella, Director, Personnel/Industrial Relations. LDI is a diversified organization comprised of 7 companies. The companies are located throughout the United States and manufacture corrugated boxes, metal fabricated products, plastic injected molded and extruded products. Another organization is a mail order company of office and industrial supplies and still another is a manufacturer/wholesaler of office and industrial supplies. Common positions include: Accountant; Actuary; Administrator; Advertising Worker; Attorney; Blue-Collar Worker Supervisor; Buyer; Chemist; Commercial Artist; Computer Programmer; Credit Manager; Customer Service Representative; Draftsperson; Chemical

Engineer; Civil Engineer; Electrical Engineer; Industrial Engineer; Mechanical Engineer; Financial Analyst; Industrial Designer; Branch Manager; Department Manager; General Manager; Operations/Production Manager; Marketing Specialist; Personnel & Labor Relations Specialist; Public Relations Worker; Purchasing Agent; Quality Control Supervisor; Sales Representative; Systems Analyst; Technical Writer/Editor; Transportation & Traffic Specialist. Principal educational backgrounds sought: Accounting; Art/Design; Business Administration; Chemistry; Communications; Computer Science; Economics; Engineering; Finance; Marketing; Mathematics. Company benefits include: medical insurance; pension plan; life insurance; tuition assistance; disability coverage; profit sharing; employee discounts; savings plan. Corporate headquarters location. Operations at this facility include: research/development; administration; service.

HOTELS AND RESTAURANTS/TOURISM

For more information on professional employment opportunities in the hotel and restaurant industry, contact the following professional and trade associations, as listed beginning on page 251:

THE AMERICAN HOTEL AND MOTEL ASSOCIATION
COUNCIL ON HOTEL, RESTAURANT AND INSTITUTIONAL
        EDUCATION
THE EDUCATION FOUNDATION OF THE NATIONAL RESTAURANT
        ASSOCIATION
MINNESOTA RESTAURANT ASSOCIATION

ARBY'S/FRANCHISE ASSOCIATES INC.
5354 Parkdale Drive, Suite 100
Minneapolis MN 55416
612/546-3391
Contact Doug Kennedy, Vice President. A major franchise of a national restaurant chain specializing in roast beef and chicken sandwiches. Common positions include: General Manager; Management Trainee. Principal educational backgrounds sought: Business Administration; Communications; Liberal Arts; Marketing; Psychology; Education. Company benefits include: medical, dental, and life insurance; profit sharing; tuition assistance; disability coverage; employee discounts; savings plan. Corporate and regional headquarters location.

BLUE HORSE
1355 University Avenue
St. Paul MN 55104
612/645-8101
Contact Personnel. One of the Twin Cities' finest restaurants.

BUFFETS INC.
10260 Viking Drive
Suite 100
Eden Prairie MN 55344
612/942-9760
Contact Personnel. An area restaurant company.

CANTEEN COMPANY OF MINNESOTA, INC.
6300 Penn Avenue South
Richfield MN 55423
612/866-0041
Contact Vicki Preese, Human Resources Manager. Corporate office for a vending machines and cafeteria company. Principal educational backgrounds sought: Food Service/Vending Training. Company benefits include: medical insurance; savings plan. Corporate headquarters location. Operations at this facility include: administration; service; sales.

CAROUSEL SNACK BARS OF MINNESOTA
9549 Penn Avenue
Minneapolis MN 55431
612/887-5399
Contact Personnel. Corporate offices for a major regional chain of snack bars. Common positions include: Restaurant Manager. Previous experience and education in food service sought. Company benefits include: medical insurance; life insurance; tuition assistance; disability coverage; profit sharing; savings plan. Corporate headquarters location.

CONSUL RESTAURANT CORPORATION
2901 Metro Drive, Suite 500
Bloomington MN 55425-1554
612/851-3333
Contact Margot McManus, Director of Human Resources. Corporate office for a restaurant company operating in the U.S. and Canada. Common positions include: Accountant; Computer programmer; Hotel Manager/ Assistant Manager; Department Manager; General Manager; Management Trainee; Marketing Specialist. Principal educational backgrounds sought: Accounting; Business Administration; Communications; Finance; Marketing; Mathematics. Company benefits include: medical insurance; dental insurance; life insurance; tuition assistance; employee discounts. Corporate headquarters location.

HYATT REGENCY MINNEAPOLIS
1300 Nicollet Mall
Minneapolis MN 55403
612/370-1234
Contact Cheri Richmond, Employment Manager. A prestigious downtown hotel with 534 rooms and suites. Hotel restaurants include The Terrace and The Willows. Internships available. Corporate headquarters location: Chicago, IL.

LUXEFORD SUITES HOTEL
1101 LaSalle Avenue
Minneapolis MN 55403
612/332-6800
Contact General Manager. An all-suite hotel at the edge of downtown Minneapolis.

MARQUETTE HOTEL
77 South 7th Avenue
Minneapolis MN 55402
612/332-2351
Contact Darcy Taul, Personnel Manager. Connected to the interior skyway of the IDS Center, this hotel offers luxury accomodations in a downtown location.

THE MINNEAPOLIS MARRIOTT CITY CENTER
30 South 7th Street
Minneapolis MN 55402
612/349-4000
Contact Joanne Jackson, Personnel Director. A 32-floor glass tower, linked to the city's skyway system.

NORTH CENTRAL FOOD SYSTEMS/HARDEES
2901 Metro Drive
Bloomington MN 55425
612/854-7944
Contact Personnel. A holding company for the owners and operators of the Hardees Restaurant fast food chain.

1 POTATO 2, INC.
5640 International Parkway
New Hope MN 55428
612/537-3833
Contact Mr. Terry Vaught, Human Resources Manager. Corporate offices for a national chain of restaurants. Common positions in Food Service; Management; Assistant Manager; District Manager. Company benefits include: medical insurance; life insurance; employee discounts; bonuses; excellent advancement opportunities. Corporate headquarters location. Operations at this facility include: research/development; administration.

PIZZA HUT
4570 West 77th Street, Suite 102
Minneapolis MN 55435
612/835-3680
Contact Kathy Danehy, Personnel Coordinator. Area offices for the well-known fast food chain. A subsidiary of Pepsico.

SOFITEL HOTEL
5601 West 78th
Bloomington MN 55439
612/835-1900
Contact Candy Lee, Personnel Director. The first North American location of the French hotel chain, offering 287 deluxe luxury suites.

INSURANCE

For more information on professional employment opportunities in the insurance industry, contact the following professional and trade associations, as listed beginning on page 251:

ALLIANCE OF AMERICAN INSURERS
AMERICAN COUNCIL OF LIFE INSURANCE
AMERICAN INSURANCE ASSOCIATION
INSURANCE INFORMATION INSTITUTE
NATIONAL ASSOCIATION OF LIFE UNDERWRITERS
NATIONAL ASSOCIATION OF LIFE UNDERWRITERS/MINNEAPOLIS
         CHAPTER
SOCIETY OF ACTUARIES

AMERICAN HARDWARE MUTUAL INSURANCE CO.
P.O. Box 435
Minneapolis MN 55440
612/935-1400
Contact Ms. Pat Iverson, Vice President, Human Resources. A leader in property and casualty insurance.

EMPLOYEE BENEFIT PLANS, INC.
435 Ford Road, Suite 500
Minneapolis MN 55426
612/546-4353
Contact Mary Rygg, Director of Human Resources. A prominent nationally managed insurance company headquartered in Minneapolis. Common positions include: Accountant; Administrator; Claim Representative; Computer Programmer; Customer Service Representative; Claims Examiner.

Principal educational backgrounds sought: Claims Experience. Company benefits include: medical, dental, and life insurance; pension plan; disability coverage. Corporate headquarters location. Operations at this facility include: administration.

FEDERATED MUTUAL INSURANCE COMPANY
121 East Park Square
Owatonna MN 55060
507/455-5200
Contact Sherry Carlson, Employment Representative. A multiple line insurance company specializing in commercial business insurance for small and medium sized business risks. Corporate headquarters location. Common positions include: Actuary; Claim Representative; Computer Programmer; Underwriter. Principal educational backgrounds sought: Business Administration; Computer Science; Finance; Liberal Arts; Marketing. Company benefits include: medical, dental and life insurance; pension plan; disability coverage; savings plan.

IDS LIFE INSURANCE CO.
P.O. Box 534
Minneapolis MN 55440
612/372-3131
Contact Personnel Department. A major insurance provider doing business as a subsidiary of IDS Financial Corporation.

ITT LIFE INSURANCE CORPORATION
P.O. Box 9302
Minneapolis MN 55440
612/545-2100
Contact Guy Courteau, Personnel Director. An area life insurance firm.

LUTHERAN BROTHERHOOD
625 4th Avenue South
Minneapolis MN 55415
612/340-7000
Contact Karen Larson, Employment Manager. A financial institution providing life, health, and disability insurance in addition to annuities and mutual funds. Common positions include: Actuary; Computer Programmer. Principal educational backgrounds sought: Computer Science; Mathematics; Actuarial Science. Company benefits include: medical, dental, and life insurance; pension plan; tuition assistance; disability coverage. Corporate headquarters location. Operations at this facility include: research/ development; administration; service.

MSI INSURANCE
Two Pine Tree Drive
Arden Hills MN 55112
612/631-7329
Contact Human Resources Specialist. A local provider of insurance services. Common positions include: Accountant; Actuary; Claim Representative; Computer Programmer; Customer Service Representative; Financial Analyst; Personnel & Labor Relations Specialist; Public Relations Specialist; Systems Analyst; Underwriter; Insurance Agent/Broker; Sales Representative; Statistician. Principal educational backgrounds sought: Accounting; Business Administration; Communications; Computer Science; Economics; Finance; Liberal Arts; Marketing; Mathematics; Training programs offered. Company benefits include: medical insurance; pension plan; life insurance; tuition assistance; disability coverage; employee discounts; savings plan. Corporate headquarters location. Operations at this facility include: regional headquarters; divisional headquarters; administration; service.

MINISTERS LIFE
A MUTUAL LIFE INSURANCE COMPANY
P.O. Box 910
Minneapolis MN 55440
612/927-7131
Contact Personnel. A life and health insurance company.

NORTH AMERICAN LIFE & CASUALTY CO.
1750 Hennepin Avenue
Minneapolis MN 55403
612/347-6500
Contact Roger Dietsch, Personnel Director. Providers of individual and mass marketed life insurance.

NORTHWESTERN NATIONAL LIFE INSURANCE CO.
20 Washington Avenue South
Minneapolis MN 55401
612/372-5432
Contact Marguerite Samuels, Human Resources Department. A leading full-service life and health insurance firm.

PHYSICIANS HEALTH PLAN OF MINNESOTA
P.O. Box 1587
Minnetonka MN 55440
612/936-1200
Contact Bob Backus, Director of Human Resources. A major area health insurance company.

ST. PAUL COMPANIES
385 Washington Street
St. Paul MN 55102
612/221-7001
Contact Personnel. A St. Paul holding company doing business through a
number of financial service and insurance industry-based subsidiaries.

SENTRY INSURANCE
1660 South Highway 100, Box 115
Minneapolis MN 55440
612/540-1100
Contact Personnel Department. A major insurance company offering all
kinds of insurance.

TITLE INSURANCE COMPANY OF MINNESOTA
400 Second Avenue South
Minneapolis MN 55401
612/371-1111
Contact Cheryl Jones, V.P. of Personnel. A major title insurer. Corporate
headquarters location.

WESTERN LIFE INSURANCE COMPANY
P.O. Box 64271
St. Paul MN 55164
612/738-4000
Contact Human Resources. Provides group health insurance. Common
positions include: Accountant; Actuary; Attorney; Benefits Analyst;
Computer Programmer; Customer Service Representative; Department
Manager; Marketing Specialist; Personnel/Benefits Specialist;
Reporter/Editor; Underwriter. Principal educational backgrounds sought:
Accounting; Business Administration; Communications; Computer Science;
Economics; Finance; Liberal Arts; Marketing; Mathematics. Company
benefits include: medical, dental, and life insurance; pension plan; tuition
assistance; disability coverage; profit sharing; employee discounts; savings
plan. Corporate headquarters location. Parent company: NV AMEV.
Divisional headquarters location.

LEGAL SERVICES

For more information on professional employment opportunities in the
legal services, contact the following professional and trade associations, as
listed beginning on page 251:

AMERICAN BAR ASSOCIATION
ASSOCIATION OF LEGAL ADMINISTRATORS
ASSOCIATION OF LEGAL ADMINISTRATORS/MINNEAPOLIS

BRANCH
FEDERAL BAR ASSOCIATION
FEDERAL BAR ASSOCIATION/MINNEAPOLIS
MINNESOTA ASSOCIATION OF LEGAL ASSISTANTS
MINNESOTA PARALEGAL ASSOCIATION
NATIONAL ASSOCIATION FOR LAW PLACEMENT
NATIONAL ASSOCIATION OF LEGAL ASSISTANTS
NATIONAL FEDERATION OF PARALEGAL ASSOCIATIONS
NATIONAL PARALEGAL ASSOCIATION
TWIN CITY PROFESSIONAL RECRUITERS ASSOCIATION

ARTHUR, CHAPMAN & McDONOUGH
500 Young Quinland Building
81 South 9th Street
Minneapolis MN 55402
612/339-3500
Contact Diane Wolf, Personnel Director. A leading Minneapolis law firm. Common positions include: Attorney; Paralegal; Legal Secretary. Company benefits include: medical insurance; life insurance; tuition assistance; disability coverage; profit sharing.

BARNA, GUZY & STEFFEN
200 Coon Rapids
Coon Rapids MN 55433
612/780-8500
Contact Dennis Fagerlee, Director of Personnel. A leading Minneapolis law firm.

BASSFORD, HECKT, LOCKART, TRUESDALE & BRIGGS
3550 Multifoods Tower
Minneapolis MN 55402
612/333-3000
Contact Rebecca Moos, Hiring Partner. A leading Minneapolis law firm.

BRIGGS & MORGAN PROFESSIONAL ASSOCIATION
W. 2200 1st National Bank Building
St. Paul MN 55101
612/291-1215
Contact Personnel. A professional legal services firm.

DORSEY WHITNEY
2200 First Bank Place East
Minneapolis MN 55402
612/340-2600
Contact Director of Personnel. A major area law firm.

FAEGRE & BENSON
2200 Norwest Center
Minneapolis MN 55402
612/336-3000
Contact Mary Pheilisticker, Director of Personnel. A major area law firm.

KINNEY & LANGE
625 Fourth Avenue South, Suite 1500
Minneapolis MN 55415
612/339-1863
Contact Kathleen Reiper, Recruitment Coordinator. A leading Minneapolis patent law firm. Common positions include: Attorney; Patent Attorney; Trademark Attorney; Intellectual Property Litigation Attorney. Principal educational backgrounds sought: Engineering; Law. Company benefits include: medical, dental, and life insurance; pension plan; disability coverage. Corporate headquarters location. Operations at this facility include: legal services.

LARKIN, HOFFMAN, DALY & LINDGREN
7900 Xerxes Avenue South
Bloomington MN 55431
612/835-3800
Contact Wilma Ruppert, Personnel Director. A major area law firm. Common positions include: Credit Manager; Marketing Specialist; Personnel and Labor Relations Specialist; Legal Related. Principal educational backgrounds sought: Accounting; Business Administration; Liberal Arts; Marketing; Legal. Training programs available. Company benefits include: medical insurance; dental insurance; pension plan; life insurance; tuition assistance; disability coverage; profit sharing; employee discounts. Corporate headquarters location.

LINDQUIST & VENNUM
4200 IDS Center, 80 South 8th Street
Minneapolis MN 55402
612/371-3211
Contact Kim Klein, Personnel. A leading Minneapolis law firm. Common positions include: Legal Secretary; Attorney. Educational backgrounds sought: Law; Legal Secretarial Training. Company benefits include: medical and life insurance; pension plan; disability coverage; profit sharing; employee discounts. Corporate headquarters location. Operations at this facility include: administration; service.

MOSS & BARNETT, P.A.
4800 Norwest Center, 90 South 7th Street
Minneapolis MN 55402
612/347-0300
Contact Anne Rogers, Personnel Administrator. A leading Minneapolis law firm.

O'CONNER & HANNAN
3800 IDS Tower, 80 South 8th Street
Minneapolis MN 55402-2254
612/341-3800
Contact Don Arbour, Attorney. A leading Minneapolis law firm.

OPPENHEIMER WOLFF & DONNELLY
3400 Plaza VII, 45 South 7th Street,
Minneapolis MN 55402
612/344-9300
Contact Gary M. Nelson, Attorney. A leading Minneapolis law firm. Common positions include: Attorney. Company benefits include: medical insurance; dental insurance; pension plan; life insurance.

OPPERMAN HEINS & PAQUIN
2200 Washington Square
100 Washington Avenue South,
Minneapolis MN 55401
612/339-6900
Contact Robert Schmidt, Attorney. A major Minneapolis law firm.

POPHAM, HAIK, SCHNOBRICH & KAUFMAN, LTD.
3300 Piper Jaffray Tower
Minneapolis MN 55402
612/333-4800
Contact Recruitment Coordinator. A major Minneapolis law firm, with offices also located in Washington D.C. and Denver, CO. Common positions include: Attorney. Company benefits include: medical insurance; pension plan; life insurance; disability coverage; profit sharing. Corporate headquarters location.

ROBINS, KAPLAN, MILLER & CIRESI
1800 Int'l Center, 900 2nd Ave. South
Minneapolis MN 55402
612/349-8500
Contact Deborah Wahl, Legal Assistant of Administration. A major Minneapolis law firm.

MANUFACTURING: MISCELLANEOUS CONSUMER

For more information on professional employment opportunities in the manufacturing industry, contact the following professional and trade associations, as listed beginning on page 251:

NATIONAL ASSOCIATION OF MANUFACTURERS

NATIONAL MACHINE TOOL BUILDERS
NATIONAL SCREW MACHINE PRODUCTS ASSOCIATION
NATIONAL TOOLING AND MACHINING ASSOCIATION
NATIONAL TOOLING AND MACHINING ASSOCIATION/
     MINNEAPOLIS CHAPTER
THE TOOLING AND MANUFACTURING ASSOCIATION

BMC INDUSTRIES INC.
2 Appletree Square
Suite 400
Minneapolis MN 55425
612/851-6000
Contact Ken Lewis, Vice-President/Personnel. A major manufacturer of precision-etched products.

BOWERS SAILS INCORPORATED
14872 DeVeau Place
Minnetonka MN 55345
612/933-6262
Contact Personnel Department. A local, regional, and national manufacturer of sailboat sails, custom bags, and custom flags and banners.

DOUGLAS CORPORATION
620 12th Avenue South
Minneapols MN 55415
612/333-8911
Contact Rhonda Ferrian, Personnel Manager. A manufacturer of product identification nameplates.

FEDERAL CARTRIDGE COMPANY
900 Bob Ehlen Drive
Anoka MN 55303
612/422-2566
Contact Cathy LaPoint. A leading manufacturer of hunting and sporting ammunition.

JEWELMONT CORPORATION
800 Boone Avenue North
Golden Valley MN 55427
612/546-3800
Contact Darlene McRae, Personnel Director. Manufacturers of jewelers' findings and materials.

MEDALLION KITCHENS OF MINNESOTA
180 Industrial Boulevard
Waconia MN 55387
612/442-5171
Contact Dick McGrady, Personnel Director. Makers of fine wood kitchen cabinets.

MID-CONTINENT CABINETRY
30 East Plato Boulevard
St. Paul MN 55107
612/297-0661
Contact Audrey Everling, Employee Benefits Coordinator. A maker of fine wood kitchen cabinets.

NATIONAL BEAUTY SUPPLIES, INC.
3109 Louisiana Avenue North
New Hope MN 55427
612/546-9500
Contact Human Resources. An area producer and distributor of beauty products.

NORTHLAND ALUMINUM PRODUCTS INC.
5005 Highway 7
St. Louis Park MN 55416
612/920-2888
Contact Manager of Human Resources. Area producers of aluminum cookware and related products. Common positions include: Accountant; Computer Programmer; Draftsperson; Chemical Engineer; Mechanical Engineer; Sales Representative; Sales Manager. Principal educational backgrounds sought: Accounting; Engineering. Company benefits include: medical, dental, and life insurance; pension plan; tuition assistance; disability coverage; employee discounts; savings plan. Corporate headquarters location. Operations at this facility include: manufacturing; research/development; administration; service; sales.

NORTHRUP KING COMPANY
7500 Olson Memorial Highway
Golden Valley MN 55427
612/593-7333
Contact Kent Vesper, Director of Corporate Development. A major manufacturer of farm supplies.

ST. PAUL BAR AND RESTAURANT EQUIPMENT COMPANY/PALM BROTHERS
2727 Nickolette
Minneapolis MN 55408
612/871-2727
Contact Mike Palm, Office Manager. A manufacturer and distributor of restaurant equipment.

SICO INCORPORATED
7525 Cahill Road
Edina MN 55439
612/941-1700
Contact Carol Friedman, Benefits Coordinator. A manufacturer of a diverse line of products, including room-service centers, stages, tables, wall-beds, and other related products. Major clients include schools and hotels.

THE TORO COMPANY
8111 Lyndale Avenue
Bloomington MN 55420
612/887-8924
Contact Dave Tourville, Senior Human Resources Representative. Engaged in the manufacture and marketing of outdoor power products for consumer and commercial uses. Products include: lawn mowers, snowblowers, trimmers, and appliances. Common positions include· Accountant; Attorney; Blue-Collar Worker Supervisor; Buyer; Computer Programmer; Credit Manager; Customer Service Representative; Draftsperson; Agricultural Engineer; Industrial Engineer; Mechanical Engineer; Mining Engineer; Metallurgical Engineer; Financial Analyst; Industrial Designer; Marketing Specialist; Purchasing Agent; Quality Control Supervisor; Sales Representative; Systems Analyst; Technical Writer/Editor; Transportation & Traffic Specialist. Principal educational backgrounds sought: Accounting; Business Administration; Computer Science; Engineering; Finance; Marketing. Company benefits include: medical, dental, and life insurance; pension plan; tuition assistance; disability coverage; profit sharing; employee discounts; savings plan; 10 paid holidays; vacations. Corporate headquarters location. Operations at this facility include: research/development; administration; service; sales. New York Stock Exchange.

VALSPAR CORPORATION
1101 South 3rd Street
Minneapolis MN 55415
612/332-7371
Contact Gary Gardner, Personnel Director. Manufacturer of paints, varnishes, lacquers, and related products.

WILSON TANNER CORPORATION
5194 W. 76th
Edina MN 55439
612/831-4567
Contact Personnel Department An area producer of videotape reels, cassette albums, trophies, as well as commercial and screen printing.

MANUFACTURING: MISCELLANEOUS INDUSTRIAL

ACROMETAL COMPANIES INC.
P.O. Box 408
Brainerd MN 56401
218/829-4719
Contact Norman Klinghagen, Human Resources. Major area manufacturer of metal spools and reels, wire handling and packaging equipment, and other industrial products. Common positions include: Accountant; Administrator; Blue-Collar Worker Supervisor; Buyer; Chemist; Industrial Engineer; Mechanical Engineer; Financial Analyst; Department Manager; General Manager; Operations/Production Manager; Purchasing Agent; Quality Control Supervisor; Sales Representative. Principal educational backgrounds sought: Accounting; Business Administration; Economics; Engineering; Finance. Company benefits include: medical insurance; dental insurance; pension plan; life insurance; tuition assistance; disability coverage; profit sharing; savings plan. Corporate headquarters location: Plymouth, MN. Operations at this facility include: Divisional headquarters; manufacturing; sales.

ADVANCE MACHINE COMPANY
14600 21st Avenue No.
Plymouth MN 55447
612/473-2235
Contact Ken Frideres, Personnel Manager. Manufacturer of floor maintenance equipment. Common positions include: Advertising Worker; Buyer; Customer Service Representative; Draftsperson; Industrial Engineer; Mechanical Engineer; Sales Representative; Technical Writer/Editor. Principal educational backgrounds sought: Business Administration; Communications; Engineering. Company benefits include: medical, dental, and life insurance; pension plan; tuition assistance; disability coverage; employee discounts; savings plan; long-term disability. Corporate headquarters location. Operations at this facility include: manufacturing; research/development; administration; service; sales.

AG-CHEM EQUIPMENT COMPANY
5720 Smetana Drive, Suite 100
Minnetonka MN 55343
612/933-9006
Contact Personnel Recruiter. A major manufacturer of farm machinery and equipment.

AMCLYDE ENGINEERED PRODUCTS
240 East Plato Boulevard
St. Paul MN 55107
612/293-4646
Contact Personnel Department. Division of AMCA International, a Fortune 500 Company, world leader in design and construction of custom engineered lifting and pulling systems.

AUTOCON INDUSTRIES INC.
995 University Avenue
St. Paul MN 55104
612/642-2967
Contact Mary L. Jarvis, Personnel Manager. A privately owned company which has been in continuous operation since 1923. Throughout its existence, Autocon's principal business has been that of supplying electrical and electronic control systems to the municipal water and wastewater markets. Autocon markets its control systems to the water and wastewater industry through independent manufacturer's representatives located in major cities throughout the country. In addition to its proprietary businesses in the water and wastewater market, Autocon markets its manufacturing capabilities as a full service contract manufacturer to original equipment suppliers. Common positions include: Accountant; Electrical Engineer; Operations/Production Manager; Purchasing Agent; Sales Representative; Systems Analyst; Programmer; Project Manager. Company benefits include: medical, dental, and life insurance; tuition assistance; disability coverage; employee discounts; 401K. Corporate headquarters location. Operations at this facility include: manufacturing; research/development; administration; service; sales.

BERGQUIST COMPANY
5300 Edina Industrial Boulevard
Edina MN 55439
612/835-2322
Contact Personnel. Manufacturers of Syltad, an insulator.

BUHLER-MIAG INC.
1100 North Xenium Lane
Plymouth MN 55441
612/545-1401
Contact Frank Lunetta, Director of Personnel. Designers and manufacturers of grain milling machinery and other agricultural equipment.

CENTURY MANUFACTURING CO.
9231 Penn Avenue South
Bloomington MN 55431
612/884-3211
Contact Steve Erbstoesser, V.P./Personnel. A major manufacturer of battery chargers and welders.

DANA CORPORATION
600 Hoover Street, NE
Minneapolis MN 55413
612/623-1960
Contact John Lunsford, Personnel Director. Producers of hydraulic pumps, motors, valves and filters.

DELTAK CORPORATION
13330 12th Avenue North
Plymouth MN 55441
612/544-3371
Contact Human Resources Department. Designers and manufacturers of specialty heat recovery steam generators and energy conversion applications. Common positions include: Accountant; Blue-Collar Worker Supervisor; Buyer; Drafter/Designer; Civil Engineer; Mechanical Engineer/Chemical Engineer; Department Manager (specialized); Operations/Production Manager; Quality Control Supervisor; Product Manager; Field Service Manager. Common positions include: Accounting; Business Administration; Engineering; Company benefits: medical insurance; dental insurance; life insurance; tuition assistance; disability coverage; profit sharing; 401k plan.

DETECTOR ELECTRONIC CORPORATION
6901 West 110th Street
Minneapolis MN 55438
612/941-5665
Contact Holly Naramore, Human Resources. Major manufacturers of fire detection equipment and providers of burner management systems. Common positions include: Accountant; Administrator; Blue-Collar Worker Supervisor; Buyer; Commercial Artist; Computer Programmer; Credit Manager; Customer Service Representative; Draftsperson; Electrical Engineer; Industrial Engineer; Mechanical Engineer; Department Manager; General Manager; Operations/Production Manager; Marketing Specialist; Personnel & Labor Relations; Purchasing Agent; Quality Control Supervisor; Sales Representative; Systems Analyst; Technical Writer/Editor. Principal educational backgrounds sought: Accounting; Art/Design; Business Administration; Communications; Computer Science; Engineering; Finance; Liberal Arts; Marketing; Mathematics. Training programs offered. Company benefits include: medical, dental, and life insurance; pension plan; tuition assistance; disability coverage; profit sharing; employee discounts; 401 K. Corporate headquarters location. Parent company: Williams Holdings Inc.

DONALDSON COMPANY INC.
P.O. Box 1299, MS 430
Minneapolis MN 55440
Contact Steve Nyguard, Manager, Employee Relations. A Fortune 1000 manufacturer of filtration systems and noise abatement products. Employs approximately 4000 persons worldwide; 700 at this location. International. Common positions include: Accountant; Buyer; Chemist; Computer Programmer; Customer Service Representative; Draftsperson; Electrical Engineer; Industrial Engineer; Mechanical Engineer; Financial Analyst; Marketing Specialist; Sales Representative; Systems Analyst. Principal educational backgrounds sought: Accounting; Business Administration; Chemistry; Computer Science; Engineering; Marketing. Company benefits include: medical, dental and life insurance; pension plan; tuition assistance; disability coverage; savings plan. Corporate headquarters location. Operations at this facility include: research/development; administration; sales. New York Stock Exchange.

ECO WATER SYSTEMS
P.O. Box 64420
St. Paul MN 55164
612/739-5330
Contact Human Resources Manager. Develops, manufactures, and markets water conditioning equipment, drinking water purifiers, chemical feed pumps, commercial and industrial water systems. Common positions include: Accountant; Blue-Collar Worker Supervisor; Buyer; Chemist; Credit Manager; Draftsperson; Chemical Engineer; Electrical Engineer; Industrial Engineer; Mechanical Engineer; Financial Analyst; General Manager; Operations/Production Manager; Purchasing Agent; Quality Control Supervisor; Principal educational backgrounds sought: Accounting; Business Administration; Computer Science; Engineering; Liberal Arts; Marketing. Company benefits include: medical insurance; dental insurance; pension plan; life insurance; tuition assistance; disability coverage; profit sharing; savings plan. Operations at this facility include: regional headquarters; manufacturing; research/development; administration; service; sales. Corporate headquarters location: Chicago, IL.

ELECTRICAL MACHINERY MANUFACTURING CO.
800 Central Avenue
Minneapolis MN 55413
612/378-8000
Contact Human Resources. Manufacturers of heavy industrial generators and related equipment.

FILMTEC CORPORATION
7200 Ohms Lane
Minneapolis MN 55439
612/835-5475
Contact Debra Schaffran, Human Resources Administrator. Manufacturers of osmosis membranes and cartridge filtration elements for desalination. A subsidiary of Dow Chemical Company.

FOLEY-BELSAW COMPANY
3300 N.E. 5th Street
Minneapolis MN 55418
612/789-8831
Contact Chris Feahr, Personnel. A manufacturer of industrial saws and related equipment.

GENERAL RESOURCE CORPORATION
201 South Third Street
Hopkins MN 55343
612/933-7474
Contact C.J. Bollhoefer, Personnel Director. A manufacturing firm operating through four subsidiaries: Air Purification Methods, Inc. produces air pollution control systems; Fluidizer, Inc. produces pneumatic conveying systems; Ammerman, Inc. produces roof ventilators, industrial fans, and auto exhaust ventilator systems; and Isomatic Corporation produces standard and custom industrial components. Corporate headquarters location. Operations include: research/development; service; sales. Common positions include: Draftsperson; Engineer; Mechanical Engineer; Purchasing Agent; General Office; Sales/Application Engineers. Principal educational backgrounds sought: Engineering. Company benefits include: medical and life insurance; tuition assistance; disability coverage; profit sharing.

GRACO INC.
P.O. Box 1441
Minneapolis MN 55440
612/623-6000
Contact Clyde Hanson, Employee Relations Manager. A manufacturer of pumping and fluid handling systems. Manufacturing plants located in Minneapolis and Chicago. Sales offices located throughout the United States. Corporate headquarters location.

HAUENSTEIN & BURMEISTER, INC.
2629 30th Avenue South
Minneapolis MN 55406
612/721-5031
Contact Marty Deckman, Vice President. A diversified manufacturer of elevator entrances and cabs, partitions and ceiling systems, hollow metal and other metal specialties, a complete school equipment line, as well as telephone and sound systems.

HUTCHINSON TECHNOLOGY
40 West Highland Park
Hutchinson MN 55350
612/587-1820
Contact Randy Dostal, Staffing Supervisor. A manufacturer of precision components for computer, military and medical markets. Common positions include: Electrical Engineer; Industrial Engineer; Mechanical Engineer; Metallurgical Engineer. Principal educational backgrounds sought: Engineering. Training programs offered; Internships offered. Company benefits include: medical insurance; dental insurance; life insurance; tuition assistance; disability coverage; profit sharing. Corporate headquarters location. Operations at this facility include: manufacturing; research/ development; administration; sales. NASDAQ.

KURT MANUFACTURING COMPANY
5280 Main Street NE
Minneapolis MN 55421
612/572-1500
Contact Mr. Kern Walker, Vice President of Human Resources. A manufacturer of industrial precision machines.

MEREEN JOHNSON MACHINE COMPANY
4401 Lyndale Avenue North
Minneapolis MN 55412
612/529-7791
Contact Personnel Department. A company engaged in manufacturing woodworking cutting machinery and plastic cutting machinery.

MINCO PRODUCTS, INC.
7300 Commerce Lane
Fridley MN 55432
612/571-3121
Contact Leanne Hyde, Personnel Administrator. Minco is a leading manufacturer of temperature sensors, heaters, and flexible interconnecting devices. Common positions include: Draftsperson; Electrical Engineer; Industrial Engineer; Mechanical Engineer. Principal educational backgrounds sought: Engineering. Training programs offered; Internships offered. Company benefits include: medical, dental and life insurance; tuition assistance; disability coverage; profit sharing. Corporate headquarters location. Operations at this facility include: regional headquarters; divisional headquarters; manufacturing; research/development; administration; service; sales.

NOVUS INC.
10425 Hampshire Avenue S.
Bloomington MN 55438
612/944-8000
Contact Personnel Department. A major corporation that manufactures and franchises a process for fixing stone damaged windshields and also manufactures and sells a plastic polish

ONAN CORPORATION
1400 73rd Avenue North East
Minneapolis MN 55432
612/574-5000
Contact Ms. Julie Lentner, Director of Staffing. Manufactures engines, generators, and related controls. Corporate headquarters location.

OSMONICS INC.
5951 Clearwater Drive
Minnetonka MN 55343
612/933-2277
Contact George McMurry, Human Resource Coordinator. Designs, manufactures, and markets fluid processing machines, systems, and components. Common positions include: Accountant; Blue-Collar Worker Supervisor; Buyer; Chemist; Draftsperson; Engineer; Ceramics Engineer; Chemical Engineer; Industrial Engineer; Mechanical Engineer; Quality Control Supervisor; Sales Representative. Principal educational backgrounds sought: Accounting; Business Administration; Chemistry; Engineering; Physics. Company benefits include: medical, dental, and life insurance; pension plan; tuition assistance; disability coverage; profit sharing; employee discounts; savings plan. Corporate headquarters location. Operations at this facility include: manufacturing; research/development; administration; service; sales.

PERKIN-ELMER PHYSICAL ELECTRONICS
6509 Flying Cloud Drive
Eden Prairie MN 55344
612/828-6100
Contact Harold Haug, Director of Personnel. Manufacturers of research instruments, including surface analysis equipment.

RAMSEY TECHNOLOGY, INC.
501 90th Avenue, NW
Minneapolis MN 55433
612/783-2500
Contact Sheryl Pupkes, Personnel Director. A firm involved in the manufacture of industrial instruments for measurement, display and control of process variables. Common job categories at this facility include: Draftsperson; Non-exempt clerical positions; Hourly production i.e, Machinist, Assembler, Sheet Metal Worker, and Mechanical Engineer.

208/The Minneapolis-St. Paul JobBank

Principal educational backgrounds sought: Engineering. Internships offered. Company benefits include: medical insurance; dental insurance; life insurance; tuition assistance; disability coverage; profit sharing. Corporate headquarters location: Houston, Texas. Parent company: Baker Hughes, Inc. Operations at this facility: divisional headquarters; manufacturing; research/development; administration; service; sales. New York Stock Exchange.

REMMELLE ENGINEERING
1211 Pierce Butler Route
St. Paul MN 55104
612/645-3451
Contact Director of Personnel. A manufacturer of special die tools.

RESEARCH INC.
P.O. Box 24064
Minneapolis MN 55424
612/941-3300
Contact Human Resources. Designer and manufacturer of industrial infrared heating equipment, process control systems and computer terminals. Common positions include: Draftsperson; Electrical Engineer; Mechanical Engineer; Sales Representative. Principal educational backgrounds sought: Engineering; Mathematics. Company benefits include: medical, dental and life insurance; tuition assistance; disability coverage; profit sharing; savings plan. Corporate headquarters location. Operations at this facility include: manufacturing; research/development; administration; service; sales. Company is listed on NMS-NASDAQ.

ROBBINS AND MYERS/ELECTRO CRAFT
6950 Washington Avenue South
Eden Prairie MN 55344
612/942-3600
Contact Personnel Department. A local, regional, and national producer of ac/dc servo motors and controls for industrial uses. Established since 1963.

ROSEMOUNT INC.
12001 Technology Drive
Eden Prairie MN 55344
612/941-5560
Contact Personnel Department. A leader in the design and manufacture of precision measurement and control instrumentation for aerospace and process control industries.

S-T INDUSTRIES, INC.
301 Armstrong Boulevard North
St. James MN 56081
507/375-3211
Contact Michael J. Smith, Treasurer. Manufactures and distributes precision measuring tools. Common positions include: Accountant; Administrator; Advertising Worker; Blue-Collar Worker Supervisor; Buyer; Computer Programmer; Credit Manager; Customer Service Representative; Draftsperson; Electrical Engineer; Industrial Engineer; Mechanical Engineer; Department Manager; Operations/Production Manager; Marketing Specialist; Personnel & Labor Relations Specialist; Purchasing Agent; Quality Control Supervisor; Systems Analyst. Principal educational backgrounds sought: Accounting; Art/Design; Business Administration; Computer Science; Engineering; Marketing. Company benefits include: medical and life insurance; pension plan; disability coverage. Corporate headquarters location. Operations at this facility include: manufacturing; research/development; administration; service; sales.

SLP MACHINE INCORPORATED
1262 McKay Drive
Ham Lake MN 55304
612/434-3535
Contact Personnel Department. An area producer of machined metal parts.

ST. CLOUD FIRE EQUIPMENT INCORPORATED
P.O. Box 1516
St. Cloud MN 56302
612/252-5562
Contact Personnel Department. A major area producer of fire protection equipment.

SNYDER GENERAL CORPORATION
Box 1551
Minneapolis MN 55440
612/553-5330
Contact Human Resources. An international company that engineers, manufactures, sells and services heating, ventilating, and air conditioning products. Snyder General, headquartered in Minneapolis, MN, is in charge of the commercial products line of equipment. Common positions include: Accountant; Draftsperson; Electrical Engineer; Mechanical Engineer. Principal educational backgrounds sought: Accounting; Engineering. Company benefits include: medical insurance; dental insurance; pension plan; life insurance; tuition assistance; disability coverage; employee discounts; savings plan; reimbursement accounts. Corporate headquarters location: Dallas, TX. Divisional headquarters location.

TSI INCORPORATED
P.O. Box 64394
St. Paul MN 55164
612/483-0900
Contact Personnel Department. A company involved in the production of particle research instruments, hot wire-hot film anemometry, laser velocimetry, and mass flow transconductors

TENNANT COMPANY
701 North Lilac Drive
Minneapolis MN 55440
612/540-1396
Contact Ms. Kathryn DesBles, Employment Specialist. Major manufacturers of floor maintenance equipment and floor coating materials. Common positions at this facility include: Accountant; Administrator; Buyer; Customer Service Representative; Chemist; Computer Programmer; Production Engineer; Industrial Engineer; Financial Analyst; Marketing Specialist; Sales Representative; Systems Analyst; General Administrative Support Worker. Principal educational backgrounds sought: Accounting; Chemistry; Computer Science; Engineering; Finance; Liberal Arts; Marketing. Company benefits include: medical insurance; dental insurance; pension plan; life insurance; tuition assistance; disability coverage; profit sharing. Corporate headquarters location. Operations at this facility include: global, regional headquarters; manufacturing; research/development; administration; sales. American Stock Exchange.

TESCOM CORPORATION
12616 Industrial Boulevard
Elk River MN 55330
612/441-6330
Contact Bruce Tyler, Personnel. A major manufacturer of industrial control systems.

THERMO KING CORPORATION
314 West 90th Street
Minneapolis MN 55420
612/887-2200
Contact Personnel Department. An area leader in refrigeration and air conditioning for buses and tractor-trailer centers.

3M
3M Center
St. Paul MN 55144-1000
612/733-0687
Contact Staffing Representative/Student Programs. A diversified manufacturing firm. Products include: chemicals and abrasives; printing products; magnetic and pressure-sensitive tape; office copiers and other

information-processing products; pharmaceuticals; and medical and surgical products. Corporate headquarters location.

THE TRANE COMPANY/
BUILDING AUTOMATION SYSTEMS DIV.
20 Yorkton Court
St. Paul MN 55117
612/490-3586
Contact Sandra Fellman, Human Resource Supervisor. Manufactures and markets computerized energy automation systems, which are used in commercial industry. Common positions include: Accountant; Buyer; Computer Programmer; Credit Manager; Department Manager; Draftsperson; Electrical Engineer; Financial Analyst; Operations/Production Manager; Marketing Specialist; Personnel and Labor Relations Specialist; Purchasing Agent; Quality Control Supervisor; Systems Analyst. Principal educational backgrounds sought: Accounting; Computer Science; Electrical Engineering. Company benefits include: medical insurance; dental insurance; pension plan; life insurance; tuition assistance; disability coverage; employee discounts; savings plan. Corporate headquarters location: New York, NY. Parent Company: American Standard, Inc. Operations at this facility include: divisional headquarters; manufacturing; administration; service; sales.

TWIN CITY FAN & BLOWER COMPANY
550 Kasota Avenue S.E.
Minneapolis MN 55414
612/331-4104
Contact Personnel Department. An area manufacturer of ventilation fans and blowers.

XERXES CORPORATION
7901 Xerxes Avenue
Minneapolis MN 55431
612/887-1800
Contact Office Manager. Major manufacturers of industrial storage tanks. Corporate headquarters location.

ZIEGLER INC.
901 West 94th Street
Minneapolis MN 55420
612/888-4121
Contact Personnel Director. Major manufacturers of farm and garden machinery.

MISCELLANEOUS SERVICES

BACHMAN'S INC.
6010 Lyndale Avenue South
Minneapolis MN 55419
612/861-7600
Contact Ruth Thompson, Director of Personnel. A major area florist.

THE BARBERS/
HAIRSTYLING FOR MEN & WOMEN, INC.
300 Industrial Boulevard NE
Minneapolis MN 55413
612/331-8500
Contact Manager of Human Resources. Franchisor of Cost Cutters and City Looks Beauty Salons. Also owns corporate salons. Common positions include: Accountant; Advertising Worker; Buyer; Computer Programmer; Credit Manager; Customer Service Representative; Draftsperson; Financial Analyst; Department Manager; Operations/Production Manager; Marketing Specialist; Public Relations Specialist; Purchasing Agent; Reporter/Editor; Sales Representative; Technical Writer/Editor; Stylist. Principal educational backgrounds sought: Accounting; Business Administration; Communications; Computer Science; Finance; Marketing. Internships offered. Company benefits include: medical insurance; dental insurance; life insurance; disability coverage; employee discounts; 401K. Operations at this facility include: administration; service; sales.

CBM INDUSTRIES, INC.
13220 County Road 6
Minneapolis MN 55441
612/559-4456
Contact Human Resources Department. A cleaning, maintenance and security service specializing in the care and security of commercial buildings.

MARSDEN BUILDING MAINTENANCE CO.
1717 University Avenue
St. Paul MN 55104
612/641-1717
Contact Mary Marsden, Director of Human Resources. A contract janitorial company. Common positions include: Accountant; Blue-Collar Worker Supervisor; Computer Programmer; Department Manager; Operations/ Production Manager; Trainer. Principal educational backgrounds sought: Accounting; Business Administration; Communications; Computer Science; Liberal Arts. Company benefits include: medical and dental insurance; disability coverage; bonus program. Corporate headquarters location.

PINKERTON'S INC.
7300 France Avenue South
Edina MN 55435
612/831-7143
Contact Personnel Manager. Regional office of the national private protection company that employs guards, investigators, and branch office staff. Corporate headquarters location: New York, NY.

NEWSPAPERS

For more information on professional employment opportunities in the newspaper industry, contact the following professional and trade associations, as listed beginning on page 251:

AMERICAN NEWSPAPER PUBLISHERS ASSOCIATION
AMERICAN SOCIETY OF NEWSPAPER EDITORS
THE DOW JONES NEWSPAPER FUND
INTERNATIONAL CIRCULATION MANAGERS ASSOCIATION
MINNESOTA PRESS CLUB
NATIONAL NEWSPAPER ASSOCIATION
NATIONAL PRESS CLUB
THE NEWSPAPER GUILD
TWIN CITIES NEWSPAPER GUILD

ABC NEWSPAPER
P.O. Box 99
Anoka MN 55303
612/421-4444
Contact Jeff Athmann, General Manager. A major newspaper and commercial printer. Common positions include: Advertising Worker; Commercial Artist; Reporter/Editor; Sales Representative. Principal educational backgrounds sought: Communications; Marketing. Company benefits include: medical insurance; dental insurance; pension plan; life insurance; tuition assistance; profit sharing. Corporate headquarters location: Princeton, MN. Operations at this facility include: manufacturing; administration; service; sales.

BUTLETIC PUBLISHING CORPORATION
7163 East Point Douglas Road
Cottage Grove MN 55016
612/459-3434
Contact Human Resources. An area publisher of newspapers and shopping guides.

CITY PAGES
401 North 3rd Street
Minneapolis MN 55401
612/375-1015
Contact Genel Kampf, Office Manager. An alternative-news weekly
newspaper.

COWLES MEDIA CO.
329 Portland Avenue
Minneapolis MN 55415
612/375-7000
Contact Personnel. Publisher of the Minneapolis Star and Tribune
newspapers.

MINNEAPOLIS STAR TRIBUNE
425 Portland Avenue
Minneapolis MN 55488
612/673-4000
Contact Cathy Veidel, Employment Supervisor. A major daily newspaper
with a daily circulation of 381,808.

MINNESOTA SUBURBAN NEWSPAPERS INC.
7831 East Bushlake Road
Bloomington MN 55439
612/831-1200
Contact Al Holt, Personnel Director. Parent company for a group of
suburban Minneapolis newspapers.

POST PUBLISHING CO.
8801 Bass Lake Road,
New Hope MN 55428
612/536-7500
Contact Alan Holz, Personnel Director. Publishers of a group of nine local
newspapers, including the Brooklyn Center Post, Brooklyn Park Post, East
Minneapolis and East Suburban Shopping Guide, the Plymouth Post, and the
New Hope-Golden Valley Post.

SAINT PAUL PIONEER PRESS
345 Cedar Street
St. Paul MN 55101
612/228-5002
Contact Vickie Erkson, Human Resources Representative. A major area
newspaper publisher. Common positions include: Reporter/Editor;
Customer Service Representative; Sales Representative. Principal
educational backgrounds sought: Business Administration; Communications;
Marketing; Journalism. Internships offered. Company benefits include:
medical, dental, and life insurance; pension plan; tuition assistance.
Corporate headquarters location: Miami, FL. Parent company: Knight-

Ridder, Inc. Operations at this facility include: manufacturing. New York Stock Exchange.

PAPER, PACKAGING & FOREST PRODUCTS/
CONTAINERS & GLASS PRODUCTS

For more information on professional employment opportunities in the paper, packaging and forest products industries, contact the following professional and trade associations, as listed beginning on page 251:

AMERICAN PAPER INSTITUTE
TECHNICAL ASSOCIATION OF THE PULP AND PAPER INDUSTRY
TECHNICAL ASSOCIATION OF THE PULP AND PAPER INDUSTRY/
    MINNESOTA SECTION

APOGEE ENTERPRISES INC.
7900 Yerxes Avenue South, Suite 1944
Minneapolis MN 55431
612/835-1874
Contact Human Resources Department. An area producer of glass, glazing and related products.

BAILEY NURSERIES INC.
1325 Bailey Road
St. Paul MN 55119
612/459-9744
Contact Irene Golberg, Personnel Manager. A large wholesale grower of nursery products to include evergreens, trees, shrubs, bedding plants, annuals, perennials, etc. Principal educational backgrounds sought: Horticulture and Agriculture. Training programs offered; Internships offered. Company benefits include: medical, dental, and life insurance; pension plan; tuition assistance; disability coverage; profit sharing; employee discounts; savings plan; 401K; 125 Plan. Corporate headquarters location. Operations at this facility include: divisional headquarters; manufacturing; research/development; administration; service; sales.

BEMIS COMPANY
625 Marquette Avenue
Minneapolis MN 55402
612/340-6000
Contact Vanessa M. Johnson, Corporate Manager, Personnel. Administrative headquarters of the manufacturer of flexible packaging and specialty coated and graphics products. Common positions include: Chemical Engineer; Electrical Engineer. Principal educational backgrounds sought: Accounting; Engineering; Finance. Company benefits include: medical

insurance; dental insurance; pension plan; life insurance; tuition assistance; disability coverage; and savings plan. Corporate headquarters location. New York Stock Exchange.

BOISE CASCADE OFFICE PRODUCTS
7509 Boone Avenue North
Brooklyn Park MN 55428
612/424-9600
Contact Neal Bailey, General Manager. A wholesale distributor of office products.

CARDINAL IG COMPANY
12301 Whitewater Drive
Minnetonka MN 55343
612/935-1722
Contact Personnel. Manufacturers of insulated glass units.

INLAND CONTAINER
3900 Highway 101
Shakopee MN 55379
612/445-4201
Contact Pat Holloway, Personnel Director. Manufacturer of corrugated boxes.

LESLIE PAPER/TWIN CITY DIVISION
P.O. Box 1351
Minneapolis MN 55440
612/540-0700
Contact Ruth Shatis, Personnel. Wholesalers of printing and writing paper.

LIBERTY CARTON COMPANY
870 Louisiana Avenue South
Minneapolis MN 55426
612/540-9600
Contact Personnel Director. A manufacturer of corrugated and solid fiber boxes.

LYMAN LUMBER COMPANY
300 Morse Avenue
P.O. Box 40
Excelsior MN 55331
612/474-0844
Contact Personnel Office. An aggressive, progressive leader in the lumber and building materials industry with several divisions in the Metro area, two in Wisconsin, and one in North Carolina. Common positions include: Accountant; Architectural Designer/Engineer; Blue-Collar Worker/ Supervisor; Buyer; Credit Manager; Customer Service Representative; Draftsperson; Branch Manager; Department Manager; Management

Trainee; Operations/Production Manager; Personnel & Labor Relations Specialist; Purchasing Agent; Sales Representative; Truck Driver; Yard Worker. Principal educational background sought: Accounting and Engineering. Company benefits include: medical, dental, and life insurance; pension plan; tuition assistance; disability coverage; profit sharing; employee discounts. Corporate headquarters. Operations at this facility include: administration.

MACKAY ENVELOPE COMPANY
2100 Southeast Elm Street
Minneapolis MN 55414
612/331-9311
Contact Personnel. A major area manufacturer of envelopes. Common positions include: Accountant; Blue-Collar Worker Supervisor; Credit Manager; Customer Service Representative; Sales Representative. Principal educational backgrounds sought: Accounting; Marketing. Company benefits include: medical, dental, and life insurance; pension plan; tuition assistance; disability coverage; profit sharing; savings plan. Corporate headquarters location. Operations at this facility include: manufacturing.

PACKAGING CORPORATION OF AMERICA
1821 North East Marshall Street
Minneapolis MN 55418
612/789-3511
Contact Dick Johnson, Office Manager. Manufacturers of corrugated shipping containers. Corporate headquarters location: Evanston, IL.

PENTAIR INDUSTRIES
1700 West Highway 36
St. Paul MN 55113
612/636-7920
Contact Duke Fuehrer, Manager, Staffing & Development. Corporate offices of a diverse firm with operations in paper mills and the manufacturing of portable and stationary woodworking tools, pumps, lubrication systems, jacks, electrical enclosures and sporting ammunition and accesories.

QUALITY PARK PRODUCTS
2520 Como Avenue
St. Paul MN 55108
612/645-0251
Contact Personnel Director. Wholesalers and manufacturers of envelopes.

SCHERER BROS. LUMBER CO.
9th Avenue NE and Mississippi River
Minneapolis MN 55413
612/379-9633
Contact Personnel. A lumber company.

SMEAD MANUFACTURING COMPANY
600 East Smead Boulevard
Hastings MN 55033
612/437-4111
Contact Janie Darsow. A die cut paper manufacturing firm. Common positions include: Accountant; Administrator; Blue-Collar Worker Supervisor; Buyer; Computer Programmer; Credit Manager; Customer Service Representative; Draftsperson; Industrial Engineer; Mechanical Engineer; Financial Analyst; Industrial Manager; Branch Manager; Department Manager; General Manager; Operations/Production Manager; Marketing Specialist; Personnel and Labor Relations Specialist; Quality Control Supervisor; Sales Representative; Systems Analyst; Transportation & Traffic Specialist; Purchasing Agent. Principal educational backgrounds sought: Accounting; Business Administration; Computer Science; Engineering; Marketing; Liberal Arts. Company benefits include: medical insurance; pension plan; life insurance; tuition assistance; disability coverage; savings plan. Corporate headquarters location. Operations at this facility include: manufacturing.

TAPEMARK CO.
150 East Marie Avenue E
St. Paul MN 55118
612/455-1611
Contact Personnel. Producers of adhesive papers and labels.

PACESETTER
354 West County Road D
New Brighton MN 55112
612/636-0050
Contact Personnel Department. Largest manufacturer of energy products in the United States.

PETROLEUM AND MINING

For more information on professional employment opportunities in the petroleum and mining industries, contact the following professional and trade associations, as listed beginning on page 251:

AMERICAN ASSOCIATION OF PETROLEUM GEOLOGISTS
AMERICAN GAS ASSOCIATION
AMERICAN GEOLOGICAL INSTITUTE
AMERICAN INSTITUTE OF MINING, METALLURGY & PETROLEUM
AMERICAN INSTITUTE OF MINING, METALLURGY & PETROLEUM/
    MINNESOTA
AMERICAN NUCLEAR SOCIETY

AMERICAN PETROLEUM INSTITUTE
AMERICAN SOCIETY OF TRIBOLOGISTS & LUBRICATION
 ENGINEERS
AMERICAN SOCIETY OF TRIBOLOGISTS & LUBRICATION
 ENGINEERS/TWIN CITIES
CLEAN ENGERGY RESEARCH INSTITUTE
GEOLOGICAL SOCIETY OF AMERICA
MINNESOTA PETROLEUM COUNCIL
PETROLEUM EQUIPMENT INSTITUTE
SOCIETY OF EXPLORATION GEOPHYSICISTS

GREAT NORTHERN IRON ORE PROPERTIES
West 2081 First National
St. Paul MN 55101
612/224-2385
Contact Personnel Director. A major trust company involved in leasing land
for use in the mining of iron ore.

PRINTING/GRAPHIC ARTS/PHOTOGRAPHY

**For more information on professional employment opportunities in the
printing industry, contact the following professional and trade associations,
as listed beginning on page 251:**

ASSOCIATION OF GRAPHIC ARTS
BINDING INDUSTRIES OF AMEICA
NATIONAL ASSOCIATION OF PRINTERS AND LITHOGRAPHERS
PRINTING INDUSTRIES OF AMERICA
PRINTING INDUSTRY OF MINNESOTA
TECHNICAL ASSOCIATION OF THE GRAPHIC ARTS

A & A PLATE SERVICE INCORPORATED
1113 Washington Avenue South
Minneapolis MN 55415
612/339-7549
Contact Personnel Department. An established manufacturer of litho
negatives & plates.

ACME TAG COMPANY
2838 Fremont Avenue South
Minneapolis MN 55408
612/872-0333
Contact Donald J. Renner, Manager Sales-Executive. Manufacturer of all
kinds of tags, printed gum labels, printed pressure sensitive labels.

BLACK'S PHOTOGRAPHY
1201 West Broadway
Minneapolis MN 55411
612/588-7861
Contact Sheila Handy, Career Development Coordinator. A retail and photofinishing specialty company serving all types of photographers. Common positions include: Accountant; Administrator; Buyer; Computer Programmer; Store Manager; Operations/Production Manager; Marketing Specialist; Personnel and Labor Relations Specialist; Transportation & Traffic Specialist. Principal educational backgrounds sought: Business Administration; Communications; Finance; Liberal Arts; Marketing; Retail; Photofinishing. Company benefits include: medical, dental, and life insurance; pension plan; tuition assistance; some disability coverage; employee discounts. Corporate headquarters location. Operations at this facility include: regional headquarters; administration; service; sales.

BROWN AND BIGELOW/ATWATER GROUP
345 East Plato Boulevard
St. Paul MN 55107
612/293-7000
Contact Lori Glanz, Personnel Director. A major area commercial lithographer, specializing in the manufacture of playing cards and calendars.

BUREAU OF ENGRAVING
500 South 4th Street
Minneapolis MN 55415
612/339-8721
Contact Mary Shearer, Director of Personnel. A diversified printer and engraver, employing over 1000.

CHECK TECHNOLOGY CORP.
1284 Corporate Center Drive
Eagan MN 55121
612/454-9300
Contact Personnel. Produces micro-computer controlled printing systems to print and assemble financial documents, including personal checks.

COLWELL INDUSTRIES INC.
123 North 3rd Street
Minneapolis MN 55401
612/340-0365
Contact Personnel. A printer of magazines and catalogs. The company also manufactures color merchandising programs and graphic arts supplies.

DATA CARD CORPORATION
11111 Bren Road West
Minnetonka MN 55343
612/933-1223
Contact Personnel. A producer of embossing systems for plastic cards.

DELUXE CORPORATION
1005 Gramsie Road
Shoreview MN 55126
612/481-4100
Contact David Broza, Employment Specialist. Deluxe Corporation began business in 1915, printing checks for financial institutions and their customers. Since its beginning, Deluxe's service has helped it become the nations's largest supplier of checks, deposit tickets and other magnetic-ink encoded transaction forms. In addition to check and related products Deluxe has also expanded into new markets. Its Business Systems group has become a major supplier of short-run computer forms, business forms and related office products to small businesses and professional practices. The Company's Consumer Specialty Products group markets greeting cards, stationery, pre-inked stamps, and a variety of related products to households. Deluxe has more than 80 service and production facilities located nationwide. The company's headquarters are in St. Paul, Minnesota. Deluxe Corporation is a major, top 500 Fortune Company with diverse job opportunities. The company hires in a variety of areas including engineering, electronics, data processing, accounting, management training, sales, marketing, and communications. Common positions include: Accountant; Computer Programmer; Customer Service Representative; Electrical Engineer; Mechanical Engineer; Management Trainee; Marketing Specialist; Sales Representative - Trainee. Principal educational backgrounds sought: Business Administration; Liberal Arts; Marketing; (mostly liberal arts). Company benefits include: medical insurance; dental insurance; pension plan; life insurance; tuition assitance; disability coverage; profit sharing; employee discounts; savings plan; stock purchase; vision care. Corporate headquarters location. Operations at this facility include: regional headquarters; divisional headquarters; manufacturing; research/development; administration; service; sales. New York Stock Exchange.

HOLDEN BUSINESS FORMS CO.
607 Washington Avenue North
Minneapolis MN 55401
612/339-0241
Contact Human Resources Director. A major area manufacturer of custom business forms. Common positions include: Accountant; Administrator; Blue-Collar Worker Supervisor; Computer Programmer; Credit Manager; Customer Service Representative; Department Manager; General Manager; Management Trainee; Operations/Production Manager; Personnel and Labor Relations Specialist; Purchasing Agent; Sales Representative; Systems Analyst. Principal educational backgrounds sought: Business Administration;

Communications; Computer Science; Printing. Training programs offered. Company benefits include: medical insurance; dental insurance; life insurance; pension plan; tuition assistance; disability coverage; profit sharing. Corporate headquarters location. Operations at this facility include: regional headquarters; manufacturing; administration; sales. Other locations: 301 South Church Street, Rockford IL 61101; 1800 Timberlake Drive, Arlington TX 76010.

INNOVEX
1313 South 5th Street
Hopkins MN 55343
612/938-4155
Contact Personnel. Producers of photographic processing equipment and chemicals.

INSTANT WEB INC.
7951 Powers Boulevard
Chanhassen MN 55317
612/474-0961
Contact Personnel. A leading commercial printing company.

JAPS-OLSON COMPANY
30 North 31st Avenue
Minneapolis MN 55411
612/522-4461
Contact Bob Murphy, President. Printing, packaging and mailing. Employs 200.

LE SUEUR PUBLISHING INCORPORATED
101 Bridge Street
Le Sueur MN 56058
612/665-3332
Contact Tom Fraundinst, Publisher. A commercial printer.

LIFETOUCH NATIONAL SCHOOL STUDIOS
7800 Picture Drive
Minneapolis MN 55439
612/835-3400
Contact Personnel Department. Engaged in portrait photography. Common position include: Sales Representative; Portrait Photographer. Principal educational background sought (but will train): Business Administration. Company benefits include: medical, dental, and life insurance; employee stock ownership plan. Corporate headquarters location: Minneapolis MN. Regional headquarters location. Operations at this facility include: manufacturing; research/development; administration; service; sales.

MAIL ADVERTISING INCORPORATED
618 N 3rd Street
Minneapolis MN 55401
612/338-5687
Contact Mr. Lee Brewer, Human Resources. A local, regional, and national commercial printing and mailing corporation.

McGILL/JENSON INC.
655 North Fairview Avenue
St. Paul MN 55104
612/645-0751
Contact Ross Hooge, Human Resources Director. A major commercial letterpress printer.

MERRILL CORP.
One Merrill Circle
St. Paul MN 55108
612/646-4501
Contact Personnel. A commercial printing company.

NORTH STAR GRAPHICS
8610 81st Street
Cottage Grove MN 55016
612/459-1362
Contact Personnel Director. An offset printing company.

PAKO CORPORATION
6550 Wedgewood Road
Maple Grove MN 55369
612/559-7600
Contact Patricia A. Nott, Manager of Human Resources. Manufacturers of graphic arts equipment and distributors of photographic equipment parts and services. Common positions include: Accountant; Blue-Collar Worker Supervisor; Buyer; Chemist; Claim Representative; Credit Manager; Customer Service Representative; Draftsperson; Chemical Engineer; Electrical Engineer; Industrial Engineer; Mechanical Engineer; Financial Analyst; Branch Manager; Department Manager; General Manager; Marketing Specialist; Purchasing Agent; Sales Representative; Transporation & Traffic Specialist. Principal educational backgrounds sought: Accounting; Business Administration; Engineering; Finance; Liberal Arts; Marketing. Company benefits include: medical, dental, and life insurance; pension plan; tuition assistance; disability coverage; savings plan. Corporate and regional headquarters location.

THE PRESS INC.
18780 West 78th Street
Chanhassen MN 55317
612/937-9764
Contact Darlene Shelley, Personnel Manager. A nationwide four-color printing company. Common positions include: Accountant; Administrator; Blue Collar Worker Supervisor; Credit Manager; Customer Service Representative; Dietician; Financial Analyst; Department Manager; Operations/Production Manager; Personnel and Labor Relations Specialist; Purchasing Agent; Sales Representative. Principal educational backgrounds sought: Accounting; Business Administration; Communications; Marketing. Company benefits include: medical insurance; dental insurance; pension plan; life insurance; tuition assistance; disability coverage; savings plan; credit union. Corporate, regional headquarters location. Operations at this facility include: manufacturing; administration; service; sales.

PROEX PHOTO SYSTEMS
7101 Ohms Lane
Edina MN 55439
612/893-1915
Contact Director of Human Resources. A retail, one-hour photo finishing firm. Operates nineteen retail one-hour labs in the Minneapolis-St. Paul area, ten portrait studios and a specialty lab. Corporate headquarters location. Common positions include: Manager; Assistant Manager; Manager Trainee; Photofinishing Laboratory Technician; Photographer. Principal educational backgrounds sought: Business Administration; Communications; Liberal Arts; Photo-technology; Management. Company benefits include: medical insurance; dental insurance; life insurance; tuition assistance; disability coverage; employee discounts; 401K plan.

QUEBCOR PRINTING
1999 Shepard Road
St. Paul MN 55116
612/690-7200
Contact David Hoogesteger, Personnel Director. A printing, publishing, and creative services company with an emphasis on catalogs and magazines.

REAL ESTATE

For more information on professional employment opportunities in the real estate industry, contact the following professional and trade associations, as listed beginning on page 251:

APARTMENT OWNERS AND MANAGERS ASSOCIATION
BUILDING OWNERS AND MANAGERS ASSOCIATION
INSTITUTE OF REAL ESTATE MANAGEMENT

INTERNATIONAL ASSOCIATION OF CORPORATE REAL ESTATE
    EXECUTIVES
INTERNATIONAL ASSOCIATION OF CORPORATE REAL ESTATE/
    EXECUTIVES/ST. PAUL
INTERNATIONAL REAL ESTATE INSTITUTE
NATIONAL ASSOCIATION OF REAL ESTATE INVESTMENT TRUSTS
NATIONAL ASSOCIATION OF REALTORS

CSM CORPORATION
2561 Territorial Road
St. Paul MN 55114-1500
612/646-1717
Contact Personnel. Property managers for both commerical and residential properties.

THE CENTER COMPANIES
400 South Highway 169, Suite 800
Minneapolis MN 55426
612/525-1200
Contact James Wherley, Personnel Director. Engaged in real estate development.

HILLCREST DEVELOPMENT
1111 Third Avenue South, Suite 440
Minneapolis MN 55404
612/371-0123
Contact Leoda Swanson, Controller. A Minneapolis real estate leasing and development company.

NORTHLAND INSURANCE
3500 West Eightieth Street
Suite 280
Bloomington MN 55431
612/831-1000
Contact Bill Hastings, Personnel Director. A commercial and real estate property management firm.

OPUS CORPORATION
9900 Bren Road East
800 Opus Center
Minnetonka MN 55343
612/936-4622
Contact Joe Braun, Human Resources Manager. A privately held construction and development company that provides single-source and vertically integrated design/build and real estate development services to commercial, industrial, and institutional customers in the Northwest region of the United States. Common positions include: Accountant; Attorney;

Computer Programmer; Marketing Specialist; Personnel & Labor Relations Specialist; Project Manager; Tax Accountant; Real Estate Manager; Construction Engineer. Principal educational backgrounds sought: Accounting; Business Administration; Computer Science; Engineering; Finance; Marketing; Real Estate. Training programs offered. Company benefits include: medical insurance; life insurance; tuition assistance; disability coverage; profit sharing; employee discounts; 401K. Corporate headquarters location. Operations at this facility include: regional headquarters; administration; service; sales.

RUBBER AND PLASTICS

For more information on professional employment opportunities in the rubber and plastics industries, contact the following professional and trade associations, as listed beginning on page 251:

SOCIETY OF PLASTIC ENGINEERS
SOCIETY OF PLASTIC ENGINEERS/MINNESOTA CHAPTER
SOCIETY OF PLASTICS INDUSTRY

CARLISLE PLASTICS, INC.
1401 West 94th Street
Minneapolis MN 55431
612/884-7281
Contact Donna Schmidtbauer, Human Resources Manager. A major area plastics firm.

DIVERSIFOAM PRODUCTS
9091 County Road 50
Rockford MN 55373
612/477-5854
Contact Carl Mura, Personnel. A manufacturer of polystyrine insulation.

INTERPLASTIC CORPORATION
1225 Wolters Boulevard
Vadnais Heights MN 55110
612/331-6850
Contact Personnel. Producers of synthetic resins and companion items, polythylene containers and sheet molding compound.

McCOURTNEY PLASTICS INC.
7309 West 27th Street
Minneapolis MN 55426
612/929-3312
Contact Peter W. Olson, Human Resources Manager. A manufacturer of plastic injection molding. Common positions include: Accountant; Claim Representative; Customer Service Representative; Customer Service Manager; Draftsperson; Industrial Engineer; Mechanical Engineer; Operations/Production Manager; Purchasing Agent; Sales Representative. Company benefits include: medical insurance; dental insurance; pension plan; life insurance; tuition assistance; disability coverage. Corporate headquarters location.

MINNESOTA RUBBER
3630 Wooddale Avenue
St. Louis Park MN 55416
612/927-1400
Contact Human Resources Representative. Producers of precision molded rubber parts. Common positions include: Accountant; Advertising Worker; Blue-Collar Worker Supervisor; Chemist; Computer Programmer; Credit Manager; Customer Service Representative; Draftsperson; Electrical Engineer; Industrial Engineer; Mechanical Engineer; Department Manager; General Manager; Operations/Production Manager; Personnel & Labor Relations Specialist; Purchasing Agent; Quality Control Supervisor; Sales Representative; Systems Analyst. Company benefits include: medical, dental, and life insurance; tuition assistance; disability coverage; profit sharing; savings plan. Corporate headquarters location. Parent company: Quadion Corporation. Operations at this facility include: regional headquarters; divisional headquarters; manufacturing; research/development; administration; service; sales.

NORWESCO INC.
1650 West 82nd, Suite 1000
Bloomington MN 55431
612/885-5900
Contact Personnel. Manufacturers of a wide range of plastic parts.

PIRELLI
4079 Pepin Avenue
Red Wing MN 55066
612/388-0771
Contact Lowell Peterson, Director of Personnel. A major manufacturer of rubber products.

PLASTECH RESEARCH INC.
P.O. Box 7
Rush City MN 55069
612/358-4771
Contact David Bloomquist, Director of Personnel. A manufacturer of assorted plastic products, including injection moldings.

PLASTICS INC.
P.O. Box 64610
St. Paul MN 55164-0610
612/227-7371
Contact Phil Hosier, Director of Human Resources. A miscellaneous plastic products manufacturer, producing plastics for such diverse uses as turntables, take-out food utensils, and microwave items.

SHELLER-GLOBE ENGINEERED POLYMERS CO.
1020 East Maple Avenue
Mora MN 55051
612/679-3232
Contact John Ohnemus, Human Resources Manager. An area injection-molded plastics manufacturer. Common positions include: Accountant; Computer Programmer; Credit Manager; Customer Service Representative; Industrial Engineer; Mechanical Engineer; Operations/Production Manager; Personnel & Labor Relations Specialist; Purchasing Agent. Principal educational backgrounds sought: Accounting; Engineering. Company benefits include: medical, dental, and life insurance; pension plan; tuition assistance; disability coverage; savings plan. Corporate headquarters location: Toledo, OH. Parent company: Sheller-Globe Corporation. Operations at this facility include: manufacturing; sales.

UFE INC.
1850 South Greeley Street
P.O. Box 7
Stillwater MN 55082-0007
612/439-1561
Contact Jim Rogosheske, Staffing Manager. An engineering and manufacturing source for precision thermoplastic components serving diverse markets. Common positions include: Mechanical Engineer. Principal educational backgrounds sought include: Engineering. Company benefits include: medical, dental, and life insurance; pension plan; tuition assistance; disability coverage; profit sharing; savings plan. Corporate headquarters location. Operations at this facility include: research/development; administration; sales.

TRANSPORTATION

For more information on professional employment opportunities in the transportation industry, contact the following professional and trade associations, as listed beginning on page 251:

AIR LINE EMPLOYEES ASSOCIATION
AIR TRANSPORT ASSOCIATION OF AMERICA
AMERICAN INSTITUTE OF AERONAUTICS AND ASTRONAUTICS
AMERICAN SOCIETY OF TRAVEL AGENTS
AMERICAN TRUCKING ASSOCIATION
ASSOCIATION OF AMERICAN RAILROADS
AUTOMOTIVE SERVICE ASSOCIATION
AUTOMOTIVE SERVICE ASSOCIATION/MINNESOTA
AVIATION MAINTENANCE FOUNDATION
FUTURE AVIATION PROFESSIONALS OF AMERICA
GREATER METROPOLITAN AUTOMOBILE DEALERS ASSOCIATION
        OF MINNESOTA
INSTITUTE OF TRANSPORTATION ENGINEERS
MARINE TECHNOLOGY SOCIETY
MINNESOTA TRUCKING ASSOCIATION
MOTOR VEHICLE MANUFACTURERS ASSOCIATION
NATIONAL AERONAUTIC ASSOCIATION OF USA
NATIONAL AUTOMOTIVE DEALERS ASSOCIATION
NATIONAL INSTITUTE FOR AUTOMOTIVE SERVICE EXCELLENCE
NATIONAL MARINE MANUFACTURERS ASSOCIATION
PROFESSIONAL AVIATION MAINTENANCE ASSOCIATION
PROFESSIONAL AVIATION MAINTENENCE ASSOCIATION/
        MINNESOTA
SHIPBUILDERS COUNCIL OF AMERICA

AERO SYSTEMS ENGINEERING
358 East Fillmore Street
St. Paul MN 55107
612/227-7515
Contact Director of Personnel. A major aerospace engineering firm serving both defense and commercial clients.

ALLSTATE LEASING INC.
1056 Gemini Road
Eagan MN 55121
612/681-4900
Contact John Waters, Controller. A major area truck leasing company.

BERGER TRANSFER
2950 Long Lake Road
St. Paul MN 55113
612/788-9393
Contact Tom Miller, Director of Administration. An interstate trucking company.

BURLINGTON NORTHERN RAILROAD
176 East 5th Street
St. Paul MN 55101
612/298-2121
Contact Personnel Department. A major area provider of railroad transport services.

CARGILL MARINE AND TERMINAL
P.O. Box 9300
Minneapolis MN 55440-9300
612/475-7575
Contact Personnel. Company is engaged in marine terminal and stevdoring services. A subsidiary of Cargill, Inc., a diversified holding company, headquartered in Wayzata MN.

CENTURY MOTOR FREIGHT
2160 Mustang Drive
Mounds View MN 55112
612/786-9650
Contact Michelle Davis, Personnel Director. A major interstate trucking company. Corporate headquarters location.

CHRYSLER MOTORS/SERVICE & PARTS OPERATIONS
P.O. Box 1231
Minneapolis MN 55440
612/553-2551
Contact Dave Foshe, Field Operations Manager. A zone office for a major automobile and truck manufacturer. Zone conducts all business relating to service, customer relations, parts sales and distribution in a five-state area. Common positions include: Administrator; Customer Service Representative; Service & Parts District Manager. Principal educational backgrounds sought: Business Administration; Industrial Technology - Automotive. Company benefits include: medical insurance; dental insurance; pension plan; life insurance; tuition assistance; disability coverage; profit sharing; employee discounts; savings plan. Operations at this facility include: regional headquarters. New York Stock Exchange.

CUMMINS DIESEL SALES
2690 Cleveland Avenue North
St. Paul MN 55113
612/636-1000
Contact Personnel Department. A major supplier of diesel engines.

DAHLEN TRANSPORT INC.
1680 Fourth Avenue
Newport MN 55055
612/459-3344
Contact Virginia Isder, Personnel Director. An interstate trucking company.

FORD MOTOR COMPANY
966 South Mississippi River Boulevard
St. Paul MN 55116
612/699-1321
Contact Jerry Norsby, Personnel Director. Automobile assembly plant operating as a division of the well-known national automobile company.

HANSORD PONTIAC
222 Hennepin Avenue
Minneapolis MN 55401
612/371-1400
Contact Betty Schlego, Personnel Manager. A local new and used automobile dealership.

HYMAN FREIGHTWAYS
P.O. Box 64393
St. Paul MN 55164-0393
612/784-5030
Contact Ida Castle, Personnel. An interstate trucking company.

INTERNATIONAL TRAVEL ARRANGERS
2600 Eagan Woods Drive
Eagan MN 55121
612/456-9280
Contact Personnel Director. A tour wholesaler, specializing in charter air travel packages to many destinations. Common positions include: Customer Service Representative; Transportation Specialist; Travel Agent. Training programs available. Company benefits include: medical insurance; pension plan; life insurance; profit sharing; employee discounts. Corporate headquarters location.

JEFFERSON LINES, INC.
P.O. Box 978
Minneapolis MN 55440
612/332-8745
Contact Karen Lyn Peterson, Human Resource Administrator. A major inter-city bus line and travel concern. Common positions include: Customer Service Representative; Accountant; Transportation & Traffic Specialist; Payroll; Data Processing. Principal educational backgrounds sought: Accounting; Business Administration; Communications; Liberal Arts; Marketing. Company benefits include: medical insurance; dental insurance; pension plan; life insurance; tuition assistance; disability coverage; savings plan; flexible benefits. Corporate headquarters location. Operations at this facility include: divisional headquarters; administration; service; sales.

JOHNSON AUTOHOUSE
801 East Seventh Street
St. Paul MN 55106
612/774-9676
Contact General Manager. A major St. Paul automotive dealership.

LUPIENT AUTOMOTIVE GROUP
7100 Wayzata Boulevard
Golden Valley MN 55426
612/546-5636
Contact Personnel. A holding company for a group of new and used automotive retailers. Subsidiaries include: Lupient Buick, employing 60, and Lupeint Oldsmobile, employing 250.

MINNESOTA COACHES
2866 White Bear Avenue
St. Paul MN 55109
612/770-7700
Contact Betty Reige, Payroll. A major area coach line.

NAPCO INTERNATIONAL INC.
1600 South 2nd Street
Hopkins MN 55343
612/931-2460
Contact Judy Winkler, Human Resources Administrator. A major wholesaler of automotive parts and supplies. Common positions include: Accountant; Administrator; Blue-Collar Worker Supervisor; Buyer; Computer Programmer; Customer Service Representative; Draftsperson; Aerospace Engineer; Mechanical Engineer; Department Manager; Marketing Specialist; Personnel and Labor Relations Specialist; Purchasing Agent; Quality Control Supervisor. Principal educational backgrounds]sought: Accounting; Art/Design; Business Administration; Computer Science; Finance; Marketing. Company benefits include: medical insurance; dental insurance; pension plan; life insurance; tuition assistance; disability coverage; profit

sharing; employee discounts. Parent company: Venturian Corporation. Corporate, regional, divisional headquarters location. Operations at this facility include: service; sales.

NATIONAL CAR RENTAL SYSTEM, INC.
7700 France Avenue South
Minneapolis MN 55435
612/893-6069
Contact Sandra Morrison, Director of Human Resources. National, one of the leading car rental companies in the world, provides travelers with the convenience of innovative and high quality service. Common positions include: Claim Representative; Management Trainee; Sales Representative; Reservation Agent. Principal educational backgrounds sought: Business Administration; Liberal Arts. Training programs offered. Company benefits include: medical insurance; dental insurance; life insurance; tuition assistance; disability coverage; employee discounts; savings plan. Corporate headquarters location.

NORTHWEST AIRLINES
Dept. A 1470, 5101 Northwest Drive
St. Paul MN 55111-3034
612/726-2215
Contact Gary L. Walbrun, Director of Staffing. One of the nation's largest scheduled airlines, providing passenger and shipping services to more than 135 cities in 21 countries around the world. Employs over 38,000 nationwide. Common positions include: Accountant; Administrator; Attorney; Blue-Collar Worker Supervisor; Buyer; Computer Programmer; Credit Manager; Customer Service Representative; Aerospace Engineer; Civil Engineer; Electrical Engineer; Mechanical Engineer; Department Manager; General Manager; Management Trainee; Operations/Production Manager; Marketing Specialist; Personnel and Labor Relations Specialist; Public Relations Worker; Purchasing Agent; Quality Control Supervisor; Sales Representative; Technical Writer/Editor; Transportation and Traffic Specialist. Principal educational backgrounds sought depend upon the position. Company benefits include: medical, dental, and life insurance; pension plan; disability coverage; employee discounts; savings plan. Corporate headquarters location. Parent company: Wings Holdings, Inc. Operations at this facility include: manufacturing; administration; service; sales.

PAGE & AVJET
3880 East 70th Street
Minneapolis MN 55450
612/726-5700
Contact Base Manager. An aviation fixed base operation at International Airport; providing fueling, hangaring, avionics, maintenance, and parts services to the corporate aircraft market.

POLARIS INDUSTRIES, L.P.
Highway 89 South
Roseau MN 56751
218/463-2312
Contact Ray Roth, Manager of Personnel. A manufacturer of recreational vehicles (snowmobiles and four-wheelers), clutches for golf cars, and blade brakes. Operations include: manufacturing; research/development. Corporate headquarters location: Minneapolis, MN. Common positions include: Accountant; Blue-Collar Worker Supervisor; Buyer; Computer Programmer; Customer Service Representative; Draftsperson; Electrical Engineer; Industrial Engineer; Mechanical Engineer; Operations/Production Manager; Personnel and Labor Relations Specialist; Purchasing Agent; Quality Control Supervisor. Principal educational backgrounds sought: Business Administration; Computer Science; Engineering. Company benefits include: medical insurance; life insurance; tuition assistance; disability coverage; profit sharing; employee discounts; savings plan. American Stock Exchange.

SAFETRAN SYSTEMS CORPORATION
4650 Main Street NE
Minneapolis MN 55421
612/572-1400
Contact Personnel Department. A local, national, and regional producer of signal equipment cases and house metal, as well as railroad wayside signals. Common positions include: Accountant; Blue-Collar Worker Supervisor; Buyer; Computer Programmer; Customer Service Representative; Draftsperson; Electrical Engineer; Mechanical Engineer; Department Manager; General Manager; Operations/Production Manager; Purchasing Agent; Systems Analyst. Principal educational backgrounds sought: Accounting; Business Administration; Engineering; Finance. Company benefits include: medical, dental, and life insurance; pension plan; tuition assistance; disability coverage. Parent company: H.S. Investments, Inc. Operations at this facility include: divisional headquarters; manufacturing; research/development; administration; service; sales.

SOO LINE RAILROAD CO.
105 South 5th and Marquette
Minneapolis MN 55402
612/347-8000
Contact Personnel. One of the nation's leading railway companies.

TRANSPORT AMERICA
10700 Lyndale Avenue, South
Bloomington MN 55420
612/884-8854
Contact Glenn Baker, Vice President of Administration. A major irregular route truck load motor carrier with 48-state authority. Common positions include: Accountant; Computer Programmer; Department Manager; Sales

Representative; Transportation and Traffic Specialist. Principal educational backgrounds sought: Accounting; Business Administration; Communications; Computer Science; Economics; Finance; Marketing; Mathematics. Company benefits include: medical insurance; pension plan; life insurance; tuition assistance. Corporate headquarters location.

UNIVERSAL CO-OP INCORPORATED
7801 Metro Parkway
Minneapolis MN 55425
612/854-0800
Contact Brian Morrison, Vice President of Human Resources. A major wholesaler of automotive parts and supplies.

UTILITIES

For more information on professional employment opportunities in the utilities industry, contact the following professional association, as listed beginning on page 251:

AMERICAN WATER WORKS ASSOCIATION

ANOKA ELECTRIC COOPERATIVE
2022 North Ferry Street
Anoka MN 55303
612/421-3761
Contact Personnel. An area electric utility.

ARKLE/MINNEGASCO
201 South 7th Street
Minneapolis MN 55402
612/372-4664
Contact Employment/Personnel. An energy services, products and communications corporation doing business through the following subsidiaries: Minnegasco, Inc., a natural gas distribution company; Dyco Petroleum, an oil and gas exploration and production company; E.F. Johnson Company, a design, manufacturing and marketing company of radio communications products and systems, electronic components, and specialty products; and EnScan, Inc., which develops and markets energy measurement products and systems.

COOPERATIVE POWER ASSOCIATION
14615 Lone Oak Road
Eden Prairie MN 55344
612/937-8599
Contact Personnel. One of the Twin Cities' leading cooperative utility companies.

NORTHERN STATES POWER CO.
414 Nicollet Mall
Minneapolis MN 55401
612/639-1234
Contact Personnel. A leading utility.

UNITED POWER ASSOCIATION
Box 800
Elk River MN 55330
612/441-3121
Contact Michael J. DeLuca, Administrator of Employment Training. An area electric utility company. Common positions include: Accountant; Actuary; Administrator; Advertising Worker; Attorney; Blue-Collar Worker Supervisor; Buyer; Claim Representative; Computer Programmer; Credit Manager; Customer Service Representative; Dietician; Draftsperson; Economist; Agricultural Engineer; Civil Engineer; Electrical Engineer; Industrial Engineer; Mechanical Engineer; Metallurgical Engineer; Mining Engineer; Petroleum Engineer; Financial Analyst; Food Technologist; Forester; Geologist; Industrial Manager; Insurance Agent/Broker; Branch Manager; Department Manager; General Manager; Management Trainee; Operations/Production Manager; Marketing Specialist; Personnel and Labor Relations Specialist; Public Relations Specialist; Purchasing Agent; Quality Control Supervisor; Reporter/Editor; Sales Representative; Statistician; Systems Analyst; Technical Writer/Editor; Transportation and Traffic Specialist. Principal educational backgrounds sought: Accounting; Art/Design; Biology; Business Administration; Chemistry; Communications; Computer Science; Economics; Engineering; Finance; Geology; Liberal Arts; Marketing; Mathematics; Physics. Training programs offered. Company benefits offered: medical insurance; pension plan; life insurance; tuition assistance; disability coverage; profit sharing; savings plan; wellness program. Corporate headquarters location. Operations at this facility include: regional headquarters.

Professional Employment Services

ACCOUNTANTS ON CALL
45 South 7th St., Ste. 2312
Minneapolis MN 55402
Contact Jan M. Kruchoski. 612/341-9900. Specializes in the area of: accounting/finance.

AGRI CONSULTANTS
300 South Highway 169
Suite 180
Minneapolis MN 55426
Contact Mark Parsons, Owner. 612/542-8550. Employment agency. Appointment requested. Founded 1982. Specializes in the areas of: Research; Sales and Marketing. Positions commonly filled include: Agricultural Engineer; Agricultural Researcher; Marketing Specialist; Sales Representative. Company pays fee. Number of placements per year: 50.

ALTERNATIVE STAFFING, INC.
3600 W. 80th Street, #55
Bloomington MN 55431
Contact Kim Howard, President. 612/835-9977. Employment agency; temporary help agency. Free training available to enhance skills and mold a person to a specific position. Specializes in the areas of: Accounting; Computer Hardware and Software; Legal; Manufacturing; Printing and Publishing; Sales and Marketing; Secretarial and Clerical. Positions commonly filled include: Accountant; Administrative Assistant; Bookkeeper; Claims Representative; Clerk; Computer Programmer; Credit Manager; Customer Service Representative; Data Entry Clerk; Draftsperson; Executive Secretary; Factory Worker; Financial Analyst; Legal Secretary; Light Industrial Worker; Marketing Specialist; Medical Secretary; Personnel Director; Purchasing Agent; Receptionist; Sales Representative; Secretary; Stenographer; Typist; Word Processor. Company pays fee. Number of placements per year: 1000+.

ELECTRONIC SYSTEMS PERSONNEL
Suite 1800
701 4th Ave South
Minneapolis MN 55415
Contact Robert Hildreth, President. 612/338-6714. Fax: 612/342-2093. Employment agency. Appointment required. Founded 1968. Services the Data Processing industry. Specializes in the areas of: Computer Hardware and Software; Sales and Marketing. Positions commonly filled include: Computer Programmer; Data Entry Clerk; EDP Specialist; Systems Analyst; Technical Writer/Editor; Word Processor. Company pays fee.

EMPLOYMENT ADVISORS, INC. OF MINNEAPOLIS
526 Nicollet Mall
Minneapolis MN 55402
Contact Frank Ventura, Manager. 612/339-0521. Employment agency. No appointment required. Founded 1970. Specializes in the areas of: Banking; Food Industry; Insurance; Management Trainee Programs; Sales and Marketing. Positions commonly filled include: Administrative Assistant; Bookkeeper; Claim Representative; Clerk; Credit Manager; Customer Service Representative; General Manager; Hotel Manager/Assistant Manager; Insurance Agent; Office Worker; Restaurant Manager; Retail Manager; Sales Representative; Underwriter. Company pays fee; individual pays fee. Number of placements per year: 501-1000.

HAYDEN & ASSOCIATES, INC.
7825 Washington Ave. South Suite 120
Minneapolis MN 55439
Contact Lowell Singerman. 612/941-6300. FAX: 612/941-9602. Specializes in the areas of: computer science (corporate/computer security; consulting; data processing; EDP audit; operations; programming; sales; software engineering; systems; technicians; word processing sales/service); engineering (aeronautical; chemical; civil; electrical; environmental/hazardous waste; HVAC; industrial; manufacturing; mechanical; nuclear; packaging); marketing (consumer products; business products/computers; direct marketing; industrial products; international; market research; medical products; product management; sales promotion); sales (business products; computers; consumer products; industrial products; international; management; media; medical products; services/intangibles).

HILLEREN KREOFSKY ASSOCIATES
8300 Norman Center Dr. Ste. 510
Bloomington MN 55437
Contact Jerry Hilleren. 612/835-2677. FAX: 612/835-0826. Specializes in the areas of: engineering (electrical; manufacturing; mechanical); marketing (medical products); marketing (medical products); sales (computers; medical products); scientific research & development (product development; research & development).

INSURANCE PLACEMENT CENTER
3800 West 80th St., Suite 1080
Minneapolis MN 55431-4409
Contact Paul Schalekamp. 612/893-6633. FAX: 612/893-6637. Specializes in the area of: insurance (actuarial; claims; life/health; pension; property/casualty; rating; reinsurance; sales; underwriting).

JUS SECRETARIAL
403 4th Street Northwest
Suite 110
Bemidji MN 56601.
Contact Jim Otterkill, Manager. 218/751-3252. Temporary help service. No appointment required. Founded 1979. Nonspecialized. Positions commonly filled include: Accountant; Bookkeeper; Clerk; Data Entry Clerk; Driver; General Laborer; Legal Secretary; Office Worker; Receptionist; Secretary; Stenographer; Typist; Word Processing Specialist. Company pays fee. Number of placements per year: 50.

KELLY TEMPORARY SERVICES, INC.
200 South 6th Street
Minneapolis MN 55402
Contact Julie Crisps, Recruiting and Retention. 612/339-7154. Temporary help agency. No appointment required. Founded 1946. Specializes in the areas of: Secretarial and Clerical. Positions commonly filled include: Accountant; Actuary; Administrative Assistant; Bookkeeper; Claims Representative; Clerk; Commerical Artist; Computer Programmer; Customer Service Representative; Data Entry Clerk; Draftsperson; Executive Secretary; Factory Worker; General Laborer; General Manager; Legal Secretary; Light Industrial Worker; Marketing Specialist; Medical Secretary; Model; Personal Computer Operator; Public Relations Worker; Purchasing Agent; Receptionist; Sales Representative; Secretary; Stenographer; Typist; Word Processor. Company pays fee. Number of placements per year: 1000+.

THE LOVERNESS GROUP, INC.
1611 W. County Rd. B #212
Roseville MN 55113
Contact Rick Lover or Mary Ness. 612/633-1086. FAX: 612/633-0390. Specializes in the areas of: account management; art; copy; direct marketing; sales promotion.

NYCOR SEARCH, INC.
4930 77th St. W #300
Minneapolis MN 55435
Contact Paul E. Nymark. 612/831-6444. FAX: 612/835-2883. Specializes in the areas of: computer science (corporate/computer security; consulting; data processing; programming; sales; software engineering; systems; technicians); engineering (chemical; civil; electrical; environmental/hazardous waste; HVAC; industrial; manufacturing; mechanical; packaging; physics).

PALESCH AND ASSOCIATES, INC.
530 Kristen Lane
Maple Plain MN 55359
Contact Tom Palesch, President. 612/955-3390. Employment agency. Founded 1979. Specializes in the areas of: Service Center Industry; Steel

Industry. Positions commonly filled include: Operations Manager; Steel Mill Manager. Company pays fee. Number of placements per year: 50.

PERSONNEL DIRECTIONS
625 4th Avenue, So. Suite 1200
Minneapolis MN 55415
Contact Karen Cucci. 612/339-1636. FAX: 612/339-5442. Specializes in the areas of: entry level (support staff); legal (legal secretaries); office administration (administrators; clerks; receptionists; secretaries; word proccessing).

ROTH YOUNG PERSONNEL SERVICE OF MINNEAPOLIS, INC.
4530 West 77th Street
Minneapolis MN 55435
Contact Donald B. Spahr, President. 612/831-6655. Employment agency. Appointment requested. Founded 1970. Specializes in the areas of: Advertising; Distribution; Fashion; Food Manufacturing; Food Sales; Health and Medical; Hospitality; Personnel and Human Resources; Restaurants; Retail; Sales and Marketing; Supermarkets; Transportation. Positions commonly filled include: Accountant; Advertising Worker; Buyer; Customer Service Representative; Dietician; Distribution Manager; District Manager; Electrical Engineer; Financial Analyst; Food Technologist; General Manager; Hospital Administrator; Hotel Manager/Assistant Manager; Industrial Engineer; Marketing Specialist; Mechanical Engineer; Nurse; Operations/Production Specialist; Personnel and Labor Relations Specialist; Physical Therapist; Physician; Public Relations Worker; Purchasing Agent; Quality Control Supervisor; Restaurant Manager; Retail Manager; Sales Manager; Supermarket Manager; Technical Writer/Editor. Company pays fee. Number of placements per year: 150-200.

SALEM TECHNICAL SERVICES OF BLOOMINGTON
2626 East 82nd Street, Suite 355
Bloomington MN 55425
Contact Bill Fitch, Manager. 612/854-2400. Temporary help service. No appointment required. Founded 1967. Branch offices found in: Atlanta, GA; Austin, TX; Beloit, WI; Burlington, MA; Charlotte, NC; Cincinnati, OH; Cleveland, OH; Dallas, TX; Grand Rapids, MI; McLeanMilwaukee, WI; Phoenix, AZ; Golden, CO; Oak Brook, IL. Specializes in the areas of: Architecture; Computer Hardware and Software; Engineering; Manufacturing; MIS/EDP; Personnel and Human Resources; Technical and Scientific. Positions commonly filled include: Aerospace Engineer; Architect; Buyer; Ceramics Engineer; Chemist; Civil Engineer; Commercial Artist; Computer Operator; Computer Programmer; Data Entry Clerk; Draftsperson; Driver; EDP Specialist; Electrical Engineer; Industrial Designer; Industrial Engineer; MIS Specialist; Manufacturing Engineer; Mechanical Engineer; Metallurgical Engineer; Operations and Production Specialist; Personnel and Labor Relations Specialist; Purchasing Agent; Quality Control Supervisor; Reporter/Editor; Software Engineer; Systems

Analyst; Technical Illustrator; Technical Recruiter; Technical Writer/Editor; Technician; Word Processing Specialist. Number of placements per year: 201-500.

STAFF BUILDERS OF MINNESOTA
12 South 6th Street, Suite 520
Minneapolis MN 55402
612/339-0681. Temporary help service. Appointment requested. Founded 1961. Branch offices located in: Arizona; California; Connecticut; District of Columbia; Florida; Georgia; Illinois; Indiana; Kansas; Louisiana; Maryland; Massachusetts; Michigan; Oklahoma; Oregon; Pennsylvania; Rhode Island; Tennessee; Texas; Virginia; Washington. Nonspecialized. Positions commonly filled include: Accountants; Administrative Assistant; Bookkeeper; Clerk; Companion; Computer Operator; Computer Programmer; Customer Service Representative; Data Entry Clerk; Demonstrator; Draftsperson; Health Aide; Legal Secretary; Light Industrial Worker; Medical Secretary; Nurse; Office Worker; Public Relations Worker; Receptionist; Sales Representative; Secretary; Stenographer; Technician; Typist; Word Processing Specialist. Company pays fee. Number of placements per year: 1001+.

STAFF BUILDERS OF MINNESOTA
408 St. Peter, Suite 438
St. Paul MN 55102
612/291-2402. Temporary help service. Appointment requested. Founded 1961. Branch offices located in: Arizona; California; Connecticut; District of Columbia; Florida; Georgia; Illinois; Indiana; Kansas; Louisiana; Maryland; Massachusetts; Michigan; Oklahoma; Oregon; Pennsylvania; Rhode Island; Tennessee; Texas; Virginia; Washington. Nonspecialized. Positions commonly filled include: Accountants; Administrative Assistant; Bookkeeper; Clerk; Companion; Computer Operator; Computer Programmer; Customer Service Representative; Data Entry Clerk; Demonstrator; Draftsperson; Health Aide; Legal Secretary; Light Industrial Worker; Medical Secretary; Nurse; Office Worker; Public Relations Worker; Receptionist; Sales Representative; Secretary; Stenographer; Technician; Typist; Word Processing Specialist. Company pays fee. Number of placements per year: 1001+.

PERSONNEL POOL INC. OF EDINA
3400 West 66th Street
Suite 290
Edina MN 55435
612/920-8008. Temporary help service. Appointment requested. Founded 1954. Nonspecialized. Positions commonly filled include: Bookkeeper; Clerk; Computer Operator; Customer Service Representative; Data Entry Clerk; Demonstrator; Draftsperson; Electronic Assembler; Factory Worker; General Laborer; Legal Secretary; Light Industrial Worker; Medical Secretary; Officer Worker; Receptionist; Secretary; Stenographer;

Technician; Typist; Word Processing Specialist. Company pays fee. Number of placements per year: 1001+.

PERSONNEL POOL INC. OF MINNEAPOLIS
222 South 9th Street
Suite 150
Minneapolis MN 55402
612/333-7557. Temporary help service. Appointment requested. Founded 1954. Nonspecialized. Positions commonly filled include: Bookkeeper; Clerk; Computer Operator; Customer Service Representative; Data Entry Clerk; Demonstrator; Draftsperson; Electronic Assembler; Factory Worker; General Laborer; Legal Secretary; Light Industrial Worker; Medical Secretary; Officer Worker; Receptionist; Secretary; Stenographer; Technician; Typist; Word Processing Specialist. Company pays fee. Number of placements per year: 1001+.

YOUTH EMPLOYMENT PROJECT, INC.
208 City Hall
Rochester MN 55902
Contact Mary Sorensen, Executive Director. 507/ 287-2345. Employment agency; temporary help service. No appointment required. Founded 1969. Specializes in the area of: Youth. Positions commonly filled include: Child Care Specialist; Deliverer; Farm Worker; Office Helper; Restaurant Worker; Retail Salesperson; Yard Worker. Individual pays fee. Number of placements per year: 1001+.

EXECUTIVE SEARCH FIRMS OF MINNEAPOLIS/ST. PAUL

ACCOUNTANTS EXCHANGE, INC.
2233 Hamline Avenue North
Roseville Professional Center, Suite 509
Roseville MN 55113
Contact Chuck McBride, President. 612/636-5490. Executive search firm. No appointment required. Founded 1977. Specializes in the areas of: Accounting and Finance. Number of searches conducted per year: 0-50.

ADVANCE PERSONNEL RESOURCES
715 Florida Avenue, Suite 206
Minneapolis MN 55426
Contact Larry Happe, Owner. 612/546-6779. Executive search firm. Appointment requested. Founded 1976. Specializes in mid-management professional positions in Sales, Management, and Technical fields. Division

also specializes in Outplacement services and Job Search seminars. Number of searches conducted per year: 30.

COMPUSEARCH OF MINNEAPOLIS
7550 France Avenue, Suite 180
Minneapolis MN 55435
Contact Bob Hammer, General Manager, or Gary Fish, Manager. 612/830-1135. Executive search firm. Appointment required; no phone calls; unsolicited resumes accepted. Founded 1965. World's largest contingency search firm. Five hundred offices nationwide, doing business under the names "Management Recruiter", "Sales Consultants", "CompuSearch" and "OfficeMate5". Specializes in mid-management/professional positions, $25,000-75,000 per annum. Specializes in the areas of: Accounting; Administration, MIS/EDP; Advertising; Affirmative Action; Banking and Finance; Chemicals and Pharmaceuticals; Communications; Computer Hardware and Software; Construction; Electrical; Engineering; Food Industry; General Management; Health and Medical; Human Resources; Industrial and Interior Design; Insurance; Legal; Manufacturing; Operations Management; Printing and Publishing; Procurement; Real Estate; Retailing; Sales and Marketing; Technical and Scientific; Textiles; Transportation. Contingency.

ROBERT CONNELLY AND ASSOCIATES INC.
Post Office Box 24028
Minneapolis MN 55424
Contact Robert F. Olsen, President. 612/925-3039. Executive search firm. Appointment requested; no phone calls; unsolicited resumes accepted. Founded 1976. Nonspecialized. Noncontingency. Number of searches conducted per year: 51-100.

ELLS PERSONNEL SYSTEM, INC.
105 Opus Center
9900 Bren Road East
Mannetonka MN 55343
Contact Tom Gladitsch, President. 612/333-1131. Executive search firm; temporary help service. Appointment requested. Founded 1912. Specializes in the areas of: Accounting and Finance; Advertising; Banking; Clerical; Engineering; Health and Medical; Manufacturing; Personnel and Human Resources; Printing and Publishing; Sales and Marketing. Positions commonly filled include: Accountant; Administrative Assistant; Aerospace Engineer; Bank Officer/Manager; Biomedical Engineer; Bookkeeper; Civil Engineer; Clerk; Draftsperson; Electrical Engineer; General Manager; Industrial Engineer; Legal Secretary; Marketing Specialist; Mechanical Engineer; Medical Secretary; Personnel and Labor Relations Specialist; Purchasing Agent; Receptionist; Sales Representative; Secretary; Systems Analyst. Company pays fee.

RUSS FALLSTADT & ASSOC.
Suite 768-218
15500 Wayzata Boulevard
Minneapolis MN 55391
Contact Russ Fallstadt, Owner. 612/476-6023. Licensed search firm. Appointment required. Specializes in the areas of: Computer Hardware and Software; Engineer; Health and Medical; Manufacturing; Technical and Scientific. Positions commonly filled include: Aerospace Engineer; Agricultural Engineer; Biochemist/Chemist; Biomedical Engineer; Civil Engineer; Electrical Engineer; Industrial Engineer; Mechanical Engineer.

HILLEREN KREOFSKY ASSOCIATES
8300 Norman Center Drive, Suite 510
Bloomington MN 55437
Contact Jerry Hilleren, Managing Director. 612/835-2677. Executive search firm. Appointment requested; unsolicited resumes accepted. Founded 1983. Specializes in the areas of: Computer Hardware and Software; General Management; Health and Medical; Sales and Marketing. Contingency; noncontingency. Number of searches conducted per year: 101-200.

LCW GROUP
6750 France Avenue South, Suite 144
Edina MN 55435
Contact Frank Lentz, President. 612/922-7879. Executive search firm. Appointment requested. Founded 1977. Specializes in the areas of: Biotechnical; Data Processing; Engineering. Positions commonly filled include: Aerospace Engineer; Biochemist; Biologist; Biomedical Engineer; Chemical Engineer; Chemist; Computer Programmer; Electrical Engineer; Industrial Designer; MIS Manager; Mechanial Engineer; Metallurgical Engineer; Operations/Production Specialist; Physicist; Quality Control Manager; Systems Analyst. Company pays fee. Number of placements per year: 51-100.

MANAGEMENT RECRUITERS OF MINNEAPOLIS
Belzer and Brenner Office Building
7625 Metro Boulevard
Edina MN 55439
Contact Manager. 612/835-4466. Executive search firm. Appointment required; no phone calls; unsolicited resumes accepted. Founded 1965. World's largest contingency search firm. Five hundred offices nationwide, doing business under the names "Management Recruiters", "Sales Consultants", "CompuSearch" and "OfficeMates5". Specializes in mid-management/professional positions, $25,000-75,000 per annum. Specializes in the areas of: Accounting; Administration, MIS/EDP; Advertising; Affirmative Action; Banking and Finance; Chemicals and Pharmaceuticals; Communications; Computer Hardware and Software; Construction; Electrical; Engineering; Food Industry; General Management; Health and Medical; Human Resources; Industrial and Interior Design; Insurance;

Legal; Manufacturing; Operations Management; Printing and Publishing; Procurement; Real Estate; Retailing; Sales and Marketing: Technical and Scientific; Textiles; Transportation. Contingency.

PROFESSIONAL STAFFING
8120 Penn Avenue South
Minneapolis MN 55431
Contact Leo Bright, Owner/Manager. 612/884-8111. Executive search firm. Appointment required; unsolicited resumes accepted. Founded 1968. Specializes in the areas of: Administration, MIS/EDP; Communications; Electrical; Engineering; General Management; Manufacturing; Operations Management; Procurement; Sales and Marketing; Technical and Scientific. Outplacement. Job Evaluations. Contingency. Number of searches conducted per year: 0-50.

SALES CONSULTANTS OF MINNEAPOLIS
7550 France Avenue, Suite 180
Minneapolis MN 55435
Contact Bob Hammer, Manager. 612/830-1420; FAX 612/893-9254. Executive search firm. Appointment required; no phone calls; unsolicited resumes accepted. Founded 1965. World's largest contingency search firm. Five hundred offices nationwide, doing business under the names "Management Recruiters", "Sales Consultants", "CompuSearch" and "OfficeMates5". Specializes in mid-management/professional positions, $25,000-75,000 per annum. Specializes in the areas of: Accounting; Administration, MIS/EDP; Advertising; Affirmative Action; Banking and Finance; Chemicals and Pharmaceuticals; Communications; Computer Hardware and Software; Construction; Electrical; Engineering; Food Industry; General Management; Health and Medical; Human Resources; Industrial and Interior Design; Insurance; Legal; Manufacturing; Operations Management; Printing and Publishing; Procurement; Real Estate; Retailing; Sales and Marketing; Technical and Scientific; Textiles; Transportation. Contingency.

SATHE & ASSOCIATES EXECUTIVE SEARCH
5821 Cedar Lake Road
Minneapolis MN 55416
Contact Mark Sathe, President. 612/546-2100. Executive search firm. Appointment required; no phone calls; unsolicited resumes accepted. Founded 1974. Minnesota's largest locally owned retainer based search firm. Specializes in the areas of: Accounting; Administration, MIS/EDP; Advertising; Affirmative Action; Agri-Business; Banking and Finance; Civilian Goverment; Construction; Electrical; Engineering; Food Industry; General Management; Health and Medical; Human Resources; Insurance; Legal; Manufacturing; Operations Management; Real Estate; Retailing; Sales and Marketing; Technical and Scientific; Women. Noncontingency. Number of searches conducted per year: 101-200.

TBL MANAGEMENT SERVICES
151 West Burnsville Parkway, Suite 211
Burnsville MN 55337
Contact Larry Buechler, Owner. 612/890-4613. Executive search firm. Specializes in the area of: Chemicals.

WHITNEY & ASSOCIATES, INC.
2975 Multifoods Tower
33 South 6th Street
Minneapolis MN 55402
Contact David L. Whitney, President. 612/338-5600. Executive search firm. No appointment required; unsolicited resumes accepted. Founded 1978. Specializes in the areas of: Accounting; Banking; Finance. Contingency. Number of searches conducted per year: 501+.

ROTH YOUNG PERSONNEL SERVICE OF MINNEAPOLIS, INC.
4530 West 77th Street
Minneapolis MN 55435
Contact Donald B. Spahr, President. 612/831-6655. Executive search firm. Appointment requested; unsolicited resumes accepted. Founded 1970. Specializes in the areas of: Accounting; Administration, MIS/EDP; Advertising; Affirmative Action; Banking; Computer Hardware and Software; Engineering; Fashion; Finance; Food Industry; General Management; Health and Medical; Legal; Manufacturing; Personnel and Human Resources; Sales and Marketing; Technical and Scientific; Transportation; Women. Contingency. Number of searches conducted per year: 101-200.

RESUME AND CAREER COUNSELING SERVICES OF MINNEAPOLIS

PROFESSIONAL RESUME AND WRITING SERVICE
5407 Excelsior Boulevard, Suite DD
St. Louis Park MN 55416.(call)
Contact Timothy R. Boyer, Manager. 612/920-9229. Appointment requested. Founded 1958. Consulting services regarding the preparation of letters and resumes. Writing, typing, and printing services. Initial free consultation. Services commonly provided include: Personal Counseling; Printing Services, Resume Writing and Preparation.

QUALITY OFFICE SERVICES
12710 Falcon Court North
White Bear Lake MN 55110
Contact Lois M. Rather, Owner. 612/426-2516. Appointment requested. Founded 1979. Secretarial Service offering assistance in: Typing, Word Processing, Bookkeeping, Telephone Answering, Transcribing from shorthand and tapes, Consultation and Writing of Resumes, Composition of Business Letters.

WORKING OPPORTUNITIES FOR WOMEN
2700 University Avenue, Suite 120
St. Paul MN 55114
Contact Yvette Oldendorf, President. 612/647-9961. Appointment requested. Founded 1975. Nonprofit organization with two divisions: The Metropolitan Centers for Displaced Homemakers, which offers career planning and job seeking skills under contract with the State of Minnesota to eligible displaced Homemakers; The Career Center, which offers seminars, conferences, and individual counseling for women at various stages in their career development. Services commonly provided include: Career Assessment; Career Resource Library; Career Testingj; Educational Counseling; Group Counseling; Individual Career Counseling; Internships; Interview Preparation; Job Listings; Networks; Personal Counseling; Resume Writing and preparation; Workshops on: Breakthrough for women who want to advance, Impact for women in management. Special programs provided for: Disadvantaged; Displaced Homemakers; Women Unemployed. Appraisal Service for Attorneys to help them estimate cost of divorced woman to become employed.

Professional and Trade Associations

Anyone who has conducted a job search has heard the dictum, "It's not what you know, it's who you know." While the validity of this comment has just as often been exaggerated, it does contain more than a grain of truth. Connections can never replace good old hard work as the best method of finding employment, but they can't hurt.

If you don't have an uncle in high places who can set up some interviews for you with a few of his friends, don't worry. Most people don't. The important thing to remember is that in most instances, connections do not materialize out of thin air -- they are created. That means that anyone who works at it can make them.

One of the best ways to meet people in your area of interest is through professional trade associations. Trade associations exist so that professionals in an industry can meet, share information about trends in the field, and arrange new business. Many of them regularly publish newsletters and magazines that will help you stay abreast of the current state of your industry. In addition, many associations hold regular meetings, and these meetings may present you the opportunity not only to learn more about the field you hope to enter, but also to establish connections.

With this in mind, we have included this directory of professional associations. Many of the addresses listed are for headquarters offices only. Inquire about local chapters in your area.

ACCOUNTING

INSTITUTE OF INTERNAL AUDITORS/TWIN CITIES CHAPTER
Barb Grondahl
363 97 1/2th Street
Bloomington MN 55420
612/884-9032

NATIONAL ASSOCIATION OF ACCOUNTANTS
Elizabeth Andrews
c/o Larson Allen Wiershire & Company
1800 Interchange Tower
600 South Highway 169
Minneapolis MN 55426
612/546-2211

For more information, contact:

AMERICAN INSTITUTE OF CERTIFIED PUBLIC ACCOUNTANTS
1211 Avenue of the Americas
New York NY 10036
212/575-6200

THE EDP AUDITORS ASSOCIATION
P.O. Box 88180
Carol Stream IL 60188
708/682-1200

INSTITUTE OF INTERNAL AUDITORS
P.O. Box 140099
249 Maitland Avenue
Orlando FL 32889
407/830-7600

NATIONAL ASSOCIATION OF ACCOUNTANTS
10 Paragon Drive
Box 433
Montvale NJ 07645
201/573-9000

NATIONAL SOCIETY OF PUBLIC ACCOUNTANTS
1010 North Fairfax Street
Alexandria VA 22314
703/549-6400

ADVERTISING, MARKETING, PUBLIC RELATIONS

AMERICAN ADVERTISING FEDERATION
John Francis
4248 Park Glen Road
Minneapolis MN 55416
612/929-1445

AMERICAN MARKETING ASSOCIATION
Gerry Ford, Vice President of Membership
c/o West Publishing Company
50 West Kellogg Blvd
St. Paul MN 55164

PUBLIC RELATIONS SOCIETY OF AMERICA
David Schoeneck, Director
c/o Grayco and Company
P.O. Box 1441
Minneapolis MN 55440
612/623-6000

For more information, contact:

AMERICAN ADVERTISING FEDERATION
1400 K Street NW
Suite 1000
Washington DC 20005
202/898-0089

AMERICAN ASSOCIATION OF ADVERTISING AGENCIES
666 Third Avenue
New York NY 10017
212/682-2500

AMERICAN MARKETING ASSOCIATION
250 South Wacker Drive
Suite 200
Chicago IL 60606
312/648-0536

BUSINESS-PROFESSIONAL ADVERTISING ASSOCIATION
Metroplex Corporate Center
100 Metroplex Drive
Edison NJ 08817
201/985-4441

PUBLIC RELATIONS SOCIETY OF AMERICA
33 Irving Place
New York NY 10003
212/995-2230

TELEVISION BUREAU OF ADVERTISING
477 Madison Avenue
New York NY 10022-104
212/486-1111

APPAREL AND TEXTILES

AMERICAN APPAREL MANUFACTURERS ASSOCIATION
2500 Wilson Boulevard
Suite 301
Arlington VA 22201
703/524-1864

AMERICAN TEXTILE MANUFACTURERS INSTITUTE
1801 K Street NW
Suite 900
Washington DC 20006
202/862-0500

NORTHERN TEXTILE ASSOCIATION
230 Congress Street
Boston MA 02110
617/542-8220

TEXTILE RESEARCH INSTITUTE
Box 625
Princeton NJ 08540
609/924-3150

BANKING/SAVINGS AND LOAN

BANK ADMINISTRATION INSTITUTE/MINNEAPOLIS CHAPTER
Harvey Becker, President
c/o New Hope State Bank
4301 Winneteka Avenue North
New Hope MN 55428
612/535-6100

**INDEPENDENT BANKERS ASSOCIATION OF AMERICA/
SAUK CENTER OFFICE**
P.O. Box 267
1168 South Main Street
Sauk Center MN 56378-1653
612/352-6546

INSTITUTE OF FINANCIAL EDUCATION
Barbara S. Kowal
c/o TCF Banking and Savings FA
801 Marquette Avenue
Minneapolis MN 55402
612/370-7451

MINNESOTA BANKING ASSOCIATION
700 Peavey Building
730 2nd Avenue South
Minneapolis MN 55402
612/338-7851

For more information, contact:

AMERICAN BANKERS ASSOCIATION
1120 Connecticut Avenue NW
Washington DC 20036
202/663-5221

BANK ADMINISTRATION INSTITUTE
60 Gould Center
Rolling Meadows IL 60008
609/424-3233

INDEPENDENT BANKERS ASSOCIATION OF AMERICA
One Thomas Circle NW
Suite 950
Washington DC 20005
202/659-8111

INSTITUTE OF FINANCIAL EDUCATION
111 East Wacker Drive
Chicago IL 60601
312/644-3100

NATIONAL COUNCIL OF SAVINGS INSTITUTIONS
1101 15th Street NW
Suite 400
Washington DC 20005
202/857-3100

BOOK AND MAGAZINE PUBLISHING

AMERICAN BOOKSELLERS ASSOCIATION
137 West 25th Street
New York NY 10001
212/463-8450

ASSOCIATION OF AMERICAN PUBLISHERS
220 East 23rd Street
New York NY 10010
212/689-8920

MAGAZINE PUBLISHERS ASSOCIATION
575 Lexington Avenue
New York NY 10022
212/752-0055

WRITERS GUILD OF AMERICA EAST, INC.
555 West 57th Street
New York NY 10019
212/245-6180

WRITERS GUILD OF AMERICA WEST, INC.
8955 Beverly Boulevard
West Hollywood CA 90048
213/550-1000

BROADCASTING

NATIONAL ASSOCIATION OF BROADCASTERS
STP-TV
3415 University Avenue
St. Paul MN 55114
612/646-5555

WOMEN IN RADIO AND TV/NORTH STAR CHAPTER
Mary McCarten, President
c/o WCCO-TV
90 South 11th Street
Minneapolis MN 55403
612/330-2620

For more information, contact:

BROADCAST EDUCATION ASSOCIATION
1771 N Street NW
Washington DC 20036
301/424-5355

CABLE TELEVISION ASSOCIATION
1724 Massachusetts Avenue NW
Washington DC 20036
202/775-3550

INTERNATIONAL RADIO AND TV SOCIETY
420 Lexington Avenue
Suite 531
New York NY 10170
212/867-6650

NATIONAL ASSOCIATION OF BROADCASTERS
1771 N Street NW
Washington DC 20036
202/429-5300

NATIONAL ASSOCIATION OF BUSINESS & EDUCATIONAL RADIO
1501 Duke Street
Suite 200
Alexandria VA 22314
703/739-0300

TELEVISION BUREAU OF ADVERTISING
477 Madison Avenue, 10th Floor
New York NY 10022-5892
212/486-1111

WOMEN IN RADIO AND TV, INC.
1101 Connecticut Avenue NW
Suite 700
Washington DC 20036
202/429-5102

CHARITABLE, NON-PROFIT, HUMANITARIAN

NATIONAL ASSOCIATION OF SOCIAL WORKERS
480 Concordia Avenue
St.Paul MN 55103
612/293-1935

For more information, contact:

NATIONAL ASSOCIATION OF SOCIAL WORKERS
7981 Eastern Avenue
Silver Spring MD 20910
301/565-0333

CHEMICALS & RELATED: PROCESSING, PRODUCTION, DISPOSAL

**AMERICAN INSTITUTE OF CHEMICAL ENGINEERING/
TWIN CITIES CHAPTER**
Greg Conrad, Section Chair
c/o Ecolab
940 Loan Oak Road
Eagan MN 55121
612/688-1689

MINNESOTA WATER POLLUTION CONTROL ASSOCIATION
520 Lafeyette Rd.
St. Paul MN 55155
612/296-7202

For more information, contact:

AMERICAN CHEMICAL SOCIETY
Career Services
1155 16th Street NW
Washington DC 20036
202/872-4600

AMERICAN INSTITUTE OF CHEMICAL ENGINEERING
345 East 47th Street
New York NY 10017
212/705-7338

AMERICAN INSTITUTE OF CHEMISTS
7315 Wisconsin Avenue
Suite 518 E
Bethesda MD 20814
301/652-2447

**ASSOCIATION OF STATE & INTERSTATE
WATER POLLUTION CONTROL ADMINISTRATORS**
444 North Capital Street NW
Suite #330 N
Washington DC 20001
202/624-7782

WATER POLLUTION CONTROL FEDERATION
601 Wythe Street Avenue NW
Alexandria VA 22314
703/684-2400

COLLEGES AND UNIVERSITIES/EDUCATION

MINNESOTA ASSOCIATION OF SCHOOL ADMINISTRATORS
Dale G. Jensen, Executive Director
1884 Como Avenue
St. Paul MN 55108
612/645-6272

For more information, contact:

AMERICAN ASSOCIATION OF SCHOOL ADMINISTRATORS
1801 North Moore Street
Arlington VA 22209
703/528-0700

ASSOCIATION OF AMERICAN UNIVERSITIES
One Dupont Circle NW
Suite 730
Washington DC 20036
202/466-5030

COMMUNICATIONS

**UNITED STATES TELEPHONE ASSOCIATION/
NORTH STAR CHAPTER**
Audrey Regenscheid, Secretary
6900 151st Street
Apple Valley MN 55124
612/891-2558

For more information, contact:

COMMUNICATIONS WORKERS OF AMERICA
1925 K Street NW
Washington DC 20006
202/728-2300

UNITED STATES TELEPHONE ASSOCIATION
900 19th Street NW
Suite 800
Washington DC 20006
202/835-3100

COMPUTERS: HARDWARE, SOFTWARE AND SERVICES

**ASSOCIATION FOR COMPUTING MACHINERY/
TWIN CITIES CHAPTER**
Box 1054
Minneapolis MN 55458

IEEE COMPUTER SOCIETY/ST. PAUL CHAPTER
William Gorder, Chairman
c/o IBM Corporation
37th Street and Highway 52 North
Rochester MN 55901

For more information, contact:

**ADAPSO/THE COMPUTER SOFTWARE AND SERVICES INDUSTRY
ASSOCIATION**
1616 N. Ft. Meyer Drive
Suite 1300
Arlington VA 22209
703/522-5055

ASSOCIATION FOR COMPUTING MACHINERY
11 West 42nd Street
New York NY 10036
212/869-7440

IEEE COMPUTER SOCIETY
1730 Massachusetts Avenue NW
Washington DC 20036
609/722-4089

CONSTRUCTION

MINNESOTA ASSOCIATION OF HOME BUILDERS
2905 Northwest Blvd.
Suite 50
Minneapolis MN 55441
612/559-4122

For more information, contact:

BUILDING OFFICIALS AND CODE ADMINISTRATORS INTERNATIONAL
4051 West Flossmoor Road
Country Club Hills IL 60477
312/799-2300

CONSTRUCTION INDUSTRY MANUFACTURERS ASSOCIATION
1111 East Wisconsin Avenue
Milwaukee WI 53202
414/272-0943

INTERNATIONAL CONFERENCE OF BUILDING OFFICIALS
5360 South Workman Road
Whittier CA 90601
213/699-0541

NATIONAL ASSOCIATION OF HOME BUILDERS
15th & M Streets NW
Washington DC 20005
202/822-0200

ELECTRICAL AND ELECTRONICS

AMERICAN ELECTROPLATERS AND SURFACE FINISHERS SOCIETY/UPPER MIDWEST BRANCH
Jon Philips
c/o Nico Plating
2929 First Avenue South
Minneapolis MN 55408
612/822-2185

ELECTROCHEMICAL SOCIETY/ TWIN CITIES CHAPTER
Harvey Kalweit
3M Company
3M Center, 208-1-01
St. Paul MN 55144
612/624-1019

INTERNATIONAL BROTHERHOOD OF ELECTRICAL WORKERS/ LOCAL 160
2522 Marshall Street NE
Minneapolis MN 55418
612/781-3126

MINNESOTA ELECTRONICS SALES AND SERVICES ASSOCIATION
4205 East 54th Street
Minneapolis MN 55417-2245
612/866-9762

NATIONAL ELECTRONICS SALES AND SERVICES ASSOCIATION
2708 West Berry Street, Suite 3
Ft. Worth TX 76109
817/921-9061

For more information, contact:

AMERICAN ELECTROPLATERS AND SURFACE FINISHERS SOCIETY
12644 Research Parkway
Orlando FL 32826
407/281-6441

ELECTROCHEMICAL SOCIETY
10 South Main Street
Pennington NJ 08534
609/737-1902

ELECTRONIC INDUSTRIES ASSOCIATION
2001 Pennsylvania Avenue NW
Washington DC 20006
202/457-4900

ELECTRONICS TECHNICIANS ASSOCIATION
602 North Jackson
Greencastle IN 46135
317/653-8262

INSTITUTE OF ELECTRICAL AND ELECTRONICS ENGINEERS
345 East 47th Street
New York NY 10017
212/705-7900

INTERNATIONAL BROTHERHOOD OF ELECTRICAL WORKERS
1125 15th Street NW
Washington DC 20005
202/833-7000

NATIONAL ELECTRICAL MANUFACTURERS ASSOCIATION
2101 L Street NW
Suite 300
Washington DC 20037
202/457-8400

ENGINEERING AND ARCHITECTURE

AMERICAN INSTITUTE OF ARCHITECTS/MINNEAPOLIS CHAPTER
275 Market Street
Suite 54
Minneapolis MN 55405
612/338-6763

AMERICAN SOCIETY OF HEATING, REFRIGERATING, AND AIR CONDITIONING ENGINEERS
Scott Williams
c/o MCE & Associates
625 Fourth Avenue South
Suite 1325
Minneapolis MN 55415
612/339-4941

AMERICAN SOCIETY OF PLUMBING ENGINEERS
Dean Parker, VP/Membership
9944 West 74th Street
Eden Prairie MN 55343
612/942-5533

INSTITUTE OF INDUSTRIAL ENGINEERS
Cathy Lou Pedresan
14300 Judicial Rd.
MS H-9
Burnsville MN 55337
612/892-4573

For more information, contact:

AMERICAN INSTITUTE OF ARCHITECTS
1735 New York Ave NW
Washington DC 20006
202/626-7300

AMERICAN SOCIETY FOR ENGINEERING EDUCATION
11 Dupont Circle NW
Suite 200
Washington DC 20036
202/293-7080

AMERICAN SOCIETY OF CIVIL ENGINEERS
345 East 47th Street
New York NY 10017
212/705-7496

**AMERICAN SOCIETY OF HEATING, REFRIGERATING
AND AIR CONDITIONING ENGINEERS**
1791 Tullie Circle NE
Atlanta GA 30329
404/636-8400

AMERICAN SOCIETY OF LANDSCAPE ARCHITECTS
4401 Connecticut Avenue
5th Floor
Washington DC 20008
202/686-2752

AMERICAN SOCIETY OF NAVAL ENGINEERS
1452 Duke Street
Alexandria VA 22314
703/836-6727

AMERICAN SOCIETY OF PLUMBING ENGINEERS
3617 Thousand Oaks Boulevard
Suite #210
Westlake Village CA 91362-3625
805/495-7120

AMERICAN SOCIETY OF SAFETY ENGINEERS
1800 East Oakton Street
Des Plaines IL 60018
708/692-4121

ILLUMINATING ENGINEERING SOCIETY OF NORTH AMERICA
345 East 47th Street
New York NY 10017
212/705-7926

INSTITUTE OF INDUSTRIAL ENGINEERS
25 Technology Park/Atlanta
Norcroff GA 30092
404/449-0460

NATIONAL ACADEMY OF ENGINEERING
2101 Constitution Avenue NW
Washington DC 20418
202/334-3200

NATIONAL SOCIETY OF PROFESSIONAL ENGINEERS
1420 King Street
Alexandria VA 22314
703/684-2800

SOCIETY OF FIRE PROTECTION ENGINEERS
60 Batterymarch Street
Boston MA 02110
617/482-0686

UNITED ENGINEERING TRUSTEES
345 East 47th Street
New York NY 10017
212/705-7000

FABRICATED METAL PRODUCTS/PRIMARY METALS

AMERICAN CASTE METALS ASSOCIATION/TWIN CITIES CHAP.
Pat Ponath, Secretary/Treasurer
c/o Northern Iron Corporation
867 Forest Street
St. Paul MN 55106
612/778-3308

For more information, contact:

AMERICAN POWDER METALLURGY INSTITUTE
105 College Road East
Princeton NJ 08540
609/452-7700

ASSOCIATION OF IRON AND STEEL ENGINEERS
Three Gateway Center
Suite 2350
Pittsburgh PA 15222
412/281-6323

NATIONAL ASSOCIATION OF METAL FINISHERS
401 North Michigan Avenue
Chicago IL 60601
312/644-6610

FINANCIAL SERVICES/MANAGEMENT CONSULTING

**AMERICAN MANAGEMENT ASSOCIATION/MINNEAPOLIS
CHAPTER**
Jackie Olsen
8400 Normandale Lake Blvd.
Suite 975
Minneapolis MN 55437
612/835-5401

AMERICAN SOCIETY OF APPRAISERS/TWIN CITIES CHAPTER
Steven J. Wall, President
Steven Wall Appraisal Company
17981 South Shore Lane West
Eden Prairie MN 55346
612/934-5153

INSTITUTE OF FINANCIAL EDUCATION/MINNESOTA CHAPTER 50
Barbara S Kowal
c/o TCF Banking and Savings, FA
801 Marquette Avenue
Minneapolis MN 55402
612/370-7451

MINNESOTA CONSUMER FINANCE CONFERENCE
800 Norwest Center
St. Paul MN 55101
612/227-1745

**NATIONAL ASSOCIATION OF CREDIT MANAGEMENT/
NORTH CENTRAL CHAPTER**
P.O. Box 59149
Minneapolis MN 55459-0149
612/341-9600

TWIN CITIES CASH MANAGEMENT ASSOCIATION
Jerry Bishop
c/o St. Paul Companies
385 Washington Street
St. Paul MN 55102
612/221-8091

For more information, contact:

AMERICAN FINANCIAL SERVICES ASSOCIATION
919 18th Street NW
3rd Floor
Washington DC 20006
202/296-5544

AMERICAN MANAGEMENT ASSOCIATION
Management Information Service
135 West 50th Street
New York NY 10020
212/586-8100

AMERICAN SOCIETY OF APPRAISERS
P.O. Box 17265
Washington DC 20041
703/478-2228

ASSOCIATION OF MANAGEMENT CONSULTING FIRMS
230 Park Avenue
Suite 544
New York NY 10036
212/697-9693

FEDERATION OF TAX ADMINISTRATORS
444 North Capital Street NW
Washington DC 20001
202/624-5890

FINANCIAL ANALYSTS FEDERATION
1633 Broadway
Room 1602
New York NY 10019
212/957-2860

FINANCIAL EXECUTIVES INSTITUTE
10 Madison Avenue
P.O. Box 1938
Morristown NJ 07962
201/898-4600

INSTITUTE OF FINANCIAL EDUCATION
111 East Wacker Drive
Chicago IL 60601
312/946-8800

INSTITUTE OF MANAGEMENT CONSULTANTS
230 Park Avenue
Suite 544
New York NY 10169
212/697-8262

NATIONAL ASSOCIATION OF BUSINESS ECONOMISTS
28790 Chagrin Boulevard
Suite 300
Cleveland OH 44122
216/464-7986

NATIONAL ASSOCIATION OF CREDIT MANAGEMENT
8815 Centre Park Drive
Suite 200
Columbia MD 21045-2117
301/740-5560

NATIONAL ASSOCIATION OF REAL ESTATE INVESTMENT TRUSTS
1129 20th Street NW
Suite 705
Washington DC 20036
202/785-8717

NATIONAL CORPORATE CASH MANAGEMENT ASSOCIATION
Wisconsin Avenue
Suite 1250 West
Bethesda MD 20814
301/907-2862
SECURITIES INDUSTRY ASSOCIATION
120 Broadway
New York NY 10271
212/608-1500

FOOD: PROCESSING, PRODUCTION, AND DISTRIBUTION

DAIRY COUNCIL OF MINNESOTA
2015 Rice Street
St. Paul MN 55113
612/488-0261

UNITED FOOD AND COMMERCIAL WORKERS UNION/LOCAL 653
Ronald N. Zwieg
505 North Highway 169
Suite 755
Plymouth MN 55441
612/525-1500

For more information, contact:

AMERICAN ASSOCIATION OF CEREAL CHEMISTS
3340 Pilot Knob Road
St. Paul MN 55121
612/454-7250

AMERICAN SOCIETY OF AGRICULTURAL ENGINEERS
2950 Niles Road
St. Joseph MI 49085
616/429-0300

AMERICAN SOCIETY OF BREWING CHEMISTS
3340 Pilot Knob Road
St. Paul MN 55121
612/454-7250

DAIRY AND FOOD INDUSTRIES SUPPLY ASSOCIATION
6245 Executive Boulevard
Rockville MD 20852
301/984-1444

NATIONAL AGRICULTURAL CHEMICALS ASSOCIATION
1155 15th Street NW
Suite 900
Washington DC 20005
202/296-1585

NATIONAL DAIRY COUNCIL
6300 North River Road
Rosemont IL 60018
708/696-1020

**UNITED FOOD AND COMMERCIAL
WORKERS INTERNATIONAL UNION**
1775 K Street NW
Washington DC 20006
202/223-3111

GENERAL MERCHANDISE: RETAIL AND WHOLESALE

NATIONAL RETAIL MERCHANTS ASSOCIATION
100 West 31st Street
New York NY 10001
212/244-8780

HEALTH CARE AND PHARMACEUTICALS/HOSPITALS

AMERICAN ACADEMY OF FAMILY PHYSICIANS/
MINNESOTA CHAPTER
2221 University Avenue SE
Suite 426
Minneapolis MN 55414
800/999-8198

CARE PROVIDERS OF MINNESOTA
2850 Metro Drive
Suite 200
Minneapolis MN 55425
612/854-2844

MEDICAL GROUP MANAGEMENT ASSOCIATION/MINNEAPOLIS
Bonnie Porte, Clinic Administrator
1250 Medical Arts Building
Minneapolis MN 55402
612/333-2888

MINNESOTA DENTAL ASSOCIATION
649 Lowry Medical Arts Building
St. Paul MN 55102
612/222-7817

MINNESOTA OCCUPATIONAL THERAPY ASSOCIATION
P.O. Box 26532
Minneapolis MN 55426
612/938-3123

MINNESOTA STATE PHARMACEUTICAL ASSOCIATION
2550 University Avenue West
Suite 320 North
St. Paul MN 55114
612/644-3566

MINNEAPOLIS VETERINARY MEDICAL ASSOCIATION
2469 University Avenue
St. Paul MN 55114
612/645-7533

NATIONAL MEDICAL ASSOCIATION/MINNEAPOLIS-ST. PAUL CHAPTER
Dr. Cassius McEllis
710 East 24th Street
Suite A-208
Minneapolis MN 55404

For more information, contact:

AMERICAN ACADEMY OF FAMILY PHYSICIANS
8880 Ward Parkway
Kansas City MO 64114
816/333-9700

AMERICAN ACADEMY OF PHYSICIAN ASSISTANTS
950 North Washington Street
Alexandria VA 22314
703/836-2272

AMERICAN ASSOCIATION FOR CLINICAL CHEMISTRY
2029 K Street NW, 7th Floor
Washington DC 20006
202/857-0717

AMERICAN COLLEGE OF HEALTHCARE EXECUTIVES
840 North Lake Shore Drive
Chicago IL 60611
312/943-0544

AMERICAN DENTAL ASSOCIATION
211 East Chicago Avenue
Chicago IL 60611
312/440-2500

AMERICAN HEALTH CARE ASSOCIATION
1201 L Street NW
Washington DC 20005
202/842-4444

AMERICAN MEDICAL ASSOCIATION
515 North State Street
Chicago IL 60610
312/464-5000

AMERICAN OCCUPATIONAL THERAPY ASSOCIATION
P.O. Box 1725
1383 Picard Drive
Rockville MD 20850
301/948-9626

AMERICAN PHARMACEUTICAL ASSOCIATION
2215 Constitution Avenue NW
Washington DC 20037
202/628-4410

AMERICAN PHYSICAL THERAPY ASSOCIATION
1111 North Fairfax Street
Alexandria VA 22314
703/684-2782

AMERICAN SOCIETY FOR BIOCHEMISTRY AND MOLECULAR BIOLOGY
9650 Rockville Pike
Bethesda MD 20814-3996
301/530-7145

AMERICAN SOCIETY OF HOSPITAL PHARMACISTS
4630 Montgomery Avenue
Bethesda MD 20814
301/657-3000

AMERICAN VETERINARY MEDICAL ASSOCIATION
930 North Meacham Road
Schaumburg IL 60196
708/605-8070

CARDIOVASCULAR CREDENTIALING INTERNATIONAL
2801 Far Hills #205
Dayton OH 45419
513/293-0315

MEDICAL GROUP MANAGEMENT ASSOCIATION
104 Imverness Terrace East
Inglewood CO 80112
303/799-1111

NATIONAL HEALTH COUNCIL
350 Fifth Avenue
Suite 318
New York NY 10118
212/268-8900

NATIONAL MEDICAL ASSOCIATION
1012 Tenth Street NW
Washington DC 20001
202/347-1895

HOTEL AND RESTAURANT RELATED

MINNESOTA RESTAURANT ASSOCIATION
871 Jefferson Avenue
St. Paul MN 55102
612/222-7401

For more information, contact:

THE AMERICAN HOTEL AND MOTEL ASSOCIATION
295 Lafayette Street, 7th Floor
New York NY 10012
212/941-5858

COUNCIL ON HOTEL, RESTAURANT AND INSTITUTIONAL EDUCATION
1200 17th Street NW
Washington DC 20036
202/331-5990

THE EDUCATION FOUNDATION OF THE NATIONAL RESTAURANT ASSOCIATION
250 South Wacker Drive
14th Floor
Chicago IL 60606
312/715-1010

INSURANCE

NATIONAL ASSOCIATION OF LIFE UNDERWRITERS/ MINNEAPOLIS CHAPTER
Rhonda Toles, Executive VP
1405 North Lilac Drive, #21
Minneapolis MN 55422-4528

For more information, contact:

ALLIANCE OF AMERICAN INSURERS
1501 Woodfield Road
Suite 400 West
Schaumburg IL 60173-4980
708/330-8500

AMERICAN COUNCIL OF LIFE INSURANCE
1001 Pennsylvania Avenue NW
Washington DC 20004
202/624-2000

AMERICAN INSURANCE ASSOCIATION
1130 Connecticut Avenue NW
Suite 1000
Washington DC 20036
202/828-7100

INSURANCE INFORMATION INSTITUTE
110 William Street
New York NY 10038
212/669-9200

NATIONAL ASSOCIATION OF LIFE UNDERWRITERS
1922 F Street NW
Washington DC 20006
202/331-6000

SOCIETY OF ACTUARIES
475 North Martingale Road
Suite 800
Schaumburg IL 60173
708/706-3500

LEGAL SERVICES

**ASSOCIATION OF LEGAL ADMINISTRATORS/
MINNEAPOLIS BRANCH**
Nancy Josephson
c/o Cousineau, McGuire, Shaughnessy & Anderson
1550 Utica Avenue
Suite 600
Minneapolis MN 55416-1523
612/546-8400

FEDERAL BAR ASSOCIATION/MINNEAPOLIS
Mary Carlson, President
Assistant U.S. Attorney
110 South Fourth Street
Minneapolis MN 55401
612/348-1500

MINNESOTA ASSOCIATION OF LEGAL ASSISTANTS
Barbara Johnson
P.O.Box 15165
Grain Exchange Building
Minneapolis MN 55415
612/339-7663

MINNESOTA PARALEGAL ASSOCIATION
Tracy Blanshan
c/o Kennedy Law Office
724 South West First Avenue
Rochester MN 55902

TWIN CITY PROFESSIONAL RECRUITERS ASSOCIATION
Donna Oman
c/o Maslon, Edelman, Borman & Brand
1800 Midwest Plaza
Minneapolis MN 55402
612/339-8015

For more information, contact:

AMERICAN BAR ASSOCIATION
750 North Lake Shore Drive
Chicago IL 60611
312/988-5000

ASSOCIATION OF LEGAL ADMINISTRATORS
175 East Hawthorne Road
Suite 325
Vernon Hills IL 60061-1428
708/816-1212

FEDERAL BAR ASSOCIATION
1815 H Street NW
Suite 408
Washington DC 20006
202/638-0252

NATIONAL ASSOCIATION FOR LAW PLACEMENT
1666 Connecticut Avenue
Suite 450
Washington DC 20009
202/667-1666

NATIONAL ASSOCIATION OF LEGAL ASSISTANTS
1601 South Main
Suite 300
Tulsa OK 74119
918/587-6828

NATIONAL FEDERATION OF PARALEGAL ASSOCIATIONS
104 Wilmot Road
Suite 201
Deerfield IL 60015-5195
708/940-8800

NATIONAL PARALEGAL ASSOCIATION
P.O. Box 406
Solebury PA 18963
215/297-8333

MISCELLANEOUS ASSOCIATIONS

AMERICAN FEDERATION OF SMALL BUSINESS
407 South Dearborn Street
Chicago IL 60605
312/427-0206

NATIONAL COOPERATIVE BUSINESS ASSOCIATION
1401 New York Ave. NW
Suite #1100
Washington DC 20005
202/638-6222

NATIONAL SMALL BUSINESS UNITED
1155 15th Street NW
Suite 710
Washington DC 20005
202/293-8830

MISCELLANEOUS MANUFACTURING

**NATIONAL TOOLING AND MACHINING ASSOCIATION/
MINNEAPOLIS CHAPTER**
Joann Hiebel
104 Union Plaza
333 Washington Avenue North
Minneapolis MN 55401
612/339-4030

For more information, contact:

NATIONAL ASSOCIATION OF MANUFACTURERS
1331 Pennsylvania Avenue, NW
Suite 1500
Washington DC 20004-1703
202/637-3000

NATIONAL MACHINE TOOL BUILDERS
7901 Westpark Drive
McLean VA 22102
703/893-2900

NATIONAL SCREW MACHINE PRODUCTS ASSOCIATION
6700 West Snowville Road
Brecksville OH 44141
216/526-0300

NATIONAL TOOLING AND MACHINING ASSOCIATION
9300 Livingston Road
Fort Washington MD 20744
301/248-1250

THE TOOLING AND MANUFACTURING ASSOCIATION
1177 South Dee Road
Park Ridge IL 60068
312/693-2347

NEWSPAPER PUBLISHING

MINNESOTA PRESS CLUB
1313 Nicollat Mall
Minneapolis MN 55403
612/338-4466

TWIN CITIES NEWSPAPER GUILD
922 Plymouth Building
12 S. Sixth St.
Minneapolis MN 55402
612/339-7031

For more information, contact:

AMERICAN NEWSPAPER PUBLISHERS ASSOCIATION
P.O. Box 17407
Dulles Airport
Washington DC 20041
703/648-1000

AMERICAN SOCIETY OF NEWSPAPER EDITORS
P.O. Box 17004
Washington DC 20041
703/648-1144

THE DOW JONES NEWSPAPER FUND
P.O. Box 300
Princeton NJ 08543-0300
609/520-4000

INTERNATIONAL CIRCULATION MANAGERS ASSOCIATION
11600 Sunrise Valley Drive
Reston VA 22091
703/620-9555

NATIONAL NEWSPAPER ASSOCIATION
1627 K Street NW
Suite 400
Washington DC 20006
202/466-7200

NATIONAL PRESS CLUB
529 14th St. NW
Washington DC 20045
202/662-7500

THE NEWSPAPER GUILD
Research and Information Department
8611 Second Avenue
Silver Spring, MD 20910
301/585-2990

PAPER PRODUCTS AND PACKAGING/CONTAINERS

**TECHNICAL ASSOCIATION OF THE PULP AND PAPER INDUSTRY/
MINNESOTA SECTION**
Jim Lunden, Chairman
c/o Boise Cascade Corporation
2425 Terminal Road
St. Paul MN 55113
612/633-8220

For more information, contact:

AMERICAN PAPER INSTITUTE
260 Madison Avenue
New York NY 10016
212/340-0600

TECHNICAL ASSOCIATION OF THE PULP AND PAPER INDUSTRY
P.O. Box 105113
Atlanta GA 30348
404/446-1400

PETROLEUM AND ENERGY RELATED/MINING AND DRILLING

**AMERICAN INST. OF MINING, METALLURGY & PETROLEUM/
MINNESOTA**
Robert Schafer
c/o Solidification Incorporated
7233 Winneteka Avenue North
Minneapolis MN 55428
612/535-1065

AMERICAN NUCLEAR SOCIETY/MINNESOTA
Laura McCarten
c/o Northern States Power- Prairie Island
414 Nicolet Mall
Minneapolis MN 55401
612/388-6758

**AMERICAN SOCIETY OF TRIBOLOGISTS & LUBRICATION
ENGINEERS/TWIN CITIES**
Bernard Eliot
c/o Senex-Land O'Lakes
Mail Stop 570
P.O. Box 64089
St. Paul MN 55164
612/451-4611

MINNESOTA PETROLEUM COUNCIL
350 St. Peters Street
Suite 1025
St. Paul MN 55102
612/227-8341

For more information, contact:

AMERICAN ASSOCIATION OF PETROLEUM GEOLOGISTS
Box 979
Tulsa OK 74101
918/584-2555

AMERICAN GAS ASSOCIATION
1515 Wilson Boulevard
Arlington VA 22209
703/841-8400

AMERICAN GEOLOGICAL INSTITUTE
4220 King Street
Alexandria VA 22302
703/379-2480

AMERICAN INSTITUTE OF MINING, METALLURGICAL AND PETROLEUM
345 East 47th Street
New York NY 10017
212/705-7695

AMERICAN NUCLEAR SOCIETY
555 North Kensington Avenue
La Grange Park IL 60525
708/352-6611

AMERICAN PETROLEUM INSTITUTE
1220 L Street NW
Washington DC 20005
202/682-8000

AMERICAN SOCIETY OF TRIBOLOGISTS AND LUBRICATION ENGINEERS
840 Busse Highway
Park Ridge IL 60068-2376
708/825-5536

CLEAN ENERGY RESEARCH INSTITUTE
P.O. Box 248294
Coral Gables FL 33124
305/284-4666

GEOLOGICAL SOCIETY OF AMERICA
3300 Penrose Place
P.O. Box 9140
Boulder CO 80301
303/447-2020

PETROLEUM EQUIPMENT INSTITUTE
6514 East 69th Street
P.O. Box 2380/74101
Tulsa OK 74133-1719
918/494-9696

SOCIETY OF EXPLORATION GEOPHYSICISTS
P.O. Box 702740
8801 South Yale
Tulsa OK 74170-2740
918/493-3516

PRINTING

PRINTING INDUSTRY OF MINNESOTA, INC.
450 North Syndicate
Suite 200
St. Paul MN 55104
612/646-4826

For more information, contact:

ASSOCIATION OF GRAPHIC ARTS
5 Penn Plaza
20th Floor
New York NY 10001

BINDING INDUSTRIES OF AMERICA
70 East Lake Street
Chicago IL 60601
312/372-7606

PRINTING INDUSTRIES OF AMERICA
100 Dangerfield Road
Alexandria VA 22314
703/519-8100

TECHNICAL ASSOCIATION OF THE GRAPHIC ARTS
Box 9887
Rochester NY 14623
716/272-0557

REAL ESTATE

BUILDING OWNERS AND MANAGERS ASSOCIATION
121 South 8th Street
Suite 610
Minneapolis MN 55402-2841
612/338-8627

INTERNATIONAL ASSOCIATION OF CORPORATE REAL ESTATE EXECUTIVES/ST. PAUL CHAPTER
Sam VanTassel
Real Estate Rep.
Ashland Oil/Super America
1240 WEst 98th Street
Bloomington MN 55431
612/887-6100

For more information, contact:

APARTMENT OWNERS AND MANAGERS ASSOCIATION
65 Cherry Plaza
Watertown CT 06795
203/274-2589

BUILDING OWNERS AND MANAGERS ASSOCIATION
1521 Ritchie Highway
Arnold MD 21012
301/261-2882

INSTITUTE OF REAL ESTATE MANAGEMENT
430 North Michigan Avenue
Chicago IL 60611
312/661-1930

INTERNATIONAL ASSOCIATION OF CORPORATE REAL ESTATE EXECUTIVES
440 Columbia Drive
Suite 100
West Palm Beach FL 33409
407/683-8111

INTERNATIONAL REAL ESTATE INSTITUTE
8383 East Evans Road
Scottsdale AZ 85260
602/998-8267

NATIONAL ASSOCIATION OF REAL ESTATE INVESTMENT TRUSTS
1129 20th Street NW
Suite 705
Washington DC 20036
202/785-8717

NATIONAL ASSOCIATION OF REALTORS
430 North Michigan Avenue
Chicago IL 60611
312/329-8200

RUBBER AND PLASTICS

SOCIETY OF PLASTICS ENGINEERS/MINNESOTA CHAPTER
Lorna Lemke
c/o Plastic Products Company
30355 Akerson Street
Lindstrom MN 55045
612/462-7900

For more information, contact:

SOCIETY OF PLASTICS INDUSTRY
355 Lexington Avenue
New York NY 10017
212/370-7340

SOCIETY OF PLASTIC ENGINEERS
14 Fairfield Drive
Brookfield Centre CT 06804
203/775-0471

TRANSPORTATION/SHIPPING/AUTOMOTIVE

AUTOMOTIVE SERVICE ASSOCIATION/MINNESOTA
100 East 146 Street
Suite 121
Burnsville MN 55337
612/462-2227

GREATER METROPOLITAN AUTOMOBILE DEALERS ASSOCIATION OF MINNESOTA
7701 York Ave South
Suite 230
Edina MN 55435
612/831-8019

MINNESOTA TRUCKING ASSOCIATION
Suite 134 North
1821 University Avenue
St. Paul MN 55104
612/646-7351

PROFESSIONAL AVIATION MAINTENANCE ASSOCIATION/ MINNESOTA
Matthew Morris, President
Thief River Falls Technical College
Highway 1 East
Thief River MN 56701

For more information, contact:

AIR LINE EMPLOYEES ASSOCIATION
5600 South Central Ave
Chicago IL 60638
312/767-3333

AIR TRANSPORT ASSOCIATION OF AMERICA
1709 New York Ave NW
Washington DC 20006
202/626-4000

AMERICAN INSTITUTE OF AERONAUTICS AND ASTRONAUTICS
555 West 57th Street
Suite 1200
New York NY 10019
212/247-6500

AMERICAN SOCIETY OF TRAVEL AGENTS
1101 King Street
Alexandria VA 22314
703/739-2782

AMERICAN TRUCKING ASSOCIATION
2200 Mill Road
Alexandria VA 22314
703/838-1700

ASSOCIATION OF AMERICAN RAILROADS
50 F Street NW
Washington DC 20001
202/639-2100

AUTOMOTIVE SERVICE ASSOCIATION
P.O. Box 929
Bedford TX 76021-0929
817/283-6205

AUTOMOTIVE SERVICE INDUSTRY ASSOCIATION
444 North Michigan Avenue
Chicago IL 60611
312/836-1300

AVIATION MAINTENANCE FOUNDATION
P.O. Box 2826
Redmond WA 98073
206/828-3917

FUTURE AVIATION PROFESSIONALS OF AMERICA
4291 J. Memorial Drive
Atlanta GA 30032
1-800/GET-JOBS

INSTITUTE OF TRANSPORTATION ENGINEERS
Suite 410
525 School Street NW,
Washington DC 20024
202/554-8050

MARINE TECHNOLOGY SOCIETY
1825 K Street NW
Suite 218
Washington DC 20009
202/775-5966

MOTOR VEHICLE MANUFACTURERS ASSOCIATION
7430 2nd Avenue
Suite 300
Detroit MI 48202
313/872-4311

NATIONAL AERONAUTIC ASSOCIATION OF USA
1815 Fort Meyer Drive
Suite 700
Arlington, VA 22209-1805
703/527-0226

NATIONAL AUTOMOTIVE DEALERS ASSOCIATION
8400 Westpark Drive
McLean VA 22102
703/821-7000

NATIONAL INSTITUTE FOR AUTOMOTIVE SERVICE EXCELLENCE
13505 Dulles Technology Drive
Herndon VA 22071-3415
703/742-3800

NATIONAL MARINE MANUFACTURERS ASSOCIATION
401 North Michigan Avenue
Suite 1150
Chicago IL 60611
312/836-4747

PROFESSIONAL AVIATION MAINTENANCE ASSOCIATION
500 Northwest Plaza
Suite 809
St. Ann MO 63034
314/739-2580

SHIPBUILDERS COUNCIL OF AMERICA
4301 North Fairfax Drive
Suite 330
Arlington VA 22203
703/276-1700

UTILITIES

AMERICAN WATER WORKS ASSOCIATION
6666 West Quincy Avenue
Denver CO 80235
303/794-7711

Index

A

D

E

F

G

H

I

M

P

Q

R

S

Alphabetical Index to Employment Services

Alphabetical Index to Professional Associations

A

M

N

P

AVAILABLE AT YOUR LOCAL BOOKSTORE

Knock 'em Dead With Great Answers to Tough Interview Questions

Will you have the answers when the recruiter asks: Why do you want to work here? What can you do for us that someone else cannot? How much money do you want? Why do you want to change jobs? In *Knock 'em Dead*, Martin Yate gives you not only the best answers to these and scores of more difficult questions, but also the best way to answer--so that you'll be able to field any tough question, and get the job and salary that you deserve. 6x9 inches, 204 pages, paperback, $7.95.

Resumes that Knock 'em Dead

In *Resumes that Knock 'em Dead*, Martin Yate reviews the marks of a great resume: what type of resume is right for each applicant, what always goes in, what always stays out, and why. Every single resume in *Resumes that Knock 'em Dead* was used by a real individual to successfully obtain a job. No other book provides the hard facts for producing an exemplary resume. 8 1/2x11 inches, 216 pages, $7.95.

Cover Letters that Knock 'em Dead

Cover Letters that Knock 'em Dead shows not just how to write a "correct" cover letter, but how to write a cover letter that offers a powerful competitive advantage in today's tough job market. *Cover Letters that Knock 'em Dead* gives the essential information on composing a cover that wins attention, interest and job offers. 8 1/2x11 inches, 184 pages, $7.95.

ALSO OF INTEREST...

The JobBank Series

There are now 18 *JobBank* books, each providing extensive, up-to-date employment information on hundreds of the largest employers in each job market. Recommended as an excellent place to begin your job search by *The New York Times, The Los Angeles Times, The Boston Globe, The Chicago Tribune*, and many other publications, *JobBank* books have been used by hundreds of thousands of people to find jobs.

Books available: *The Atlanta JobBank--The Boston JobBank--The Chicago JobBank--The Dallas-Ft. Worth JobBank--The Denver JobBank--The Detroit JobBank--The Florida JobBank--The Houston JobBank--The Los Angeles JobBank--The Minneapolis JobBank--The New York JobBank--The Ohio JobBank--The Philadelphia JobBank--The Phoenix JobBank--The St. Louis JobBank--The San Franciso JobBank--The Seattle JobBank--The Washington DC JobBank*. Each book is 6x9 inches, over 250 pages, paperback, $12.95.

If you cannot find a book at your local bookstore, you may order it directly from the publisher. Please send payment including $3.75 for shipping and handling (for the entire order) to : Bob Adams, Inc., 260 Center Street, Holbrook, MA 02343. Credit card holders may call 1-800-USA-JOBS (in Massachusetts, 617-767-8100). Please first check at your local bookstore.